COPYRIGHT AND ANONYMITY IN THE CREATIVE USER-GENERATED WORLD

This book explores the relationship between copyright law, online anonymity, and creative user-generated content (CUGC).

Presenting original empirical findings, the book evaluates the co-existence of copyright law and normative systems regulating a CUGC landscape made up of artists, photographers, and writers, and makes novel recommendations for copyright reform. It takes a multi-jurisdictional approach across Anglo-American and EU legal systems, using the UK, USA, and Germany as representative jurisdictions for legal analysis. Qualitative findings are drawn from creators and communities on Reddit and 4chan.

Copyright subsists in much CUGC, but pervasive anonymity makes it difficult for the law to regulate it effectively. Simultaneously, anonymity offers creative benefits in a way that highlights flaws in traditional justifications of copyright. Comparisons between community norms and copyright law identify practical differences but also fundamental compatibilities in terms of ownership expectations. However, the simultaneous existence of legal and normative enforcement mechanisms complicates matters for creators and potential users, with negative implications for creativity and copyright law. While existing reform efforts have made suggestions to create a UGC exception, these overlook and undermine the role of CUGC creators as copyright holders. This can be addressed through the consideration of a framework of supplementary CUGC guidelines when developing such reforms.

This valuable resource for researchers and students provides a distinct perspective in framing CUGC creators as copyright holders, examining online anonymity as a pivotal factor influencing regulation.

Copyright and Anonymity in the Creative User-Generated World

Rachel Maguire

•HART•
OXFORD • LONDON • NEW YORK • NEW DELHI • SYDNEY

HART PUBLISHING
Bloomsbury Publishing Plc
Kemp House, Chawley Park, Cumnor Hill, Oxford, OX2 9PH, UK
1385 Broadway, New York, NY 10018, USA
Bloomsbury Publishing Ireland Limited, 29 Earlsfort Terrace, Dublin 2, D02 AY28, Ireland

HART PUBLISHING, the Hart/Stag logo, BLOOMSBURY and the Diana logo are trademarks of Bloomsbury Publishing Plc

First published in Great Britain 2025

A catalogue record for this book is available from the British Library.

Library of Congress Cataloging-in-Publication data

Names: Maguire, Rachel, author.

Title: Copyright and anonymity in the creative user-generated world / Rachel Maguire.

Description: Oxford ; New York : Hart Publishing, 2025. | Includes bibliographical references and index. | Summary: "This book explores the relationship between copyright law, online anonymity, and creative user-generated content (CUGC). It evaluates the co-existence of copyright law and normative systems regulating a CUGC landscape made up of artists, photographers, and writers, and makes novel recommendations for copyright reform. It takes a multi-jurisdictional approach across Anglo-American and EU legal systems; qualitative findings are drawn from creators and communities on Reddit and 4chan. This valuable resource for researchers and students provides a distinct perspective in framing CUGC creators as copyright holders, using original empirical research and examining online anonymity as a pivotal factor influencing regulation"—Provided by publisher.

Identifiers: LCCN 2024057443 (print) | LCCN 2024057444 (ebook) | ISBN 9781509982325 (hardback) | ISBN 9781509982363 (paperback) | ISBN 9781509982332 (Epub) | ISBN 9781509982349 (pdf)

Subjects: LCSH: Copyright. | Internet—Security measures. | Data protection—Security measures. | Intellectual property. | Law reform.

Classification: LCC K1420.5 .M25 2025 (print) | LCC K1420.5 (ebook) | DDC 346.04/82—dc23/eng/20241203

LC record available at https://lccn.loc.gov/2024057443

LC ebook record available at https://lccn.loc.gov/2024057444

ISBN:	HB:	978-1-50998-232-5
	ePDF:	978-1-50998-234-9
	ePub:	978-1-50998-233-2

Typeset by Compuscript Ltd, Shannon

For product safety related questions contact productsafety@bloomsbury.com

To find out more about our authors and books visit www.hartpublishing.co.uk. Here you will find extracts, author information, details of forthcoming events and the option to sign up for our newsletters.

For Helen

ACKNOWLEDGEMENTS

Thanks to Chris Reed for his excellent supervisory efforts and the rest of the staff in the Centre for Commercial Law Studies at QMUL who provided academic guidance and administrative support during the doctoral studies that form the basis of the book. Similarly thanks to the Herchel Smith Fund for making it financially possible.

Thanks to my examiners, Jonathan Griffiths and Andres Guadamuz, for their helpful comments and guidance.

Thanks to the creators and online communities that contributed and helped along the way.

Thanks to my friends and family for showing enthusiasm despite not having the slightest interest in copyright law.

Extra special thanks go to James and to my mother, Helen.

CONTENTS

LIST OF ABBREVIATIONS

CDPA	Copyright, Designs and Patents Act 1988
CUGC	Creative user-generated content
DMCA	Digital Millennium Copyright Act
IP	Intellectual property
TDM	Text and data mining
UGC	User-generated content
UrhG	Urheberrechtsgesetz (Germany Copyright Law)
USC	United States Code

TABLE OF CASES

USA

TABLE OF LEGISLATION

Nigeria

UK

USA

International

1

Introduction

I. Introduction

Sharing content online and interacting with content shared by others is a widespread daily activity, and one that takes place in an environment where obscured identities are commonplace. This content is better known as user-generated content (UGC)[1] and a significant category of it is *creative* user-generated content (CUGC): art, photography, poetry, film, stories as a handful of examples. In the offline world these types of creative output attract the protection of copyright, but despite a long-standing interest in the implications of UGC for copyright law, the scholarship has largely overlooked the fact that UGC creators can own copyright, preferring to focus on UGC's relationship with the traditional copyright industries. This in turn means that the wider implications of this for our understanding of creativity and copyright have not been fully explored.

This book aims to understand how copyright law, creativity and online anonymity interact in the context of CUGC to better understand copyright law in practice. In doing so, it aims to engage with existing copyright debates by interrogating narratives and rhetoric in copyright theory, by contributing to the growing body of empirical copyright studies and by exploring whether reform is required. Using the specific context of CUGC communities, this book therefore provides a detailed exploration of the legal and normative regulation of the CUGC world. To understand how these works are shared and used we need an accurate exploration and evaluation of how these regulatory systems work *in reality*. To do this, the book compares various elements of copyright law – doctrinal and theoretical – with CUGC community and creator norms in relation to creative practices and the sharing and use of their work. The book uses these comparisons to develop a critique of copyright law and to interrogate reform narratives. The discussion draws in part from original qualitative findings from creative communities on 4chan and Reddit. The book also recognises that a key element of understanding the regulation of CUGC is to consider the role of online anonymity, which is shown to be a pervasive and immutable characteristic of the CUGC environment.

[1] User-generated content (UGC) is content that is uploaded to a third-party service (such as a social media platform) by its users without payment. Because of the lack of payment, this content is often described as 'amateur', but this is somewhat of a misnomer as it does not indicate a lower level of quality and fails to reflect the fact that some people sharing UGC are also creative professionals.

By examining the interrelationship between copyright, creativity and anonymity, the book builds a wide-ranging critique of copyright law in the digital age. It highlights that copyright subsists in much CUGC, but that anonymity makes it difficult for copyright law to regulate this environment effectively. Simultaneously, anonymity provides creative benefits, often more effectively than copyright, despite the latter's reliance on creativity-focused justificatory narratives. In considering the normative regulation of CUGC, the book demonstrates that anonymity does not mean that CUGC is in the public domain and that although community ownership norms deviate from copyright (and sometimes each other) in significant ways, the values underpinning those norms are largely compatible with copyright law. It is also shown that copyright is part of the enforcement system of community norms, but conflicts with normative expectations of acceptable uses of CUGC, thereby complicating matters for creators and potential users in a way that is anathema to its aims. Consequently, it is argued that a better approach is needed, and is possible.

The book takes a normative position that using the concept of creativity to guide copyright law is coherent, and therefore the law should respond to these critiques. Current UGC reform debates focused on making copyright less restrictive through the use of copyright exceptions are compelling but largely overlook the role of the CUGC creator as copyright owner, and thereby risk entrenching the problem reform seeks to address. An argument for supplementary guidelines is therefore put forward to ensure that the needs of CUGC creators and users are better met.

II. Copyright in the Digital World

Academic attention on copyright in the digital world is nothing new. Since the late 1990s, there has been a significant body of literature exploring the implications for copyright of what is created and shared online and using digital technologies. Those original scholars of the creative digital world wrote of open-source software, of mashups, of memes, of read-write culture.[2] These discussions identified tensions between these creative and cultural practices and the model of creativity implicit

[2] See, eg: M Chon, 'New Wine Bursting from Old Bottles: Collaborative Internet Art, Joint Works, and Entrepreneurship' (1996) 75 *Oregon Law Review* 257; R Tushnet, 'Legal Fictions: Copyright, Fan Fiction, and a New Common Law' (1996) 17 *Loyola of Los Angeles Entertainment Law Journal* 651; J Boyle, *Shamans, Software, and Spleens: Law and the Construction of the Information Society* (Cambridge, MA, Harvard University Press, 1997); L Lessig, *Free Culture: The Nature and Future of Creativity* (New York, Penguin Books, 2005); M Deuze, 'Participation, Remediation, Bricolage: Considering Principal Components of a Digital Culture' (2006) 22 *The Information Society* 63; JD Litman, *Digital Copyright* (Amherst, NY, Prometheus Books, 2006); A Bruns, 'The Future Is User-Led: The Path towards Widespread Produsage' (2008) 11 *Fibreculture Journal*: eleven.fibreculturejournal.org/fcj-066-the-future-is-user-led-the-path-towards-widespread-produsage/; L Lessig, *Remix: Making Art and Commerce Thrive in the Hybrid Economy* (New York, Bloomsbury Academic, 2008).

within copyright, aligning with broader critiques of the conceptions of authorship and of originality within the law that do not reflect the historical reality,[3] or are not sustainable from a post-structuralist viewpoint.[4] Instead, they argued that the 'author' is better understood as an interpreter of pre-existing concepts, works and culture[5] and that copyright law should be less restrictive.

This book relies on this heritage of copyright literature as its foundation but is also clear that continued attention to the way that copyright and online creativity interact is essential. The creative user-generated world is not static. While read-write culture remains a significant part of this phenomenon, platforms change, the way people interact online evolves and the divide between the online and offline worlds reduces. The technology also advances, as we have seen most recently, with the rise in accessibility of generative AI technology and its integration into creative practices.

Fundamental to the discussion in this book, and in contrast to the majority of the existing UGC literature, is the framing of CUGC creators as a legitimate stakeholder in copyright discourse, not just as a user but also as a copyright owner. Also important is the position that online creativity such as UGC is not a fringe activity in our wider cultural landscape. Online activities are no longer 'other', they are a fully integrated element of our lives; we no longer need to talk of *going* online, we *are* online. This means that online creativity, and therefore CUGC, is not just a phenomenon of cyberspace, but one of culture, society and the economy more generally. Often this has been overlooked because UGC has been framed as an amateur or purely non-commercial endeavour, so has been viewed in some way as less weighty a consideration in copyright reform debates.

This book fundamentally disagrees with that viewpoint. Vast amounts of content that we would recognise as traditionally creative such as art, photography and writing can be found on UGC platforms, and this exposes large numbers of people to more cultural and creative works than they would ever see through traditional channels. For example, there are 22 million subscribers to Reddit's r/Art community, and in January 2024 there were 1.22 billion visits to Reddit.[6] Simultaneously, while the blurred line between consumer and creator has been recognised for decades, to describe CUGC as amateur or non-commercial based purely on the fact that it is UGC is an oversimplification. The blurring between

[3] M Woodmansee, *The Author, Art and the Market: Rereading the History of Aesthetics* (New York, Columbia University Press, 1996).

[4] P Jaszi, 'On the Author Effect: Contemporary Copyright and Collective Creativity' (1991) 10 *Cardozo Arts & Entertainment Law Journal* 293; M Biagioli, P Jaszi and M Woodmansee, *Making and Unmaking Intellectual Property: Creative Production in Legal and Cultural Perspective* (Chicago, IL, University of Chicago Press, 2011).

[5] RJ Coombe, *The Cultural Life of Intellectual Properties: Authorship, Appropriation, and the Law* (Durham, NC, Duke University Press, 1998); P Levy, *Cyberculture*, R Bononno trans (Minneapolis, MN, University of Minnesota Press, 2001).

[6] 'Web Users of Reddit.Com 2024' (*Statista*): www.statista.com/statistics/1310710/redditcom-monthly-users.

non-commercial and commercial creative practices is much more pronounced in a UGC environment that facilitates branding and marketing and overlooks the fact that this part of creative activity is increasingly commercialised. Even where CUGC is shared as a purely non-commercial endeavour, the digital world creates an effective environment for developing creative skills and ideas, with many serious, high-quality creators, or those aspiring to be, sharing creative UGC online. UGC creators experience other people sharing, altering and commercialising their work on a regular basis, rarely with express permission to do so. That there has been so little detailed consideration of their rights in their creative work and the approaches to regulating CUGC is a missed opportunity and means that there is a significant gap in the UGC-based copyright critiques and reform suggestions.

It is also important to acknowledge that copyright does not occur in a vacuum in the digital world; it operates alongside environmental factors such as community norms and a pervasive layer of anonymity, as will both be established and explored in later chapters. If we are interested in understanding how copyright works, or how it should work, in the CUGC environment, then we can only properly do so if we consider how these core factors interact or interfere with the law.

III. Defining Key Concepts

This book is broadly about the interrelationships between three things: copyright law, creativity and anonymity. While 'copyright' is straightforward in the sense that we can – and will – look to the doctrine to understand it, the other concepts need some more specific attention. While these will be explored in more depth and in more focused context in the chapters that follow, the discussion below frames the book's core approach to understanding 'anonymity' and 'creativity'.

A. Anonymity

The over-used trope of online anonymity is that of nameless hackers, trolls and scammers, with people choosing to obscure their names for nefarious purposes. However, the reality of online anonymity is more complex than this, both in terms of its consequences and what it actually looks like. While the book acknowledges the potential for negative or harmful consequences, its starting point is to view online anonymity as more complex a phenomenon. The chapters that follow consider the ways that online anonymity affects copyright law, creative practices and community norms, and shows that its effects span a spectrum from negative through to positive. Therefore, it is essential that our understanding of online anonymity starts from a neutral normative position.

It is also essential to clarify what is meant by online anonymity; the trope described above frames it as simply not using a real name but this focus on individual choices about names is overly simplistic. Despite its etymology, anonymity encompasses more than just namelessness. Such a traditional understanding of the term fails to reflect what anonymity actually conceals: it is not simply our names, but our broader identities.[7] Consequently, anonymity in this book is more accurately understood through the connected ideas of unreachability,[8] 'untraceability',[9] unidentifiability,[10] or unavailability of information[11] or of identity knowledge.[12] There are a wide range of forms of identity knowledge, with Marx outlining nine types including information about an individual such as their name or username, typification information such as gender or race, or geographical information such as home or email addresses.[13] The more identity knowledge is – or becomes – available, the greater a picture of an individual can be pulled together, even if this does not include a direct link back to their 'real name' or an offline identity. This demonstrates that knowing, or not knowing the name of an individual, is not a definitive measure of anonymity, and that the understanding of anonymity that underpins this book must necessarily be more nuanced.

Part of this nuance is that being anonymous to any extent online is not necessarily a static state of being, nor one that is a result of the choice of an individual to be anonymous or not. Smith Ekstrand uses a model of anonymity that focuses on the *receiver* of identity information. The anonymity status of an individual in this sense is constructed based on how the receiver of that information perceives the source, whether they are interested in knowing the identity of the source and whether they are able to discover this.[14] As Noguiera Silva and Reed explain, the ability to discover identity information through searching online means that any anonymity status is ephemeral and out of the control of the individual.

Simultaneously, however, it is clear that individuals have some impact on what identity information is available. We see this in choices such as using a pseudonym, sharing selfies or using 'throwaway' accounts that do not link back to other posts. This book distinguishes between these choices as identity *practices* in contrast to the identity *statuses* discussed above. Individuals participate in anonymity practices through their initial choices as to how to present themselves, but the degree of anonymity that they ultimately have is not definitively set by these choices.

[7] H Nissenbaum, 'The Meaning of Anonymity in an Information Age' (1999) 15 *The Information Society* 141, 141–42.

[8] ibid 142.

[9] DG Post, 'Pooling Intellectual Capital: Thoughts on Anonymity, Pseudonymity, and Limited Liability in Cyberspace The Law of Cyberspace' [1996] *University of Chicago Legal Forum* 139, 150.

[10] GT Marx, 'What's in a Name? Some Reflections on the Sociology of Anonymity' (1999) 15 *The Information Society* 99, 100.

[11] G Bachmann, M Knecht and A Wittel, 'The Social Productivity of Anonymity' (2017) 17 *ephemera: theory & politics in organization* 241, 247.

[12] G Marx, 'Internet Anonymity as a Reflection of Broader Issues Involving Technology and Society' (2004) 11 *Asia-Pacific Review* 142, 143.

[13] ibid 143–44.

[14] V Smith Ekstrand, 'The Many Masks of Anon: Anonymity As Cultural Practice and Reflections in Case Law' (2013) 18 *Journal of Technology Law & Policy* 1, 5.

This further informs us that, in terms of identity status, there is not a binary distinction between being anonymous and being identified as identity knowledge can be accumulated in different ways, some provided intentionally by the individual and others provided passively or sought out separately by the receiver. It is therefore more accurate to frame anonymity as one end of a spectrum with full identification at the other, whereby individuals use varying 'layers of cloaking' to reach different degrees of anonymity.[15] Where pseudonymity fits in with this requires some specific clarification. Nissenbaum includes pseudonymity within the general anonymity spectrum, somewhere below full anonymity and above full identification, but this is not an uncontested view. Rather, others have argued that while anonymity is a state, pseudonymity is an identity practice,[16] or that anonymity and pseudonymity are fundamentally different 'modes of being' online.[17] This book chooses to talk about pseudonymity as an identity practice where it involves an individual's choice, for example to employ a username instead of their real name; a partially identifiable identity status is instead subsumed into the wider discussion of anonymity.

The final element of nuance to address is that an individual can be anonymous or identified in different spheres and different ways. For example, Bachmann distinguishes between social, technical, discursive and legal anonymity.[18] As will be seen in later chapters, identifiability in the social and legal spheres is particularly relevant to the discussion in the book. Consequently, our discussions of anonymity here are focused on those spheres and particularly whether the individual could be (a) traced, reached or identified to their offline identity, and/or (b) traced, reached or identified to their other online activities by other users.

B. Creativity

Creativity as a concept can be interpreted in various ways. For example, Cohen identifies that legal narratives around creativity in copyright are often focused on creativity as production of works, rather than any particular quality of that work or the process behind production.[19] Conversely, psychology scholars understand creativity as a characteristic of either a person or an end product.[20] Some discuss

[15] Nissenbaum (n 7) 155.

[16] B Hogan, 'Pseudonyms and the Rise of the Real-Name Web' in J Hartley, J Burgess and A Bruns (eds), *A Companion to New Media Dynamics* (Chichester, Wiley-Blackwell, 2013) 293; E Van der Nagel and J Frith, 'Anonymity, Pseudonymity, and the Agency of Online Identity: Examining the Social Practices of r/Gonewild' (2015) 20 *First Monday*: firstmonday.org/ojs/index.php/fm/article/view/5615.

[17] L Knuttila, 'User Unknown: 4chan, Anonymity and Contingency' (2011) 16 *First Monday*: firstmonday.org/ojs/index.php/fm/article/view/3665.

[18] Bachmann, Knecht and Wittel (n 11) 247.

[19] JE Cohen, 'Creativity and Culture in Copyright Theory' (2007) 40 *UC Davis Law Review* 1151, 1152.

[20] BA Hennessey and TM Amabile, 'Creativity' (2010) 61 *Annual Review of Psychology* 569.

creativity as an activity ('creative enterprises'),[21] others as a neurological,[22] social or psychological process.[23] There is also a 'common-sense understanding'[24] where creativity is most likely to be understood in relation specifically to artistic, literary and similar contexts.

This book's approach to creativity navigates these multiple, sometimes overlapping, meanings by using the concept of 'creativity' as an umbrella term that will be adapted to the different contexts explored in the chapters that follow. This is achieved by referring to the creative process, creative practices, the creative product and creative ability or characteristics. However, for practical reasons of scope, and also because this falls within the everyday understanding of creativity without controversy, the focus of this book is specifically on artistic and literary creativity in the format of user-generated content.

IV. Overview of Chapters

Chapter two explores the creative and legal positions of user-generated content. The first part of the chapter explores the world of UGC by describing core elements of the environment, with particular reference to the field sites of Reddit and 4chan. These elements include categories of UGC, interactions with UGC, and pervasive anonymity. It also specifically highlights the link between UGC and creativity by focusing on a significant part of this phenomenon: the online sharing of artistic, photographic and literary works (creative UGC).

The second part of the chapter explores the relationship between copyright and CUGC. It undertakes a doctrinal analysis to demonstrate that copyright will subsist in much CUGC, and that copyright law will regulate many of the interactions with it once it is shared online. It then explores the challenges faced by copyright in acting as an effective regulator of CUGC, in particular those resulting from online anonymity. It argues that pervasive online anonymity undermines copyright in UGC as it restricts or confuses protection, licensing and enforcement attempts and reduces legal certainty.

Chapter three looks at the relationships between creativity and both copyright law and anonymity. It commences with an exploration of the creativity rhetoric that underpins arguments supporting copyright law and its expansion. The chapter argues that using the concept of creativity to guide what copyright law looks like is normatively coherent, but that there is a disconnect between copyright's current conception of creativity and creativity in reality. It demonstrates this disconnect

[21] P Ganley, 'The Internet, Creativity and Copyright Incentives' (2005) 10 *Journal of Intellectual Property Rights* 188.

[22] E Reuveni, 'Copyright, Neuroscience and Creativity' (2013) 64 *Alabama Law Review* 735.

[23] TM Amabile, *Creativity in Context*, 2nd edn (New York, Routledge, 2018).

[24] RW Weisberg, 'On the Usefulness of "Value" in the Definition of Creativity' (2015) 27 *Creativity Research Journal* 111, 116.

by examining who benefits from copyright law and how the law reflects creative processes, in particular in relation to authorship and incentives.

The chapter further explores creativity in the anonymous online world. Presenting qualitative findings, it explores the impact of pervasive online anonymity on CUGC creator practices and identifies several creative benefits. Based on this anonymous creativity, the chapter develops a critique of copyright, highlighting that anonymity practices while creating challenges for copyright law are often advantageous for creativity, and furthermore benefit creativity in ways that copyright law fails to.

Chapter four presents qualitative findings on social norms regarding 'ownership' of shared content found in online creative communities on 4chan and Reddit. It explores the relationship between pervasive anonymity and the concepts of ownership or exclusive rights over CUGC. It demonstrates that while sharing CUGC in the anonymous online environment could be interpreted as an act that is politically or practically incompatible with the exclusive rights that copyright provides, it is inaccurate to view such acts as a dedication to the public domain.

The chapter goes on to outline the normative rules that instead regulate interactions with CUGC once it is shared online, comparing these to the regulatory framework provided by copyright law. This part of the discussion explores concepts of originality, authorship, rights and justification narratives. While it identifies significant differences between the two systems, in particular the comparative permissiveness of the norms system, the chapter also highlights that these differences do not equate to a fundamental incompatibility of values that would preclude coherent copyright reform to narrow the gap.

Chapter five presents qualitative findings about how the social norms identified in chapter four are communicated and enforced. It describes, explains and evaluates fours steps of this process: communication and interpretation of norms; deterrence of transgression; detection of transgression; and remedies or sanctions for transgression. The role of anonymity within these processes is also explained, finding that it causes some practical problems for individuals but offers benefits to community-level approaches.

The chapter then goes on to evaluate the efficiency of the norms system as a regulator of the use of CUGC. It highlights that the system is flawed as it lacks clarity and certainty, and this could undermine the CUGC sharing community. It also argues that these issues are further entrenched by the confusion caused by the simultaneous applicability of different rules under copyright law.

Chapter six interrogates the need for copyright reform based on the findings in previous chapters. It begins by detailing an argument for reform, first linked to the needs of the CUGC environment specifically, and secondly linked to broader critiques of copyright, underpinned by the interrelationship between copyright, creativity and anonymity.

The chapter then goes on to consider what copyright reform should look like. It explores the potential of existing reform narratives, including those focused specifically on UGC, to address the flaws identified in the existing system.

The chapter argues that a generally more permissive copyright system would be supported by the findings in this book, but that existing UGC reform proposals largely overlook the role of CUGC creator as copyright owner, and thereby risk entrenching the problem reform seeks to address. As such, this chapter suggests supplementary guidelines to fill this gap.

The concluding chapter, chapter seven, summarises the key findings set out in the book and reiterates the overall argument in relation to the gaps and flaws in copyright law as it stands. It ends by putting forward practical suggestions for CUGC creators, CUGC communities and CUGC users to help them navigate and mitigate the complexities of sharing and using CUGC in the current copyright regime and by considering the future of CUGC.

V. Methods

The book emerges from a range of methodologies, combining doctrinal and secondary research with empirical work. In relation to doctrinal research, the jurisdictional focus of the book is the United Kingdom (UK), the United States (US) and Germany (as harmonised with European Union (EU) law). Of course, this does not fully reflect the transnational context of CUGC, where CUGC creators from anywhere in the world can share their work on websites run from different countries to then be viewed by a global audience. It is also acknowledged that this approach likely overlooks some of the nuances of copyright law in other jurisdictions. However, the choice of jurisdictions was made for practical reasons as it would not be possible to include every possible applicable legal system. The jurisdictions chosen reflect the demographic data for the chosen field sites at the start of the project, with the UK, the US and Germany in the top five contributing countries at the time.[25] Furthermore, the chosen jurisdictions reflect both common and civil law traditions and represent some of the most influential legal systems in global copyright law and policy, particularly the US and the EU.

The qualitative findings in the book draw from two related research studies, whose methods are outlined here. Both studies comprised observational work focused on discussion threads posted on creative communities on the websites Reddit and 4chan. The first study also comprised online interviews with 12 creators from those creative communities.

The first study ('the main study') explored the relationship between copyright law, creativity and anonymity in online communities, looking specifically at what motivated CUGC creators to create and share their work, views on how their CUGC could be used once shared online and how these were enforced, and views

[25] '4chan.com Traffic Statistics' (*Alexa*, 2018): web.archive.org/web/20180417214612/https://www.alexa.com/siteinfo/4chan.com; 'Reddit.com Traffic Statistics' (*Alexa*, 2016): web.archive.org/web/20161009191623/https://www.alexa.com/siteinfo/reddit.com.

on copyright and related concepts. After this study was completed, the online creative world experienced a significant shift, as generative AI technology became widespread and has been increasingly used to produce the sorts of creative outputs this book is exploring. As a result, another study ('the AI study') was undertaken to supplement the main study by exploring the impact of those tools on the first study's findings. In both studies, the focus was on CUGC that could be categorised as either (static, two-dimensional) art, photography, or literary or dramatic writing.

The interviews took place between December 2017 and April 2018. The observational work for the main study took place between January and August 2018. However, due to the archive nature of the internet, data was collected from discussion threads posted between 1 September 2016 and 31 August 2018. The AI study took place over four weeks in June and July 2024, with data collected from discussion threads posted from 1 January 2024 and 4 July 2024.

The observational work in both studies used the same research design, underpinned by netnographic methods and principles. These are designed to guide in-depth research into social media and online communities using the data that is shared freely online.[26] The main study collected and analysed 356 discussion threads (217 from Reddit and 139 from 4chan) and also comprised online interviews with 12 creators from those creative communities. The second study analysed 73 discussion threads (44 from Reddit and 29 from 4chan). A reflexive thematic analysis of the data was undertaken, using NVIVO software to facilitate the coding process and theme development.

A. Field Sites

Choosing appropriate field sites for research into CUGC is not a simple task: there is a huge range of potentially relevant websites, communities, forums and platforms that could all provide interesting, meaningful data. Reddit and 4chan were chosen as field sites from a long list of options based on five selection criteria: widespread sharing of creative UGC; relevant types of creativity; sufficient levels of regular interaction with shared creative works within a community and discussions about creative topics; significantly sized; and strong normative attitudes towards use of pseudonyms or anonymity.

Reddit is a popular website where users can share written comments, images and video. Posts to Reddit are organised based on a user-rating system, so posts that receive more 'up-votes' are more prominent on the website. Users have a username (styled as *u/username*), and this is most commonly a pseudonym rather than a real name. Users only need to provide an email address to sign up. The site is arranged into a wide variety of communities, known as subreddits

[26] R Kozinets, *Netnography: Redefined* (London, SAGE Publications, 2015) 67, 79.

(styled as *r/name*). These can be set up by any user and so there are many hundreds of thousands, if not millions, of subreddits at any one time. These cover almost any topic you can think of, from the surreal and esoteric (*r/breadstapledtotrees* – dedicated to sharing images of bread stapled to trees), to the general (*r/politics*). A large number of subreddits focus on creative activities and interests. Subreddits can be made private, but most popular subreddits are open for anyone to join or just to access, even without being signed up to a Reddit account. While it is possible to 'follow' specific users and to view all their posts and comments by clicking on their profile, the focus of interactions on Reddit is community-based discussion. This makes it a convenient field site to gather discussion threads on particular topics.

4chan is an image-based bulletin board-style website, split into various 'boards' dedicated to specific topics, including several dedicated to creative activities. Within each of these boards, users can post images and text, either starting a new thread on a topic or adding to an existing thread. Users can post anonymously (with the username showing only as 'Anonymous') or they can choose to provide a username to accompany their post. There is no need to have an account to view or post, and users can change their username with each post if they wish – it is as simple as changing what they type into the relevant box when making the post. The only way to maintain a verifiable, linked identity across posts is with the use of a specific function called a tripcode. Most posts are anonymous, and the acceptability of use of tripcodes is limited to certain narrow contexts. The specific boards are generated by 4chan, so users cannot create new ones. There is no archive function on the 4chan website, so inactive threads are deleted to make space for new ones when they fall to the bottom of the board.[27]

It should be noted that 4chan has a reputation for being controversial. It is not a 'mainstream' website in the way that others such as Reddit or Instagram are and is most often associated with online behaviours such as trolling, doxing and harassment, and a high tolerance for racism, misogyny and the alt right.[28] It is certainly the case that some of the discussions collected as data for the studies included abusive, offensive or otherwise irreverent content, but the creative boards on 4chan attract far less attention for this as they are neither as controversial nor as political as the more popular and better known boards such as */b/* (the 'random' board, which has very few rules) or */pol/* ('politically incorrect'). Instead, 4chan was selected as a field site due to its value as a creative space – many of the most famous internet memes such as LOLcats, began life on 4chan[29] – and particularly

[27] There are, however, some external websites that archive 4chan posts.

[28] A Nagle, *Kill All Normies: Online Culture Wars from 4Chan and Tumblr to Trump and the Alt-Right* (Lanham, John Hunt Publishing, 2017) 14, 15; M Tuters, E Jokubauskaitė and D Bach, 'Post-Truth Protest: How 4chan Cooked Up the Pizzagate Bullshit' (2018) 21 *M/C Journal*: journal.media-culture.org.au/index.php/mcjournal/article/view/142; A Zelenkauskaite et al, 'Shades of Hatred Online: 4chan Duplicate Circulation Surge during Hybrid Media Events' [2021] *First Monday*: firstmonday.org/ojs/index.php/fm/article/view/11075.

[29] Knuttila (n 17).

as it has an unusually high culture of anonymity for its users. Like Reddit, it also provided practical benefits to data collection due to the way that interactions are structured within communities. Other popular platforms such as Instagram, TikTok and Facebook were discounted due to their heavy focus on posts from individuals, collated via hashtag, rather than community discussion.

Within the two selected field sites, specific communities were chosen to observe and collect data from. This was straightforward on 4chan, where the number of creative boards is relatively low. Therefore, all the creative boards that met the selection criteria outlined above were included in the study. These were oekaki (drawing), known as /i/; artwork/critique, known as /ic/; and photography, known as /p/, with most of the data ultimately coming from /ic/ and /p/ in both studies. Selecting subreddits was a more complicated task as there are many to choose from. For the main study, the most popular creative subreddits were identified,[30] alongside a snowball approach including the author's personal exploration of the platform, recommendations from community members and suggestions made by other subreddits. When considering their suitability, the decision-making was guided by the same criteria for choosing the platforms. For the AI study, a smaller number of subreddits – largely those observed during the main study – were included.[31] It should be noted that some of the subreddits chosen focus was on discussion of creative issues rather than sharing of CUGC. These were included because of their rich debates on relevant issues, with the assumption that there is cross-over between the users of these subreddits and those where CUGC is shared. This is the case, for example, with r/photography which is for discussion about photography but has a sister subreddit (r/photographs) for sharing.

B. Observation

Both of the studies' observational work comprised regular overviews of live community discussions alongside keyword searches to find discussion threads relevant to the research questions. In the first study this involved the use of third-party search tools built for Reddit and 4chan,[32] but in the second study keyword searches were done using the native search bar due to a change in Reddit's terms of use and a lack of an up-to-date and reliable archive for 4chan.

The approach taken necessarily means that the dataset is not a random sample. However, it was preferred over a more structured process using random sampling of a dataset created by a web scraping tool as the latter would have undermined a key element of the netnographic approach. Kozinets et al explain that such tools 'overshadow real time engagement with the cultural context' and

[30] 'Redditlist.Com – Tracking the Top 5000 Subreddits' (*redditlist*): www.redditlist.com.
[31] A list of the subreddits chosen can be found in the Appendix.
[32] Pushshift.io and archived.moe.

undermine understanding.[33] Whether a discussion thread was included in the dataset depended on whether there was sufficient interaction with the research issue for it to be considered rich data (assessed in relation to the number of participants and the depth of points made) and whether saturation had been achieved.[34]

C. Interviews

Interviewees were recruited using convenience sampling, via requests posted on relevant communities on Reddit and 4chan. Again, this approach means that it cannot be confirmed to be a representative sample. Eight of the 12 interviewees were Reddit users and four were 4chan users. In order to embed respect for anonymity and identity practices within the research design, little personal information was requested from participants. Some provided their 'real' name but others did not.[35] Information on location or gender was not requested and participants were only required to confirm they were over the age of 18. This approach aligns with online ethnographic and netnographic methodologies that reject the idea of the offline world as the 'real' world and see internet data as complete rather than partial.[36]

Interviews were semi-structured and conducted either by online instant message services (Discord, Skype Instant Message or Facebook chat) or Skype voice chat, according to the preferences of the interviewee. Instant messaging has some limitations including reduced additional social cues and increased mediacy through typing of responses,[37] but offered several benefits to the research design, including mirroring the online environment being studied, providing participants with control over their online identity practices, and attracting and facilitating participation from individuals from all over the world.

D. Limitations and Validity

Care must be taken when interpreting qualitative findings, as they are necessarily limited to the specific time, context, field sites and participants of the dataset

[33] R Kozinets, P-Y Dolbec and A Earley, 'Netnographic Analysis: Understanding Culture Through Social Media Data' in U Flick (ed), *The SAGE Handbook of Qualitative Data Analysis* (London, SAGE Publications, 2014) 267.

[34] SL Faulkner and SP Trotter, 'Data Saturation' in *The International Encyclopedia of Communication Research Methods* (Hoboken, NJ, John Wiley & Sons, 2017) 1.

[35] Interview participants have been given pseudonyms in this book that reflect the level of anonymity they chose in their interactions with me. Interview participant information can be found in the Appendix.

[36] C Hine, *Virtual Ethnography* (London, SAGE Publications, 2000) 144; Kozinets (n 26) 81.

[37] R Opdenakker, 'Advantages and Disadvantages of Four Interview Techniques in Qualitative Research' (2006) 7 *Forum: Qualitative Social Research* Art 11; N King and C Horrocks, *Interviews in Qualitative Research* (London, SAGE, 2010) 19–28.

they are based on. This means that the qualitative findings cannot be generalised to apply to all CUGC contexts, and so the book draws on findings from a range of other studies to support wider claims. There are also some limitations of the study design: first, that the sampling is not random or representative, and secondly, that it is not possible to authenticate the interview participants due to the prioritisation of their identity choices. In mitigation, two strategies were employed to ensure validity: a dataset built from more than one type of data (observational data and interview data), and prolonged and persistent observation producing thick, rich data.[38] Findings across both types of data were consistent.

E. Ethics

Ethical approval for the interviews in the main study was granted by Queen Mary Ethics of Research Committee (QMERC).[39] All interview participants provided written informed consent before participation, including consent to inclusion in future publications of their anonymised data.

QMERC deemed it unnecessary to seek ethical approval for the observational element of the study as it used data from publicly accessible online discussion threads. Conversely, ethical approval was sought for observational work in the AI study, and granted by the Royal Holloway, University of London Research Ethics Committee.[40] Regardless of whether approval was sought for the observational work in the studies, steps were taken to ensure it was conducted in an ethical manner. These steps focused on two key ethical issues: the inability for informed consent to be given by those who have contributed to discussion threads online, and the possibility that those contributors may be under 18 or vulnerable.

While online discussion threads are publicly accessible, the scholarship on this area highlights that much of what is shared online is seen as within a specific context or community and that external uses of this can go beyond a user's expectations.[41] There can also be concerns about creating a permanent record of online posts within the dataset, which undermines the inherent ephemerality of 4chan (where there is no archive and threads are deleted when new ones are posted) and the ability for Reddit users to delete posts whenever they like. The research design minimised and mitigated these risks in several ways.

[38] JM Morse, 'Critical Analysis of Strategies for Determining Rigor in Qualitative Inquiry' (2015) 25 *Qualitative Health Research* 1212, 1214–16.

[39] Approval reference number: QMERC2017/54.

[40] Project ID: 4167.

[41] A Markham, 'The Methods, Politics, and Ethics of Representation in Online Ethnography' in NK Denzin and YS Lincoln (eds), *Collecting and Interpreting Qualitative Materials*, 3rd edn (Thousand Oaks, CA, SAGE Publications, 2008) 274; Kozinets (n 26) 131.

First, the data was anonymised so no usernames or otherwise identifying details are included in this book and they were redacted on collection in the AI study. To prevent the potential for posts to be linked back to individual users by searching online, no direct quotations from discussion posts are included in this book. Instead, quotations are only included when provided by interview participants who provided express consent. The dataset of discussion threads was also not made publicly accessible. Secondly, to further minimise the potential for research findings to be linked to individual users, the research draws data from a number of communities, rather than just one or two. This helps to further abstract the findings from specific individuals or communities. Thirdly, in the case of Reddit (where membership numbers are available), communities were chosen as field sites as they are very large and therefore it is more reasonable to expect that individuals understand that their posts will reach a wide audience.

The research did not specifically target vulnerable participants or under 18s, but due to the online nature of the research, it cannot be guaranteed that some of the discussion comments collected as data would not come from people in this group. Reddit's minimum user age is 13, while on 4chan it is 18, but there are no mechanisms within the sites to enforce this. As the study topic is not sensitive, the risk to these individuals is low, but was minimised by discarding any data that suggests that the person writing it fell within this category (for example, mentioning that they are in high school). The risk was further minimised by the mitigations outlined for informed consent.

2

Understanding (Creative) User-Generated Content and Copyright

I. Introduction

Creative user-generated content (CUGC) is the core focus of this book and therefore this chapter provides a necessary exploration of the creative and legal positions that relate to this type of content. The first part of the chapter explores the world of user-generated content, focusing on the creative part of this phenomenon: the online sharing of artistic, photographic and literary works. To do this, it explores core elements of this environment including types of CUGC, how CUGC is interacted with, and the pervasive anonymity that characterises the CUGC environment. This provides initial context for the discussions that follow, both within this chapter and those that follow.

The second part of the chapter explores the relationship between copyright law and CUGC. It highlights that, from a doctrinal perspective, copyright subsists in much CUGC, and that copyright law therefore regulates many interactions with CUGC. However, it also outlines the challenges faced by copyright in acting as an effective regulator of those interactions. The chapter argues that pervasive online anonymity undermines this in a variety of ways, demonstrating that while within the letter of the law copyright protection is available, it will often be an ineffective and flawed system where anonymity is widespread. Consequently, this raises some practical questions to be addressed in later chapters.

II. The User-Generated Content Environment

What follows in this part of the chapter is a description of the CUGC environment, which aims to provide some essential clarity and context about what it is, specifically, that is meant when the book talks about CUGC. However, this is not necessarily straightforward: the general UGC environment is diverse and complex, making efforts to put forward a definitive or exhaustive description challenging if not impossible. The approach here relies mostly on examples from the field sites, 4chan and Reddit, but in many cases they will have a broader application to other online platforms, and efforts are focused on providing clarity on those elements of the UGC environment relevant to the focus of this book.

A. Creative UGC

Let us first start with what we should understand by 'creative UGC'. Unpicking this is valuable for several reasons. First, it should help to convince you that CUGC is worth the specific consideration this book gives it by demonstrating that it is a common and significant form of UGC. Secondly, by outlining some of the characteristics and variations of CUGC, it provides some general context and background knowledge that will be important for discussions later in the book. And thirdly, it provides the opportunity to contextualise some methodological decisions by situating the specific types of CUGC focused on in this book within a broader understanding of UGC. To achieve this, it outlines the *what*, the *where* and the *who* of sharing CUGC.[1]

So, ***what*** is creative UGC, as opposed to non-creative UGC? UGC comes in many forms. It can be a post discussing an article on an online news website, it can be a photograph of someone's dinner shared on Instagram, it can be computer code added to Github, it can be a watercolour painting uploaded to Reddit. It can be a contribution to Wikipedia, a heart posted under a friend's engagement announcement on Facebook, or a screenshot of a rude email posted on Facebook. Some, or maybe all of these, could be argued to be 'creative' in some way, depending on how one chooses to interpret it, but not all would be the focus of this book. To distinguish the two forms of UGC, a starting point can be to rely on an everyday understanding of 'creative', linked to the use of one's imagination and particularly to artistic production,[2] or perhaps more clearly, looking for whether the UGC is the result of *creative practice*. We could ask: would we consider the person who made that post to be a *creator*? Based on this approach, the watercolour painting would be CUGC but the heart emoji not.

However, to help unravel this a bit further, giving some examples of different types of CUGC will be valuable, as well as being helpful in illustrating some of the variation within the category. CUGC can encompass a range of branches of creativity, for example painting, drawing, video, poetry or digital art. Furthermore, within these branches it is possible to find both traditional expressions (such as photographs, stories and drawing) and non-traditional expressions (such as memes, video mashups, or Tiktok dances) of these types of creative practice. What would be less likely to be considered CUGC is content such as standard discussion posts and other everyday forms of online interaction.

As explained in chapter one, the specific forms of CUGC that were considered in the studies underpinning this book were static 2D art forms (including drawing, painting, digital painting, Photoshop artwork) and written creativity (including story-writing and scriptwriting). It is not practically feasible to consider all types of CUGC, and therefore there needed to be some focus on specific areas.

[1] See ch 3, section II.C for the *why*.
[2] 'Creative, adj', *Oxford English Dictionary* (Oxford, Oxford University Press, 2011).

These were chosen as straightforward and uncontroversial examples of CUGC, underpinned by well-known and well-understood forms of creative practice, but the author acknowledges there will certainly be some instances of UGC where categorisation is a blurrier task. While the findings in this book are drawn from specific areas, later discussions in the book wrangle with some of the greyer areas[3] and therefore give some indication of wider applicability.

It should also be noted that the increased accessibility of AI technology has not bypassed CUGC practices. Although later chapters will highlight community disdain and concerns for the impact of such technologies on creativity generally and the CUGC environment specifically, it is still the case that some CUGC will have been created using AI in some way. This could range from using generative AI services such as ChatGPT, DALL-E and Midjourney to execute the full expression of the user's idea, to the use of AI enhanced tools for creative practice, such as in photography editing. There are arguments to be made that generative AI technology cannot accurately be described as 'creative' and is better understood as a facsimile of human creativity, and therefore to consider such outputs to be CUGC would be flawed. For example, Gervais argues that generative AI technologies *produce* outputs rather than *create* them within copyright law's understanding of (human) authorship.[4] However, this book chooses not to exclude them from its consideration for a number of reasons. First, it is not always straightforward to identify whether – or to what extent – AI technology has been used in UGC and so it does not seem to be a helpful or practical way of distinguishing CUGC from other content. Secondly, the use of 'creative' to describe UGC in this context can afford to be a little more flexible in its scope as it is focused on being able to visually identify and categorise types of content, rather than Gervais whose analysis is focused on the application and analysis of legal doctrine. Furthermore, those doctrinal questions are considered in more detail in the later parts of this chapter.

Moving on to describe some CUGC in more detail, we can also see there are many ways in which it can vary. This helps us to understand what CUGC is, while also giving us an initial insight into its scale and scope. The first element of variation is in terms of the balance between how much of the output stems from the CUGC creator themselves and how much derives from existing works and content. In his copyright taxonomy of user-generated content, Gervais names three types of content that help to illustrate this: user-authored, user-derived and user-copied.[5] User-authored content is created without directly incorporating

[3] eg, does copyright subsist in snapshots, and what level of creative effort is required for community members to view UGC as art?

[4] D Gervais, 'The Machine as Author' (2020) 105 *Iowa Law Review* 2053, 2098–99; D Gervais, 'AI Derivatives: The Application to the Derivative Work Right to Literary and Artistic Productions of AI Machines' (2022) 52 *Seton Hall Law Review* 1111, 1113.

[5] D Gervais, *(Re)Structuring Copyright: A Comprehensive Path to International Copyright Reform* (Cheltenham, Edward Elgar Publishing, 2017) 131–36.

elements of existing works, for example a sketch of a creature imagined and drawn by the person who posted it. User-derived content includes elements of other works within it, for example a wallpaper design for a mobile phone created by the person posting it but including design elements from a superhero film. User-copied content is a direct copy of existing works, for example a simple repost of someone else's work such as a famous photograph or artwork. Creative UGC falling into either of the first two categories (user-authored or user-derived) comes within the remit of this book. The latter category (user-copied) is relevant to discussions relating to interactions with creative UGC.

Creative UGC created with the help of generative AI tools does not fit neatly within these categories, although there remain variations in the input of the 'user' in such AI-generated or AI-assisted outputs and in how derivative they are of previous existing works. The former is dependent on how involved the user is in the prompting of such outputs, and in the subsequent editing. The latter is reliant on the size of the training dataset[6] and the practical execution of the prompt. As will be demonstrated below, the concepts of authorship and derivation in AI-generated outputs are contentious in a legal context. However, in trying to understand and categorise the types of CUGC one might encounter, it is less significant to us at this stage due to the challenges of reliably identifying where CUGC is AI generated or AI assisted, or of the extent of user input and of the specific tool used.

Another variation within CUGC is in terms of proficiency, with a wide range of capabilities showcased. Complete beginners and first-time creators post alongside highly competent creators, with a range of abilities found on the spectrum in between. Related to this is the ***who*** of CUGC; CUGC creators vary from hobbyist to professional, with everything that falls in between, including those aspiring to be professional in the future. This book considers all forms of content and all forms of creator in this regard.

Where CUGC is shared is also open to variation and indicates the wide variety of options available to creators, some of which have already been used as examples in this chapter (Instagram, Github, Wikipedia). For the purposes of this study, the focus was on specifically creative communities on the 4chan and Reddit platforms, although CUGC is often also shared within non-creative communities.[7] For example, a satirical cartoon might be shared within a politics community, rather than (or as well as) an art community. As outlined in chapter one, the focus on community-based posting rather than individual profiles on these platforms contributed to their suitability as research field sites but does not necessarily

[6] eg, the Next Rembrandt project was only trained on 346 Rembrandt paintings and so necessarily and purposefully created something highly derivative, whereas OpenAI's DALL-E image generator was trained on 650 million images, and Stable Diffusion on 2.3 billion: 'The Next Rembrandt: Recreating the Work of a Master with AI' (*Microsoft News Centre Europe*, 13 April 2016): news.microsoft.com/europe/features/next-rembrandt.

[7] Madhumita Murgia and Ian Johnston, 'Art and Artificial Intelligence Collide in Landmark Legal Dispute' (21 January 2023): www.ft.com/content/d691d599-3cdb-48d8-9824-9b2784a17d90.

indicate substantial differences from other platforms. Those with more focus on the individual still create equivalent communities, albeit less formally structured, for example on Instagram and TikTok, hashtags can be used to contribute to particular communities.

So far it has been highlighted that CUGC can take many forms, express a variety of creative practices, can be high or low quality, made by different types of creators, and shared in a variety of ways and in a variety of places online. This potential for multifaceted variety goes some way to indicate the scale of CUGC and its scope to be a significant aspect of the UGC environment. This is further entrenched by the fact that, for the everyday social media user, this description of CUGC will be nothing particularly new or unfamiliar. The extent of involvement in and exposure to CUGC can be seen by looking at one of the creative subreddits from the study: r/Art. This subreddit currently has over 20 million members and is in the top 25 of subreddits by membership (out of hundreds of thousands).[8] It often receives several hundred posts per day, with several hundred comments on those posts.[9] While other creative communities may have lower membership, or lower participation and engagement, they nonetheless contribute cumulatively to the fact that CUGC is a major aspect of the UGC environment. It also suggests that CUGC can be significant within the wider creative environment. Considering the potential scale and reach of creative UGC communities, it seems essential to consider their value to the creative environment alongside more traditional routes to dissemination and development.[10]

B. Interactions with Creative UGC

Once shared online, other people are able to interact with CUGC. This section does the important task of setting up a taxonomy of the different elements of these interactions, as well as providing some context on stakeholders and where and how these interactions take place.

First there needs to be some explanation of the various individuals and stakeholders who interact with CUGC and it is useful for later discussions to categorise them according to the type of interaction they are involved in. Members of online communities are most often referred to as 'users' but this does not adequately reflect the range of different roles available to them. Meese rejects the use of 'user'

[8] Reddit, 'R/Art': www.reddit.com/r/Art; Subreddit Stats, 'Statistics for Every Subreddit': subredditstats.com; Statista, 'Reddit – Statistics & Facts': www.statista.com/topics/5672/reddit.

[9] Subreddit Stats, 'r/Art Stats': subredditstats.com/r/Art.

[10] Later chapters also examine the role that CUGC plays for creators and explain how they describe some common themes linking CUGC to the wider creative economy, whether through its role in their professional creative lives, or their aspirations to one day make money from their creative practices in the 'real world'.

as a blanket term in these cases, arguing that it is not a neutral term and in fact entrenches views of them as not being creators in their own right.[11] Similarly, terms that frame them through more 'active' vocabulary (such as 'prosumer') have also been criticised for over-representing the levels of actual active participation in these communities.[12] It is therefore important to be clear about the distinct roles 'users' play in interactions with CUGC.

The active roles individuals play in these interactions can be divided into *creator*, *commenter*, *remixer*, *utiliser* and *distributor*. Individuals can, and often do, play several or all of these roles at one time within a community and within an interaction. Creators are those who create and share creative UGC, while commenters are those who post feedback and comments on it (or vote on it on Reddit).[13] Utilisers (distinguished from 'users' in this more specific definition) are those who use CUGC without any substantial modification (for example, by setting a photograph as the background on their personal website). Remixers also use CUGC but in a creative way that involves modifying it to some extent. These last two roles represent ends of a continuum of use, with one end signifying there has been no change to the original content and the other signifying the content has been changed completely. Distributors are those who re-share or publish the CUGC in some form, usually online. There are other roles within the communities that do not involve interaction with CUGC, including those who post non-creative UGC, and 'lurkers' who are those who access but do not interact with the community at all. This chapter focuses on creators, utilisers, remixers and distributors[14] as they are the ones whose actions raise copyright issues.[15]

From this framework of stakeholder roles, we can derive several categories of interaction with creative UGC: remix, utilisation, remix and re-share, utilisation online, re-share and feedback and commentary. The first, 'remix', is where creative content is transformed or altered. This could include using CUGC as a prompt for a generative AI tool. The second is 'utilisation' where creative content is used

[11] J Meese, 'User Production and Law Reform: A Socio-Legal Critique of User Creativity' (2015) 37 *Media, Culture & Society* 753, 762.

[12] Van Dijck cites a study that found that over half of users are 'inactives' and one third 'passive spectators', while only 13% were 'active participants' where they create and share content; these sorts of terms are, therefore, an overly simplistic way of approaching a more nuanced selection of roles: J Van Dijck, 'Users like You? Theorizing Agency in User-Generated Content' (2009) 31 *Media, Culture &* Society 41, 44.

[13] While the latter is not a significant consideration in this chapter, it should be noted that the opportunity to get feedback, edits and suggestions from others is often a driver in the decision to share creative UGC in online communities. In the interviews conducted in the main study with UGC creators, it was seen as an important and accessible element of their creative training and this provides an insight into why these communities can be important to the creative economy.

[14] The role of commenters is not discussed in detail in this chapter, but will be indirectly discussed in ch 3 and ch 5 in reference to feedback and enforcement mechanisms respectively.

[15] It should also be noted that traditional copyright industries are potential stakeholders in these interactions, eg, where content is derived from the works they control. As previously discussed, many scholars have explored the relationship between copyright law, 'user-derived' creative content and the copyright industries, and so this is not a primary focus of this book.

for a particular purpose without being transformed or altered. If the interaction takes place online, these categories are necessarily amended to take into account the distribution aspect, becoming 'remix and re-share' (where creative content is transformed or altered, and then reposted as user-derived creative content) and 'utilisation online' (where creative content is used online in its original format for a specific purpose, rather than shared as content).[16] This utilisation could also include the use of CUGC in generative AI training datasets. Online interactions also include the further categories of 're-share', where creative content is shared again as (user-copied) creative content in its original format, and 'feedback and commentary', where people interact with creative content by commenting, discussing, and – where relevant – upvoting or liking.

These interactions can also be categorised according to where they take place. Due to the accessible nature of these platforms, interaction is not solely limited to community members. Consequently, interactions may take place within the original community where the content was posted ('intra-community', for example within the same 4chan board); outside the original community but within the same platform ('extra-community', for example on another subreddit); outside the original platform but on another platform or website ('extra-platform'); or offline. Furthermore, due to the commenting structure on 4chan and Reddit and the ability for these interactions to take place cross-platform (for example, through a re-share), interactions are not necessarily linear. This creates a network of interaction where CUGC can feature in various positions.

From the descriptions set out in this section, we can see that there is a broad range of creative UGC and a variety of ways that individuals can interact with it within a large-scale online environment made up of individuals, communities, platforms and websites and the offline world. As with the description of CUGC above, the scale and complexity of these interactions highlights the significance of this issue.

C. Anonymity

The last aspect of the CUGC environment to discuss is that of online anonymity. Online anonymity is often understood to mean that someone does not use their real name when participating in the CUGC environment. Under this narrow view, anonymity is the result of individual identity practices, that is, whether a person chooses to provide their name or not, but the reality of anonymity is more complex, with a variety of other factors and variables that need to be considered. This means that regardless of identity practices, anonymity is a pervasive characteristic of the CUGC environment.

[16] It should be noted that acts of distribution may or may not include attribution to the original creator.

First, anonymity encompasses more than just namelessness. Such a narrow understanding of the term fails to reflect what anonymity actually conceals: it is not simply our names, but our broader identities.[17] Consequently, anonymity has been more accurately defined through the connected ideas of unreachability,[18] 'untraceability',[19] unidentifiability,[20] or unavailability of information[21] or of identity knowledge.[22] Chapter one set out Marx's idea of 'identity knowledge' and the different forms that can take.[23] Beyond providing a real offline name, there are other forms of identity knowledge that are key to the CUGC context. The key examples of these are an online username or pseudonym; routes to contact (for example, an email address, or more commonly built-in platform messaging tools); patterns of behaviour such as written or artistic style;[24] and personal information about their 'typification' such as gender or race or about their geographic location.

Secondly, it is not always a result of individual choices when identity information is available. A person's identity practices will also be influenced by platform requirements (for example, Facebook's real name policy) and cultural norms. For example, there is a widespread culture of anonymity practices on some platforms, and that is particularly the case on 4chan, where the majority of users post as 'Anonymous', and on Reddit, where most users post under a pseudonym. To reveal one's identity in some way on 4chan is often met with derision or hostility.[25]

Thirdly, the identity *status* of an individual in the UGC environment, that is to say, where we consider them to fall on the spectrum between known or anonymous, does not necessarily derive from their chosen anonymity practices. The identity knowledge available about a person can be provided passively or unwittingly. For example, perhaps we can tell that they live in the UK because their street photography includes a car with UK number plates in the background. Conversely, just because identity information is available, it does not necessarily directly correlate to the identity status of an individual as the type and extent of identity information required depends on the context and purpose. For example, to be able to ascribe reputational value to someone, a consistent pseudonym may suffice, but to be able to enforce legal rights against someone, being able to link the

[17] H Nissenbaum, 'The Meaning of Anonymity in an Information Age' (1999) 15 *The Information Society* 141, 141–42.

[18] ibid 142.

[19] ibid.

[20] GT Marx, 'What's in a Name? Some Reflections on the Sociology of Anonymity' (1999) 15 *The Information Society* 99, 100.

[21] G Bachmann, M Knecht and A Wittel, 'The Social Productivity of Anonymity' (2017) 17 *ephemera: theory and politics in organization* 241, 247.

[22] G Marx, 'Internet Anonymity as a Reflection of Broader Issues Involving Technology and Society' (2004) 11 *Asia-Pacific Review* 142, 143.

[23] ibid 143–44.

[24] Nissenbaum (n 17) 141–42; Marx, 'What's in a Name?' (n 20) 101.

[25] L Knuttila, 'User Unknown: 4chan, Anonymity and Contingency' (2011) 16 *First Monday*: firstmonday.org/ojs/index.php/fm/article/view/3665.

online behaviour to a single individual and to contact them in the real world will be essential.[26]

Where there is such a specific purpose, certain significant characteristics of the CUGC environment can particularly reduce the effectiveness of identity information. The scale of this environment, the speed at which interactions take place and the multiplicity and ephemerality of participation can all undermine efforts to trace an individual. For example, a common name such as 'James Brown' without any further information is as untraceable to a real-world individual as 'anonymous' when the scale of the environment is taken into account. Furthermore, the UGC environment facilitates multiple identities in the sense of having multiple names[27] further complicating matters. Finally, the speed of interactions and the ephemerality of online participation can create problems even when you do have the ability to contact someone. For example, Reddit has a direct messaging function that would facilitate direct contact to a creator without the need for knowledge about their offline identity and contact details. However, while this enables a message to be sent it does not mean that the individual will respond. They may be asleep on the other side of the world. They may be an infrequent user of the platform, or an infrequent email checker. They may have created a 'throwaway' account[28] for a particular purpose and never log in with those details again. Consequently, we can see that anonymity in the CUGC environment is a generic and pervasive issue that can transcend the identity practices of the individuals within it.

III. The Legal Position of Creative User-Generated Content

Having outlined the variety of CUGC formats and the types of interactions with this content that can be seen in the CUGC environment, it is now possible to explore the relationship between this and copyright law. Specifically, this section addresses whether copyright subsists in such content and, therefore, whether copyright law regulates the interactions with it. It demonstrates that copyright can subsist in a significant proportion of CUGC, meaning that such content can be considered a 'work' under the law. Consequently, interactions with that work will be regulated as 'uses' under copyright law, and the individuals involved in these interactions may fall into the copyright roles of copyright owner, user or infringer.

[26] These different contexts and purposes will be explored in various places in this book. Consideration of anonymity and legal rights comes later in this chapter, for example.

[27] The idea that people create new identities far removed from their offline identities in terms of behaviour, interests and sense of self has largely now been rejected. This is only used to highlight that providing the opportunity to use multiple names allows new identities in the sense of attributing acts, rather than necessarily representing some fundamental multiplicity of self.

[28] An account created for one-off use. This will often be to post something the user feels to be embarrassing, or 'off-brand' for their usual account.

A. The Subsistence of Copyright in Creative UGC

While receiving comparatively little attention in the literature on the relationship between user-generated content and copyright law, a handful of scholars have established that copyright can subsist in (at least some forms of) user-generated content. Some studies take subsistence for granted in their discussions,[29] but other papers, including this author's own, have undertaken more detailed doctrinal analysis to show that UGC will often meet the requirements for copyright subsistence in several jurisdictions.[30] The potential for copyright subsistence in CUGC is foundational to the discussion throughout this book and so it is important to reiterate the doctrinal basis for the key assertion that copyright will subsist in a significant proportion of CUGC and that CUGC creators are often copyright holders. It also builds on previous discussions to consider whether CUGC that is AI-generated or AI-assisted is also protected. The discussion addresses subject matter, fixation and originality criteria, as well as conceptions of authorship.

In terms of subsistence, subject matter and fixation requirements under copyright law pose little concern to CUGC. Article 2(1) of the Berne Convention states that protection is available to 'every production in the literary, scientific and artistic domain'. Both the US[31] and Germany[32] have an open list approach to copyrightable subject matter, and even the UK's exclusive list of protected subject matter[33] provides protection for original literary, dramatic, musical and artistic works. The subsistence of copyright in the sort of subject matter defined as CUGC (photographs, paintings, drawings, stories, poems, etc) is therefore not contentious. To the extent that fixation is required,[34] this is similarly found to be unproblematic.

[29] J Meese and J Hagedorn, 'Mundane Content on Social Media: Creation, Circulation, and the Copyright Problem' (2019) 5 *Social Media + Society* 1.

[30] S Hetcher, 'User-Generated Content and the Future of Copyright: Part One – Investiture of Ownership' (2007) 10 *Vanderbilt Journal of Entertainment and Technology Law* 863; AG Schuler, 'Insta-Appropriation: Finding Boundaries for the Second Circuit's Fair Use Doctrine after Campbell' (2016) 85 *Fordham Law Review* 367; C Tan, *Regulating Content on Social Media: Copyright, Terms of Service and Technological Features* (London, UCL Press, 2018); M Iljadica, 'User Generated Content and its Authors' in T Aplin (ed), *Research Handbook on Intellectual Property and Digital Technologies* (Cheltenham, Edward Elgar Publishing, 2020); R Maguire, '"It Doesn't Belong to the Internet": Copyright Reform for User-Generated Content' [2022] *Intellectual Property Quarterly* 141.

[31] 17 USC s 102(a).

[32] Urheberrechtsgesetz (UrhG) 1965 (German Copyright Law) s 2(1).

[33] Set out in Copyright, Designs and Patents Act 1988 (CDPA) s 1(1).

[34] In the US, fixation is required for all works under 17 USC s102(a). Germany does not require fixation and the CJEU ruling in *Levola* clarified that no permanent form is required: Case 31/17 *Levola Hengelo BV v Smilde Foods BV* ECLI:EU: C: 2018:899; [2018] Business Law Report 2442 [40]. The UK's fixation requirements are more contested. An express requirement for fixation for literary works is set out in the CDPA 1988, s 1(1)(a). There is also an argument that there is an implicit fixation for artistic works arising from cases such as *Merchandising Corp of America Ltd v Harpbond* [1983] FSR 32. Conversely, there are also questions about the compatibility of the CDPA fixation requirements with the *Levola* ruling as part of retained law post-Brexit. Regardless of the position of fixation in the UK, it does not change the analysis on subsistence here.

Fixation is broadly construed and encompasses digital as well as physical formats,[35] meaning that in the context of CUGC, the works are all necessarily 'fixed' in some visual or textual form in the process of sharing them online, and also possibly in other formats during their creation. Iljadica raises valid questions about fixation in terms of ephemeral user-generated content such as on Snapchat and that could also extend to 4chan's model of posts being deleted to make room for new ones. However, this author has elsewhere demonstrated that these are largely misplaced in this context since it is materiality,[36] non-transitoriness,[37] or a lack of tangibility[38] rather than permanence that is essential.[39] Even were some forms of CUGC to struggle to meet fixation requirements, most would not.

For CUGC, the most significant potential barrier to copyright subsistence will be originality. While there are long-standing jurisdictional differences in definitions of originality, these have been 'substantially reduced' in recent years[40] and there are now numerous overlaps.[41] The UK traditionally applied an interpretation of originality based on labour, skill and/or judgement,[42] but now follows the EU standard of originality set out in *Infopaq*[43] that the work must be the 'author's own intellectual creation'.[44] This has been interpreted to mean that the author has made creative choices, rather than functional or technical ones.[45] This is evidently also the standard required under German law.[46] In the US, *Feist* also made clear that labour alone was insufficient and there must be 'at least some minimal degree of creativity', which will be found wherever 'the creative spark is [not] utterly lacking or so trivial as to be virtually non-existent'[47] for a work to be original, sometimes referred to as the 'modicum of creativity' doctrine.[48]

[35] CDPA, s 178; 17 USC s 101; US HRREP No 1476, 94th Cong, 2d Sess 47, 52 (1976).

[36] E Derclaye, 'Debunking Some of UK Copyright Law's Longstanding Myths and Misunderstandings' (2013) 1 *Intellectual Property Quarterly* 1, 12.

[37] 17 USC s 101.

[38] GS Donat, 'Fixing Fixation: A Copyright with Teeth for Improvisational Performers' (1997) 97 *Columbia Law Review* 1363, 1364.

[39] Maguire (n 30) 148.

[40] WW Fisher, 'Recalibrating Originality' (2016) 54 *Houston Law Review* 437, 447.

[41] EF Judge and DJ Gervais, 'Of Silos and Constellations: Comparing Notions of Originality in Copyright Law' (2009) 27 *Cardozo Arts & Entertainment Law Journal* 375, 403.

[42] *University of London Press v University Tutorial Press* [1916] 2 Ch 601; *Ladbroke (Football) v William Hill (Football)* [1964] 1 All ER 465.

[43] Case 5/08 *Infopaq Int'l A/S v Danske Dagblades Forening* ECLI:EU:C:2009:465, [2009] ECR I-6569 [37].

[44] *THJ Systems Limited & Anor v Daniel Sheridan & Anor* [2023] EWCA Civ 1354; [2024] ECDR 4 [15].

[45] Case 145/10 *Painer v Standard Verlags GmbH* EU:C:2011:798; [2012] ECDR 6 [89]; Case 403/08 and Case 429/08 *Football Association Premier League v QC Leisure and Karen Murphy v Media Protection Services Ltd* EU:C:2011:631; [2012] ECR I-9083 [98].

[46] UrhG, s 2(2).

[47] *Feist Publications, Incorporated v Rural Telephone Service Company, Incorporated,* 499 US 340 (1991) 395.

[48] While the doctrinal discussions in this book are focused on the jurisdictions of the UK, the US and Germany, it is valuable to highlight the overlaps with originality standards in other jurisdictions. For example, s 2(2)(a) of the Nigeria Copyright Act 2022 requires that 'some effort has been expended

The sort of 'user-copied' CUGC defined earlier in this chapter will not be able to meet the originality standard, but beyond this, the originality requirement has a low bar in terms of creative choices, as seen through cases where outputs that would not necessarily be understood to be 'creative' in lay terms were recognised nonetheless as original by the courts.[49] It is therefore almost certain that CUGC that is 'user-authored' will be sufficiently original. If a telephone directory is considered sufficiently creative to be original, then stories and paintings, as long as not copied, should not trouble the courts. There have been questions about the originality of one particular form of CUGC: photography, with Schuler flagging the ubiquitous snapshots of dinners and tourist attractions as concerns.[50] Is pointing a camera and pressing a button a compelling example of making sufficient creative choices to satisfy such originality requirements? However, the Court of Justice of the European Union (CJEU) recognised a generous range of potential creative choices within the making of a photograph including selecting the camera angle, lighting and positioning in *Painer*.[51] Furthermore, Germany extends copyright protection to all photographs, even if they cannot meet the originality requirements.[52]

The UK and US courts have also demonstrated that the bar for recognising originality in photographs is relatively low. Section 4(1)(a) of the Copyright, Designs and Patents Act (CDPA) 1988 is clear that protection of photographs is available regardless of artistic quality and UK case law supports a low standard of originality that most photographs could meet, for example, in *Temple Island Collections Ltd v New English Teas Ltd*,[53] a rather generic photograph of a London bus crossing Westminster Bridge was also sufficiently original due to creative choices in composition. In the US, photographs have been recognised as being capable of being original since the nineteenth century Supreme Court case of *Burrow-Giles Lithographic Co v Sarony*.[54] There is some confusion within the case law about whether simple photographs are sufficiently original,[55] but in most

on making the work, to give it an original character', overlapping with the UK's former labour, skill and effort standard. Others focus on 'creativity' requirements similar to aspects of the US standard. For example, India's Supreme Court highlighted a 'flavour of minimum standard of creativity' requirement for originality in *Eastern Book Company and Ors v DB Modak and Anr* (2008) 1 SCC 1. While China's originality standard is not clearly stated in its copyright legislation and has not received much judicial consideration, it is based on the creativity of the author (see K He, 'The Concept of Originality in Copyright Law in China and Europe' in N Lee, N Bruun and M Li (eds), *Governance of Intellectual Property Rights in China and Europe* (Cheltenham, Edward Elgar Publishing, 2016) 99–101). Japan frames originality as the manifestation of the author's personality, similar to the EU standard.

[49] See, eg: in the UK, football pools coupons in *Ladbroke v William Hill* (n 42); in the EU, football fixture lists in Case 604/10 *Football Dataco Ltd and Others v Yahoo! UK Ltd and Others* ECLI:EU:C:2012:115; [2012] ECDR 10; in the US, telephone directories in *Feist Publications* (n 47).

[50] Schuler (n 30) 371.

[51] *Painer v Standard Verlags* (n 45).

[52] UrhG, ss 72(1) and 72(2).

[53] *Temple Island Collections Ltd v New English Teas Ltd* [2012] EWPCC 1.

[54] *Burrow-Giles Lithographic Co v Sarony*, 111 US 53 (1884).

[55] See, eg: Justice Miller (obiter) in *Burrow-Giles*; *Jeweler's Circular Publishing v Keystone Publishing*, 281 F 83 (2d Cir 1922); *Bridgeman Art Library v Corel Corp*, 36 F Supp 2d 191 (SDNY 1999).

cases the photographs at issue are highly mechanical or are replicating an existing artistic work exactly. As such, it is clear that when applying the conception of originality of 'creative choices', in these three jurisdictions (Germany, the UK and US) the bar is set relatively low, and user-authored CUGC will likely be able to meet it in most cases, even when it comes to photography.

The more complex challenges for CUGC in meeting this criterion would instead be found in works that are user-derived, that is, works where the CUGC integrates previously existing works. This is the type of user-generated content that has received the most scholarly attention, with much consideration of copyright law's role in remix culture of the sort seen in fan fiction, memes and mashups.[56] However, this has largely focused on whether these forms of creativity are infringing rather than whether copyright can subsist in them. The Berne Convention requires protection for derivative works as original works under Article 2(3), and this is reflected in national law. While user-derived CUGC creators will not hold copyright over elements of their work created by other people, copyright can subsist in derivative CUGC if it meets the originality standard set in law, for example in the UK and Germany, where the CUGC is the author's own intellectual creation and in the US, where it meets the *Feist* standards. In the UK, this is even possible where the CUGC uses copyrighted elements without permission, as copyright can be held in some parts of a work even if other parts are infringing.[57] Regardless, both Germany and the US provide protection for non-infringing derivative works.[58] What this means in practice is that there will certainly be forms of derivative CUGC that may not be able to meet originality criteria, but there will also be plenty that can.

Once the copyright subsistence criteria are met, it is necessary to consider authorship and ownership of copyright. In this context, it is most likely that the CUGC creator will be considered to be the author, and therefore the holder of copyright in the work, as in this non-commercial context they are unlikely to have created it in the course of employment or to have assigned their rights to someone else.[59] The fact that CUGC may be posted under a pseudonym or anonymously, as described above, does not undermine copyright subsistence or the CUGC creator's role as author and copyright holder. There are clear provisions for the protection of anonymous works or works of unknown authorship under the UK CDPA,[60] the US Copyright Act[61] and the German Copyright Act,[62]

[56] See, eg: R Tushnet, 'User-Generated Discontent: Transformation in Practice' (2007) 31 *Columbia Journal of Law & Arts* 497; L Lessig, *Remix: Making Art and Commerce Thrive in the Hybrid Economy* (New York, Bloomsbury Academic, 2008).

[57] *ZYX Music GmbH v King* [1995] 3 All ER 1; L Bently and B Sherman, *Intellectual Property Law*, 4th edn (Oxford, Oxford University Press, 2014) 94.

[58] UrhG, s 3; 17 USC s 103.

[59] CDPA, s 90; 17 USC s 201(d); CDPA, s 11(1); 17 USC s 201(a); CDPA, s 11(2); 17 USC s 201(b).

[60] CDPA, s 9(4) and 9(5).

[61] 17 USC s 101.

[62] UrhG, s 66.

even if these have a shorter duration of protection. Furthermore, scholarship on other creative areas shows that anonymous authorship does not fundamentally undermine a creator's copyright interest in a work. Free and open-source software (FOSS) hackers[63] widely use pseudonyms but rely on their legal right to hold copyright in their work to enforce open-source licensing terms on future users.[64] While these 'copyleft' licences aim to circumvent some of the restrictive aspects of copyright, they are themselves reliant on the rights pseudonymous FOSS hackers hold over their work to enforce this 'openness'.[65] Another example is that of graffiti. For various reasons, including that their creative practice often involves elements of illegality, graffiti and street artists often sign their work using a pseudonym or not at all. Both Iljadica and Bonadio highlight that copyright subsists in these works.[66] This demonstrates that even though creators may be anonymous or pseudonymous, they are nonetheless considered the authors of their work and therefore hold copyright in it.

Whether this subsistence and authorship analysis can be applied to CUGC that has been AI-assisted or AI-generated (AI-CUGC) is a more complicated question that requires consideration of both originality and authorship issues. As a relatively new phenomenon, there understandably remains much academic debate about the answer to this question, both at a normative and a doctrinal level, and there has been little legislative or judicial clarity provided so far. It is beyond the scope of this book to explore these issues in depth, and many others have already done so more thoroughly than possible here.[67] As such, the aim here is to highlight the key issues and challenges of determining copyright subsistence in AI-assisted or AI-generated CUGC. As will be seen, the complexities of such an analysis means that it is likely that assessment of copyright subsistence will require a case-by-case approach.

Essential to navigating this issue is recognising the different ways that AI tools and machines can be used in creative practice and understanding how these alter the subsistence analysis. Ginsburg and Budiardjo helpfully distinguish between 'ordinary tools' (whose outputs reflect the users' creative choices in the way a camera does), and generative machines, either 'fully-generative machines' (which require only minimal, if any, user input) and 'partially-generative machines'

[63] 'Hackers' here refers to the original sense of the term: someone part of the computer programming subculture (playing with others' code) rather than someone who breaks into computer systems.

[64] ES Raymond, *The Cathedral & the Bazaar* (Cambridge, MA, O'Reilly Media, 2001).

[65] K Bowrey, *Law and Internet Cultures* (Cambridge, Cambridge University Press, 2005) 99.

[66] M Iljadica, *Copyright Beyond Law: Regulating Creativity in the Graffiti Subculture* (Oxford, Hart Publishing, 2016); E Bonadio, 'Street Art, Graffiti and Copyright: A UK Perspective' in E Bonadio (ed), *The Cambridge Handbook of Copyright in Street Art and Graffiti* (Cambridge, Cambridge University Press, 2019).

[67] See, eg: JC Ginsburg and LA Budiardjo, 'Authors and Machines' (2019) 34 *Berkeley Technology Law Journal* 343; G Frosio, 'Four Theories in Search of an A(I)uthor' in R Abbott (ed), *Handbook of Intellectual Property and Artificial Intelligence* (Cheltenham, Edward Elgar Publishing, 2022); DJ Gervais, 'The Human Cause' in R Abbott (ed), *Research Handbook on Intellectual Property and Artificial Intelligence* (Cheltenham, Edward Elgar Publishing, 2022).

(where the creative choices of both the designer and the user combine to produce the output).[68] It should be noted that they do not consider a category for a machine capable of autonomous creativity. They highlight that such technology does not yet exist, and that current AI machines produce only a simulation of human creativity.[69] Questions of hypothetical future machine creativity, while interesting, are similarly ignored here as they are not relevant to the discussion. Instead, the focus is on whether AI-CUGC can be protected by copyright and if so, who is considered the author and holder of the right.

Whether copyright can subsist in AI-CUGC depends on the level of human involvement and on the jurisdiction. The EU and US have made it clear that outputs that have no human input at all will not be eligible for copyright protection. This is because the current legal position is that AI machines themselves cannot be authors and copyright holders under copyright law, as authorship must be human and such machines have no legal personality.[70] This arises from originality standards that expressly or impliedly require human authorship.[71] This has been seen in the case of *Thaler v Perlmutter*,[72] where copyright protection was denied after an application to protect a piece of visual art created by 'the Creativity Machine' which its owner stated created the artwork independently. The owner, Thaler, claimed the copyright should be transferred to him as the machine owner, but this was denied by the Copyright Office as, under his description of the production process, there was no human author. The US District Court agreed. The UK varies in this regard, not because its originality standard is different, but because it is one of a handful of jurisdictions with specific legislative provisions granting copyright protection to computer-generated works.[73] While this predates the recent generative AI phenomenon by several decades and its application to this specific context has not been tested in the courts, it is generally accepted by scholars that this will allow copyright to subsist in AI outputs generated in a way that would not satisfy human authorship and originality requirements.[74]

It is clear then that an evaluation of the human contribution to AI-CUGC is the first step. This takes the form of evaluating the creative choices made by humans in the process of producing the output.[75] When it comes to Ginsburg and

[68] Ginsburg and Budiardjo (n 67) 404–16.

[69] ibid 349.

[70] ibid 400; A Guadamuz, 'Do Androids Dream of Electric Copyright? Comparative Analysis of Originality in Artificial Intelligence Generated Works' in J-A Lee, R Hilty and K-C Liu (eds), *Artificial Intelligence and Intellectual Property* (Oxford, Oxford University Press, 2021) 154; Frosio (n 67) 160–61; Gervais, 'The Human Cause' (n 67) 23.

[71] Guadamuz (n 70) 160–61; Frosio (n 67) 162–63; G Campus, 'Generative AI: Main Copyright Issues and Some (Partial) Answers in the EU AI Act' (2024) 46 *European Intellectual Property Review* 434, 434. See also: *Painer v Standard Verlags* (n 45); *Thaler v Perlmutter*, Civil Action No 22-1564, BAH (US); and *Naruto v Slater*, No 16-15469 (9th Cir 2018).

[72] *Thaler v Perlmutter* (n 71).

[73] CDPA, s 9(3).

[74] Guadamuz (n 70) 159; N Cordell, B Potts and R Dickens, 'Ownership of AI-Generated Content in the UK' (2024) 46 *European Intellectual Property Review* 470, 472.

[75] Guadamuz (n 70) 162; Y Benhamou and A Andrijevic, 'The Protection of AI-Generated Pictures (Photograph and Painting) under Copyright Law' in R Abbott (ed), *Research Handbook on Intellectual*

Budiardjo's 'ordinary tools', there is unlikely to be much difficulty in establishing sufficient human contribution for copyright to subsist. A common CUGC example would be AI technology integrated into photography editing software, or within a smartphone camera. In other, generative, forms of AI machine, a more careful consideration of human creative choices is required, but many will work on the basis of human input from a range of different people, particularly the programmer and the user, raising questions about who holds copyright. If relying on the UK's computer-generated works provision, it is similarly unclear who would be considered to be the rights-holder and a case-by-case analysis would be required.[76]

Whether the creative choices of a particular individual (developer or user) are sufficient to meet subsistence requirements would vary on a case-by-case basis. It might be difficult for a programmer to demonstrate sufficient creative choices in the output of a general generative AI tool such as ChatGPT or Midjourney, as the user has much discretion in what they want to create, compared with a narrower tool designed to offer only limited choices to the user. Simultaneously, it might be difficult for a user to reach the originality requirements if they provide only basic prompts to the tool. For example, the output from a simple prompt such as 'draw a woman riding a unicorn' will include a large number of creative elements that have been incorporated by the machine as a result of its algorithm, rather than the user's originality. Indeed, Cordell et al highlight that the US Copyright Office refused to copyright outputs from Midjourney, despite the human user's detailed and extensive prompts.[77] It should also be considered that several mainstream AI models including OpenAI (ChatGPT and DALL-E) and Midjourney have terms on ownership within their user agreements, most often allocating any rights, where they exist, to the user.[78]

What this tells us is that it is not possible to provide a definitive answer on whether AI-CUGC is protected by copyright where generative AI services are used, and a case-by-case evaluation would be essential, although not necessarily straightforward. It is also not straightforward to allocate ownership of copyright to a particular stakeholder, meaning that the CUGC creators at the heart of this book may not necessarily hold copyright even if it does exist, although terms of service may assist in this regard. Despite this, it is certainly doctrinally possible for AI-CUGC to be protected by copyright owned by the CUGC creator. The way such technology is used in the creative process varies so widely, from a simple prompt ('draw a fat cat'), through to using their own, original creative work as prompt material ('make this short story more dramatic') and editing AI-generated outputs. This means that there are many conceivable instances where copyright will subsist, particularly where there are high levels of creative choices, or in the UK due to section 9(3) CDPA.

Property and Artificial Intelligence (Cheltenham, Edward Elgar Publishing, 2022) 213–16; Gervais, 'The Human Cause' (n 67) 36; Cordell, Potts and Dickens (n 74) 473.

[76] Guadamuz (n 70) 159.

[77] Cordell, Potts and Dickens (n 74) 475.

[78] OpenAI, 'EU Terms of Use': openai.com/policies/eu-terms-of-use/; Midjourney, 'Midjourney Terms of Service': docs.midjourney.com/docs/terms-of-service.

B. Relevant Rights and the Regulation of Interactions with Creative UGC

Where copyright subsists in CUGC, it provides the CUGC creator with certain exclusive rights. The types of interactions with CUGC outlined earlier in the chapter (remix, utilisation, etc) could infringe several of these rights, in particular reproduction and distribution rights. Each of the different interactions described (except for commentary and feedback) involve reproduction of the CUGC, either in part or in full, and online interactions also include distribution. Under UK law, we find that copying a work,[79] issuing a work to the public[80] and communicating a work to the public[81] (which includes sharing via the internet)[82] are all restricted acts, which means that conducting these acts without the permission of the copyright holder constitutes copyright infringement unless they are covered by an exemption or limitation to copyright. Additionally, UK legislation provides authors with moral rights over their works, including the right to be named as the author[83] (the right to paternity or attribution) and the right to object to derogatory treatment of a work[84] (the right to integrity). While the scope of these moral rights is reduced by limitations,[85] including that the right to attribution requires the author to have asserted this in advance, and that these rights can be waived, the rights are still available to CUGC creators to some extent.

These rights are set out in the Berne Convention[86] and are also mandatory under Article 9 of the TRIPS agreement[87] (with the exception of the moral rights set out in Article 6bis of Berne). Therefore, we see similar economic rights in jurisdictions around the globe; although approaches to moral rights differ more in their scope, particularly depending on the philosophical traditions of the jurisdiction, most jurisdictions do provide moral rights protection to some extent.[88] In Germany, authors hold the exclusive right of reproduction,[89] the exclusive right of distribution[90] and the exclusive right to make the work available to the

[79] CDPA, 16(1)(a).
[80] CDPA, s 16(1)(b).
[81] CDPA, s 16(1)(d).
[82] CDPA, s 20(2)(b).
[83] CDPA, s 77(1). For infringement to be found, an author must have asserted this right in advance.
[84] CDPA, s 80(1).
[85] CP Rigamonti, 'Deconstructing Moral Rights' (2006) 47 *Harvard International Law Journal* 353, 402.
[86] Arts 9(1) and 6bis(1) of the the Berne Convention for the Protection of Literary and Artistic Works 1886 deal with the relevant exploitation and moral rights respectively.
[87] 'Agreement on Trade Related Aspects of Intellectual Property Rights'.
[88] Traditionally, common law jurisdictions are considered to have less thorough approaches to moral rights than civil law jurisdictions, however the majority do have some functioning protection for moral rights. See: G Dworkin, 'The Moral Right of the Author: Moral Rights and the Common Law Countries' (1994) 19 *Columbia-VA Journal of Law and the Arts* 229; P Goldstein, *International Copyright: Principles, Law and Practice* (Oxford, Oxford University Press, 2001) 283–84.
[89] UrhG, s 15(1)(1).
[90] UrhG, s 15(1)(2).

public,[91] including via the internet.[92] They also have the inalienable right to recognition as the author of a work[93] and the right to prevent distortion of their work.[94] In the US, copyright holders have the exclusive right to reproduce the copyrighted work, prepare derivative works and distribute copies to the public.[95] The US also provides some moral rights in narrow circumstances; authors of visual art have the right to claim authorship of their works[96] and to 'prevent any intentional distortion, mutilation, or other modification of that work, which would be prejudicial to his or her honor or reputation'.[97] However, these rights are very limited in practice[98] and do not extend to other forms of subject matter.

Where exclusive rights to restrict use exist, uses without permission would infringe copyright unless such uses fell within a permitted use, limitation or exception. As this author has argued elsewhere, the most relevant provisions to the CUGC context are permitted uses for caricature, parody or pastiche,[99] reporting on current events[100] and quotation[101] in the UK and Germany, but these are framed narrowly, which limits how much they can be relied on.[102] For example, a video comprised of copyright protected CUGC artwork as a placeholder image combined with a user's own audio track would fall within none of the permitted uses. In the US, the relevant provision would be the fair use exception which requires the user to '[alter] the original with new expression, meaning, or message'.[103] This is more flexible than the UK and German permitted uses in relation to remix activities but utilisation without remix would nonetheless remain problematic. Permitted uses, limitations and exceptions do not therefore provide a comprehensive framework capable of responding to the broad variety of CUGC interactions, and so to try to avoid copyright issues by relying on them requires careful and sometimes complex analysis on a case-by-case basis.[104]

As touched on earlier in the chapter, AI technology can also intersect with possible interactions with CUGC, and this raises questions about whether these can infringe copyright. This arises as a particular issue with CUGC as online content can easily be used to create datasets to train AI models. There are two potential ways this could infringe copyright in CUGC: first, the AI outputs themselves could

[91] UrhG, s 15(2)(2).
[92] UrhG, s 19a.
[93] UrhG, s 13.
[94] UrhG, s 14.
[95] 17 USC s 106(1)–(3).
[96] 17 USC s 106(a)(1)(A).
[97] 17 USC s 106(a)(3)(A).
[98] Goldstein (n 88) 284; NC Suhl, 'Moral Rights Protection in the United States under the Berne Convention: A Fictional Work' (2001) 12 *Fordham Intellectual Property, Media & Entertainment Law Journal* 1203; Rigamonti (n 85) 406.
[99] CDPA, s 30A; UrhG, s 51(a).
[100] CDPA, s 30(2); UrhG, s 50.
[101] CDPA, s 30(1ZA); UrhG, s 51.
[102] Maguire (n 30) 150.
[103] *Campbell v Acuff-Rose Music, Inc*, 510 US 569 (1994).
[104] Maguire (n 30) 150–51.

include elements of the CUGC above the threshold for infringement; and secondly, the inclusion of the work in the dataset itself could be considered to be an unauthorised reproduction. The first scenario is possible although not common as the outputs are created from very large datasets; OpenAI's DALL-E image generator was trained on 650 million images, and Stable Diffusion on 2.3 billion.[105] This means it is unlikely that specific elements of individual works will be identifiable in AI outputs.

In the second scenario there is necessarily some reproduction of copyright works, but whether this is unauthorised is a more complex issue. The creation of AI training datasets is covered in the EU by text and data mining (TDM) exceptions. Article 4 of the Copyright Directive[106] provides an exception for any type of beneficiary to carry out acts of reproduction for TDM purposes, unless the rights-holder has opted out.[107] The UK's TDM exception only applies to non-commercial uses.[108] Following a consultation by the Intellectual Property Office, the UK government planned an extension to the exception so it would cover any beneficiary and without an opt-out option, but this has not been implemented. The English court refused to strike out a claim brought by Getty Images against Stability AI arguing that Stability has infringed copyright by scraping images from Getty websites without consent.[109] In the US, AI models are reliant on fair use rules to avoid liability and there are currently a number of claims under way in the US that should help to bring some legal clarity to the situation.[110]

The terms of service of many CUGC platforms may, however, allow AI companies to get permission to scrape CUGC. These usually include provisions that grant the platform a licence to use its users' content and often to sublicence it. Reddit's user agreement, for example, states that users grant it 'a worldwide, royalty-free, perpetual, irrevocable, non-exclusive, transferable, and sublicensable license to use, copy, modify, adapt, prepare derivative works of, distribute, store, perform, and display' their content.[111] Reddit has used this sublicensable licence to do a deal with OpenAI to use Reddit content in its training data.[112] Similarly, Meta plans to

[105] Murgia and Johnston (n 7).

[106] Directive (EU) 2019/790 of the European Parliament and of the Council of 17 April 2019 on copyright and related rights in the Digital Single Market and amending Directives 96/9/EC and 2001/29/EC (Text with EEA relevance) [2019] OJ L130/92 (Copyright Directive).

[107] s 106 of the EU's AI Act has also created obligations for AI models to ensure that they are complying with opt-outs under the Copyright Directive: Regulation 2024/1689 of the European Parliament and of the Council of 13 June 2024 laying down harmonised rules on artificial intelligence and amending Regulations (EC) No 300/2008, (EU) No 167/2013, (EU) No 168/2013, (EU) 2018/858, (EU) 2018/1139 and (EU) 2019/2144 and Directives 2014/90/EU, (EU) 2016/797 and (EU) 2020/1828 [2024] OJ L2024/1689 (Artificial Intelligence Act).

[108] CDPA, s 29A.

[109] *Getty Images (US) Inc v Stability AI Ltd* [2023] EWHC 3090 (Ch); [2024] FSR 12.

[110] See eg: *Getty Images v Stability AI*; *Alter v OpenAI*; *Anderson v Stability AI*.

[111] Reddit, 'Reddit User Agreement': www.redditinc.com/policies/user-agreement-february-15-2024.

[112] OpenAI, 'OpenAI and Reddit Partnership' (16 May 2024): openai.com/index/openai-and-reddit-partnership/.

use content from its social media platforms, Facebook and Instagram, as training data for its own AI models.[113] In these cases, therefore, there is no infringement.

Therefore, we can see that copyright law provides CUGC creators with rights to restrict the use and distribution of their works by using copyright law, as well as potentially offering moral rights over attribution and integrity, to deal with conflict in interactions with their content. The extent to which use of CUGC by AI models infringe those rights is largely dependent on the relevant exceptions and limitations within the jurisdiction and any potential sublicences. The moral rights available, and their scope, also varies depending on the jurisdiction. The key takeaway from this discussion, however, is that the rights that arise as a result of copyright subsistence correspond to the types of interaction that occur with CUGC and, therefore, those interactions can be regulated using copyright law.

IV. Challenges for the Copyright Regulation of Creative User-Generated Content: Anonymity

Having established that copyright law may offer CUGC creators rights that are relevant to the interactions with their content, this section explores the practical effects of anonymous authorship and anonymous interactions on copyright as a system of regulation. As explained, copyright law restricts certain acts unless the 'user' has permission from the copyright holder. For the system to work efficiently and effectively, that is, to find the appropriate balance between restriction and access, two elements therefore need to be assessed. First, whether the CUGC creator is able to enforce their rights to restrict uses, and, secondly, whether those who wish to interact with CUCG can identify when permission is needed and can arrange licensing or grant permission to use a work where it is. This section explores how anonymity affects these elements.

Here it is demonstrated that, despite copyright being available to some CUGC creators, the anonymity of infringers means that enforcing these rights would be difficult. Furthermore, the anonymity of CUGC creators means that large numbers of such works are effectively orphan works, which causes problems for potential users and the efficient functioning of the copyright system. This section also demonstrates that potential legal solutions to the problems created by orphan works are unsuitable in the context of pervasive, generic anonymity in the CUGC environment. Finally, it is argued that online anonymity exacerbates the difficulties of navigating a complex global copyright landscape, particularly for amateur creators.

[113] Meta, 'Building AI Technology for the UK in a Responsible and Transparent Way' (*Meta*, 13 September 2024): about.fb.com/news/2024/09/building-ai-technology-for-the-uk-in-a-responsible-and-transparent-way/.

A. Enforcement and Anonymity: Locating Infringers

Pervasive online anonymity significantly undermines the effectiveness of copyright law as enforcing intellectual property rights in a digital world where people can access, copy and share other people's copyrighted works globally with very few – if any – costs, while their identity is hidden, is extremely difficult.[114] While discourse on this topic has most often focused on the relationship between the copyright industries and online infringers, most often file-sharers and pirates,[115] CUGC creators (as copyright holders) suffer the same problems when faced with anonymous infringers. However, they often have fewer resources to pursue or prevent infringements via other legal and technical means than commercially focused rights-holders.

For a copyright holder wanting to prevent the unauthorised use of works, or to seek remedies and damages for infringement of their rights through the courts, online anonymity makes this very difficult. Legal action for acts in the digital world takes place in the real world, and as such requires a tangible defendant (and therefore enough information to identify a person's real-world identity and how to reach them). When it is unclear who that defendant is, the rights and redress offered by copyright law are limited, if not non-existent, in practice. As access to digital technology has become widespread, this problem has played out through the entertainment industries' ongoing fight against online piracy.

However, the copyright industries have shown us that there are some possible solutions. It is possible (although not in all cases)[116] to identify a defendant by forcing internet service providers (ISPs) to reveal the identities of their customers,[117] to force ISPs to block access to specific file-sharing and torrent websites,[118] or to implement non-legal measures such as digital rights management (DRM) technology and changes of business models[119] to reduce unauthorised use of their works. Despite these successes, it has still been a case of copyright infringement

[114] AM Froomkin, 'Legal Issues in Anonymity and Pseudonymity' (1999) 15 *The Information Society* 113, 114.

[115] See, eg, S Larsson and M Svensson, 'Compliance or Obscurity? Online Anonymity as a Consequence of Fighting Unauthorised File-Sharing' (2010) 2 *Policy & Internet* 75.

[116] There are limits on the extent to which the courts will order identification through *Norwich Pharmacal* orders, and the courts will weigh up the balance of competing rights to decide whether to grant relief, eg in *Sheffield Wednesday FC & ors v Hargreaves* [2007] EWHC 2375 (QB), relief was not granted in relation to alleged defamation where the posters' rights to freedom of speech and anonymity outweighed the claimant's right to reputation.

[117] TJ McIntyre, 'Online Anonymity: Some Legal Issues' (2004) 11 *Commercial Law Practitioner* 90; 17 USC s 512(h) also facilitates this in the US.

[118] *Twentieth Century Fox and others v British Telecommunications plc* [2011] EWHC 1981 (Ch); [2012] 1 All ER 806; *Dramatico Entertainment Ltd v British Sky Broadcasting Ltd* [2012] EWHC 1152; [2012] 3 CMLR 15.

[119] eg, through subscription services like Netflix and Spotify which allow users to stream content legally.

whack-a-mole, and even with the support of a well-financed legal team, anonymous infringers remain a considerable problem for traditional copyright holders.[120]

Non-commercial copyright holders are not immune to these problems; they are as relevant for the CUGC creators in this discussion as they are for the copyright industries. Such creators do not have an in-house legal team to advise them, nor the same level of funds to access that advice elsewhere, and are less likely to have their own reliable understanding of copyright law, with numerous studies identifying misunderstandings and confusions among online creators.[121] Additionally, they are less likely to have the possibility of relying on the alternative measures available to corporate copyright holders, such as digital rights management technology. Therefore, CUGC creators dealing with anonymous copyright infringements will often face significant challenges in enforcing their rights.

B. Balancing Access and Copyright: Orphan Works

Beyond the well-explored problems facing copyright holders in the anonymous online environment, there are also CUGC-specific issues. These affect those interacting with CUGC, rather than the CUGC creator/copyright holder, as they make it harder to meet copyright requirements. This section considers one element of this difficulty: that due to the difficulties in tracing creators in the context of pervasive online anonymity, getting adequate permission to use works is very difficult, if not impossible. This means that many instances of CUGC should be considered as forms of orphan works. However, as will be seen, while orphan works are recognised as a problem in copyright logic, existing solutions are ineffective, often because they do not consider the CUGC context, with the consequence that CUGC and online anonymity raise some fundamental questions about the efficiency of copyright.

An orphan work is a copyrighted work where the rights-holder cannot be traced. Being able to trace rights-holders is essential for the effective functioning of copyright regulation, as users need to be able to negotiate licences to use works. Orphan works are seen as a problem in copyright law as they mean users must either risk liability for infringement if they choose to use the work, or simply not use it,[122] unless the law provides an adequate solution of some form.

[120] The IPO's online copyright infringement tracker found that 32% of people had illegally downloaded at least one item of online content in the three months preceding the survey: Intellectual Property Office, 'Executive Summary Online Copyright Infringement Tracker (Wave 12)' (Intellectual Property Office, 3 February 2023): www.gov.uk/government/publications/online-copyright-infringement-tracker-survey-12th-wave/executive-summary-online-copyright-infringement-tracker-survey-12th-wave.

[121] Maguire (n 30) 153–55.

[122] S van Gompel, 'The Orphan Works Chimera and How to Defeat It: A View from across the Atlantic' (2012) 27 *Berkeley Technology Law Journal* 1347, 1348; A Bunce, 'British Invasion: Importing the United Kingdom's Orphan Works Solution to United States Copyright Law' (2013) 108 *Northwestern University Law Review* 243, 245.

Horowitz points out that legal uncertainty of this sort is problematic for the rule of law, particularly in light of the high potential penalties for copyright infringement.[123] They also cause a problem for the copyright system as they make it less efficient, causing a 'structural market failure' where productive uses of works are prevented by high transaction costs of getting permission from the copyright owner.[124] In the US and the UK, particularly where copyright is based on utilitarian ideas, orphan works mean that copyright does not meet the correct balance of protection and access as works are blocked off from use by copyright.[125]

Traditional examples are often found in the museum and heritage sectors, for example where the rights-owners of archive photography cannot be identified or traced. However, we see the same issues in tracing the copyright owners of CUGC as a result of pervasive online anonymity. Of course, sharing CUGC anonymously does not automatically equate to it being an orphan work. Gervais distinguishes anonymous and pseudonymous works from orphan works,[126] and there is a long history of artists and writers choosing to obscure their identity for some purpose: George Eliot, Robert Galbraith, Banksy, to name a few. However, in the pre-digital world, and still today in traditional copyright industries, the publication and distribution of most creative works was managed by an intermediary, for example a publication house, a film studio, an agent. If someone wanted to acquire a licence to use an anonymous work in a way otherwise restricted by copyright law, they could contact the intermediary. Nowadays, creators and their works can have global reach without such intermediaries, which means potential users need to go directly to the creator to seek permission. Anonymity makes this process difficult because, in the same way that the anonymous infringer is difficult to track down, so is the anonymous creator.

So while Gervais is correct that, theoretically, 'anonymous' is just a different form of attribution, and not all anonymous works will be orphan works, in practice online anonymity creates a system which replicates orphan works' excessive transaction costs of locating copyright owners. Those transaction costs take the form of both effort and time. Some efforts could only ever be futile, for example 4chan does not provide a messaging system, so unless the CUCG creator has included a link to an external personal website or social media page, or you have some other way of finding out who they are, you cannot ask for that permission. Others could be slow or impractical, like sending a direct message to a creator on Reddit, where that user used a throwaway account, is inactive or is an irregular user. In these instances, a response could be delayed beyond a reasonable time frame for such a fast-paced creative environment. Interactions with CUGC are

[123] SJ Horowitz, 'Copyright's Asymmetric Uncertainty' (2012) 79 *University of Chicago Law Review* 331.

[124] G Colangelo and I Lincesso, 'Law versus Technology: Looking for a Solution to the Orphan Works' Problem' (2012) 20 *International Journal of Law and Information Technology* 178, 179–82.

[125] Bunce (n 122) 256.

[126] Gervais, *(Re)Structuring* (n 5) 206.

often reactive and memetic, building on and bouncing off each other[127] – for such a culture to exist efficiently, it needs to be underpinned by a quick, responsive system, otherwise this interactivity of creativity will be hindered. If you do not get a reply to your request until eight hours later because the creator was at work, or asleep in another time zone, you may well no longer be interested in using the work.

The consequences of this uncertainty also mirror that of orphan works. Copyright subsists in an eligible work automatically, and an anonymous creator can exploit their rights in their works, subject to the difficulties of dealing with anonymous infringers described above. Therefore, potential users should assume in the first instance that an unauthorised use of a work will be an infringement of copyright.[128] Lessig argues that when legal uncertainty like this exists, it restricts creativity as users are less likely to take the risk of using the work.[129] The problem with this lies in the fact that a lot of online creative culture (including but not exclusively on 4chan and Reddit) is built on ideas of sharing and remix[130] which require the use of works in ways that are potentially infringing on copyright. A combination of a presumption of copyright enforcement for infringing acts and a culture built on potentially infringing acts requires an adequate system of authorisation for uses of works. Pervasive online anonymity undermines the ability for that system to operate effectively and efficiently. Therefore, unless the law provides adequate solutions or defences for such use, CUGC, like other types of orphan works, gives users two undesirable options: use without permission, or do not use at all.

How to address the problems created by orphan works is an important concern of copyright policymakers and academics. However, in those discussions 'orphan works' are almost exclusively considered to be old works where the rights-holder has become difficult to identify and/or locate, and particularly relating to the fields of conservation, heritage and archiving; as a result, they overlook the specifics of the context of CUGC. What follows, therefore, is an analysis of the effectiveness of possible legal solutions to the CUGC orphan works problem. This includes consideration of specific mechanisms put in place for orphan works in certain jurisdictions as well as the possibility of implied licences to circumvent the problem. Beyond this, it is also possible that copyright limitations and exceptions could provide a solution for the orphan works problem, but as already explained above they cannot be reliably applied to CUGC; this will not be explored further here.

[127] P Levy, *Cyberculture*, R Bononno trans (Minneapolis, MN, University of Minnesota Press, 2001) 116.

[128] Lessig, *Remix* (n 56) 100.

[129] L Lessig, *Free Culture: The Nature and Future of Creativity* (New York, Penguin Books, 2005) 185; While Lee disputes this, arguing instead that informal practices fill these sorts of grey areas in the law, and this can lead to 'warming' rather than chilling where unauthorised uses become accepted practice, a deeper look at this idea in ch 4 and ch 5 will show this to be flawed: E Lee, 'Warming up to User-Generated Content' [2008] *University of Illinois Law Review* 1459.

[130] Levy (n 127); Lessig, *Free Culture* (n 129); Lessig, *Remix* (n 56).

i. Licensing Schemes and Statutory Provisions for Orphan Works

Treatment of orphan works varies between countries. For example, the UK runs a licensing scheme for orphan works so that anyone who wants to use a copyrighted work but cannot locate the copyright holder despite a 'diligent search' can apply to the scheme for a licence.[131] This provides a solution to the problems associated with orphan works as the licence removes the user's liability and with it any potential chilling effect. However, it is doubtful that this solution would be appropriate to the particular context of CUGC interactions for several reasons. First, to get a licence, an application form must be completed as well as evidence of a 'diligent search' provided. In terms of effort, this seems disproportionate to the likely use of the work, which is likely to be non-commercial, perhaps playful or humorous and, due to the fast-paced nature of interactions in the CUGC environment, an immediate response to the work. The application guidance explains that applications for licences to adapt works will be considered, but will only be granted where the adaption would not infringe the author's right against derogatory treatment.[132] Additionally, if the proposed use is inappropriate ('offensive, in poor taste or contentious') then the licence application is not likely to be successful.[133] This could apply to some uses, particularly on 4chan, where potentially offensive content such as pornography is widespread. Furthermore, for these types of interactions an application process that offers a response within 10 working days may be too slow in many cases. Considering these issues, it seems unlikely that this scheme would be used in the context of CUGC orphan works.

There are also provisions for dealing with orphan works in German legislation, arising as a result of the EU Orphan Works Directive.[134] In Germany, orphan works are dealt with in section 61 of the UrhG, which outlines specific uses of orphan works that are permitted following a diligent search. However, its applicability is limited to certain bodies such as heritage institutions, libraries and museums.[135] Section 61(2)(1) also restricts use to orphan works printed in books, journals, newspapers and magazines. As a result, these provisions are neither relevant to CUGC users nor the CUGC itself. Additionally, section 62(1) prohibits any alteration to orphan works, so even if they did meet the requirements, users would not be able to use the work for any remix-based activities. Therefore, these provisions are not of use in this context.

[131] The UK may also permit licensing bodies to apply to run extended collective licensing schemes under s 116B of the Enterprise and Regulatory Reform Act 2013. Such schemes would provide de facto solutions to the orphan works problem. Unfortunately, no licensing body has yet completed an application to run such a scheme.

[132] 'Orphan Works Licensing Scheme Overview for Applicants' (GOV.UK): www.gov.uk/government/publications/orphan-works-overview-for-applicants/orphan-works-licensing-scheme-overview-for-applicants.

[133] ibid.

[134] Directive 2012/28/EU of the European Parliament and of the Council of 25 October 2012 on certain permitted uses of orphan works [2012] OJ L299/5.

[135] Similar provisions were previously available in the UK under sch ZA1 of the CDPA, but have been repealed post-Brexit.

In the US, despite some attempts to pass relevant legislation,[136] there is still no specific mechanism to deal with issues arising from use of orphan works. Users can either decide not to use the work, or to use it and, if subject to copyright litigation as a result, rely on the fair use defence, which, as discussed above, is limited in its applicability. Consequently, licensing schemes and statutory provisions are not capable of providing an adequate solution in the context of CUGC.

ii. Implied Licences

Implied licences are another potential option for circumventing the CUGC orphan works problem, as if there is such a licence the user does not need to contact the CUGC creator for permission. Implied licences are unwritten and Mysoor identifies three possible ways to imply a licence: consent, custom or policy.[137] There are a few ways that sharing CUGC could be argued to form an implied licence. First, in sharing the work it could be said the copyright holder is aware of the potential uses from the general, typical conduct in those communities, and in choosing not to explicitly reserve their rights in the works, they consent to those uses, thereby creating a consent-based implied licence. Furthermore, it could be argued that the existence of easy-to-use ready-made licences such as Creative Commons licences mean that it would be simple for copyright holders wishing to restrict uses of their works to make that explicit when publishing. If they choose not to, this could potentially be argued to be the copyright holders consenting to those uses.

Secondly, there is also a possible argument for a custom-based implied licence. Sieman argues that the court may infer knowledge from 'widely known industry customs and standards'.[138] Therefore, it may be arguable that in communities where sharing, remix and reposting are fundamental activities, such uses should be viewed as widely known customs and standards. Finally, in terms of policy-based implied licences, Sieman also argues that implied licences are a way to 'insert some common sense' into the relationship between copyright law and internet practices.[139] Afori sees them as a mechanism for introducing objective policy considerations into copyright judgments.[140] This could potentially apply to the CUGC context, where it could be viewed as nonsensical or damaging to copyright for CUGC interactions to be considered infringing despite seemingly being tolerated by creators of that content.

However, implied licences are not a straightforward solution in this context. The scholarship about the value of implied licences in the digital age focuses mostly on technical infrastructure and inherent uses of the internet, such as browsing,

[136] Bunce (n 122) 246.
[137] P Mysoor, *Implied Licences in Copyright Law* (Oxford, Oxford University Press, 2021) 289.
[138] JS Sieman, 'Using the Implied License to Inject Common Sense into Digital Copyright' (2006) 85 *North Carolina Law Review* 885, 916.
[139] ibid 898.
[140] O Fischman Afori, 'Implied License: An Emerging New Standard in Copyright Law' (2009) 25 *Santa Clara Computer & High Technology Law Journal* 275, 278.

hyperlinking and indexing.[141] These differ significantly from CUGC sharing and therefore the arguments for implied licences are less compelling here. For example, Mysoor puts forward a strong argument for browsing to be permissible under a consent-based implied licence (based on her framework for identifying such licences), but is clear that wider uses, including CUGC interactions, go beyond consent as 'when a copyright owner places her work on the internet, while it is possible that her work can be downloaded, printed, adapted, reposted, and so on, these are not within her reasonable expectation that users would do'.[142] Social media platform terms of service are usually clear that their users retain copyright in their posted works and that sharing of CUGC does not provide a licence for others to carry out otherwise infringing acts, and so the argument that a consent-based licence exists is more challenging. The possible exception to this would be in cases where the CUGC was shared within communities with an express focus on one of these particular uses. For example, in *r/photoshopbattles* the entire focus of the subreddit is on altering images using Photoshop, and this is made explicit within the subreddit,[143] so uses within these parameters might be more acceptably implicitly licensed.

This focus on the technical functioning of the internet is also reflected in the existing case law, with cases often looking at issues relating to search engines and web crawlers.[144] A closer case on the facts falls outside the jurisdictional focus of this book, in the Australian case *Trumpet Winsock*.[145] It was held here that there was a limited implied licence to distribute shareware as a result of making it available but this licence did not extend to amending the work. However, this is an old case that seems to have had little consideration in other jurisdictions, is not specifically dealing with CUGC, and is limited in its scope to address common CUGC interactions such as remixing.

The use of implied licences is further complicated in the CUGC context by a lack of consistent approach across jurisdictions. In the US and Germany, implied licences have been found in relation to some search engine activities.[146] However, in the UK the scope of implied licences remains unclear. Bently et al identify that the UK courts 'have been reluctant to imply licences'.[147] The courts are rigid in their approach to implying terms into existing contracts but are more flexible in less formal circumstances.[148] Where actual consent is lacking, a licence may only be implied on public policy grounds, and this is uncommon.[149]

[141] See, eg: Sieman (n 138); Fischman Afori (n 140); Mysoor (n 137).

[142] Mysoor (n 137) 261.

[143] Reddit, 'R/PhotoshopBattles': www.reddit.com/r/photoshopbattles/.

[144] eg, in the US: *Field v Google, Inc*, 412 F Supp 2d 1106 (D Nev 2006); *Associated Press v Meltwater US Holdings, Inc*, 931 F Supp 2d 537 (SDNY 2013); In Germany: BGHZ I ZR 69/08 *Vorschaubilder*, 29 April 2010.

[145] *Trumpet Software Pty Ltd v OzEmail Pty Ltd* [1996] 34 IPR 481 (Federal Court of Australia).

[146] *Field v Google* (n 144); *Vorschaubilder* (n 144).

[147] L Bently et al, *Intellectual Property Law*, 6th edn (Oxford, Oxford University Press, 2022) 331.

[148] ibid 332.

[149] D Osborne, 'User Generated Content (UGC): Trade Mark and Copyright Infringement Issues' (2008) 3 *Journal of Intellectual Property Law & Practice* 555, 561–62.

Furthermore, even where implied licences have been found by the courts it seems that the reasoning can be easily distinguished from the CUGC context. In *Field*, the website owner was found to have granted an implied licence to Google to list his website in their search results because he chose not to use a mechanism to opt out of inclusion, despite knowing about it.[150] In *Vorschaubilder*,[151] it was held that unauthorised use of images as thumbnails by search engines was not copyright infringement if the copyright holder had not taken technical steps to prevent the copying (through a robots.txt command). In not taking such steps, the rights-holder was viewed to have consented to those acts because it was widely known how the Google Image search function operates.[152] Conversely, in *Meltwater*,[153] no implied licence was found, despite the fact the Associated Press (AP) had licensed the sections of articles to other organisations, because there was no 'interaction with AP from which it could be inferred that there was a meeting of minds between the parties that AP was granting Meltwater a non-exclusive licence'.[154] Additionally, claims that the licence was implied because AP licensees were not required to use a mechanism (like that in *Field*) to prevent web crawlers accessing their content could not be supported as this would be too burdensome for copyright holders.[155] This focus on accessing content and on the availability of straightforward measures to opt out of these automated processes differs greatly from what implied licences would need to address for CUGC, which includes a wide range of interactions, less compelling evidence and knowledge of consent and custom due to platform terms and conditions, and less straightforward or easily understood opt-out options.

What this shows is that even if there are compelling arguments for the use of implied licences in the CUGC context, this is currently not tested in law in these facts. Furthermore, the cases where implied licences have been found by the court are distinguishable from the CUGC context and demonstrate much stronger examples of consent or custom (the US and Germany), have limited applicability to CUGC interactions (Australia) or are rare (the UK).

C. Complicated Questions of Conflict of Laws

Finally, the anonymity of both creators and those interacting with CUGC makes navigating the copyright landscape difficult for the other. This is considered not just in terms of identifying an infringer, or licensing restricted uses of works, but also by adding another layer of uncertainty to an already complex interaction

[150] *Field v Google* (n 144).
[151] *Vorschaubilder* (n 144).
[152] I Stamatoudi and P Torremans, *EU Copyright Law: A Commentary* (Cheltenham, Edward Elgar Publishing, 2014) 458.
[153] *Associated Press v Meltwater* (n 144).
[154] ibid 562.
[155] ibid 563.

between globalised CUGC interactions on the internet and territorially focused copyright laws. As copyright laws are still set at the national level, we end up with the potential for different regulatory schemes from different countries to govern the same behaviour.[156] As demonstrated throughout this chapter, while copyright law has some broadly similar themes across jurisdictions, there remain many elements of difference in the scope and provision of rights. Deciding which country's laws should apply to a work shared on the internet, or to an infringement carried out online, can therefore have significant consequences for a rights-holder or user. For example, a transformative use of a copyrighted work might be able to rely on the fair use defence in the US, but that would not be available in the UK, or the sorts of moral rights available in Germany would not be available in the US. For orphan works, choosing the correct law is important as search requirements differ by country.[157]

Traditionally, international copyright law uses *lex loci protectionis*, that is, the law of the place where protection is being sought, in choice of law decisions. In practice, this is also the law of the place of the alleged infringement (*lex loci delicti*). However, in online interactions that place is difficult to define or could potentially mean that the laws of all countries apply simultaneously,[158] which is clearly an undesirable situation; it is unreasonable and impossible that an individual could know and adhere to all laws across differing countries.[159] The effect of this is legal uncertainty[160] for users and rights-holders, which in turn may lead to defensive approaches to sharing and uses of works, particularly in cases of non-professional creators who are less likely to have expert knowledge of copyright laws around the globe, or to be able to afford a lawyer to provide that. Many internet users assume that US law always applies to these scenarios because the websites are US based. However, in reality if the rights-holder and the infringer are based in the same country it is much more likely that their country of domicile is the most appropriate forum for any litigation.

Scholars have explored how other international law principles, such as *lex originis* (the law of the jurisdiction in which property originated) could better decide which law is the most closely linked in cases with global elements.[161] This does

[156] A Ohly, 'Choice of Law in the Digital Environment – Problems and Possible Solutions' in J Drexl, R Hilty and J Straus (eds), *Intellectual Property and Private International Law: Heading for the Future* (Oxford, Hart Publishing, 2005) 243; DJB Svantesson, *Private International Law and the Internet*, 3rd edn (Alphen aan den Rijn, Kluwer Law International, 2016) 3.

[157] AN Wilson, 'Jet-Setting Orphan Works: The Transnational Making Available of Works of Unknown Authorship, Anonymous Works, or Lost Authors' (2009) 23 *Emory International Law Review* 783, 790.

[158] R Matulionyte, 'The Law Applicable to Online Copyright Infringements in the ALI and CLIP Proposals: A Rebalance of Interests Needed' (2011) 2 *Journal of Intellectual Property, Information Technology and E-Commerce Law* 26, 27.

[159] C Reed, *Making Laws for Cyberspace* (Oxford, Oxford University Press, 2012) 18–19; Svantesson (n 156) 6–7.

[160] Matulionyte (n 158) 27.

[161] Ohly (n 156) 253.

little to reduce the legal uncertainty for creators and users, as it remains unclear which principle would apply. However, online anonymity makes this task significantly more difficult whichever principle is applied. Without identity knowledge of the location of the creator or user, in practice it is impossible for the anonymous CUGC creator or user to assess where protection is sought, where the work originated or where the infringement happened. Therefore, anonymity exacerbates the existing difficulties in dealing with the international nature of the interactions with CUGC.

V. Conclusion

This chapter has provided a detailed overview of the user-generated content (UGC) environment and the forms of anonymity within it, highlighting key areas of complexities. Evidently, copyright will often subsist in creative user-generated content, even where this is shared anonymously, and this provides creators with exclusive rights relevant to the types of interactions with that content.

In exploring whether these rights, in practice, have any effect, this chapter argued that there are fundamental problems that undermine the law as an effective system of regulation in an anonymous environment. Creators will find it difficult to enforce their rights against anonymous infringers, particularly without adequate legal advice. Anonymity also exacerbates legal uncertainty regarding how a work can be used and the laws that apply. Anonymous creators are essentially creating large numbers of orphan works, as users may have no practical or reliable way to get, or circumvent, the author's permission to carry out technically infringing acts. The fact that creators may not enforce their rights is irrelevant, as without explicit knowledge of this, users will have to decide whether to risk using the work. The potential solutions to orphan works are inadequate for these forms of orphan works, as where specific provisions do exist, they are formulated too narrowly or inappropriately for the types of interactions that occur. Where other solutions exist, such as fair use or implied licences, it is often difficult to predict whether they would apply, which leaves the user in the same position as they started in.

Additionally, anonymity makes it harder for creators and users to know which laws apply to their interactions online. As the scope of rights available varies according to jurisdiction, as do the potential solutions to orphan works, it is important to know which law is relevant. This is already a highly confused and complex legal area. However, anonymity in creative online communities further undermines their ability to make reasonable assessments. Copyright law is territorially focused, but as creators and users are abstracted from their identity, and therefore physical location, identifying relevant law becomes even more difficult.

Therefore, copyright law and online anonymity are shown to be mismatched on a practical level. This raises key questions to be considered in subsequent chapters. Why do creators choose anonymous identity practices, when this perpetuates anonymity online and undermines the system that is supposed to regulate it? Are there benefits to being anonymous that exceed those of copyright law, or is the claimed link between copyright law and creativity in this sense exaggerated or inaccurate? How do these issues link to the needs and desires of creative user-generated content (CUGC) creators, users and communities? What implications does this have for copyright law and what should be done about it?

3

Optimising Creativity: Copyright and Anonymity

I. Introduction

This chapter is about the relationships between creativity and both copyright law and anonymity. It starts with an exploration of the creativity rhetoric that underpins arguments supporting copyright law and its expansion. The chapter argues that using the concept of optimising creativity to guide what copyright law looks like is normatively coherent, but that there is an apparent disconnect between copyright's current conception of creativity and creativity in reality. It demonstrates this disconnect by examining who benefits from copyright law and how the law reflects creative processes, in particular in relation to authorship and incentives.

The chapter further explores creativity in the anonymous online world. Presenting qualitative findings, it explores the impact of pervasive online anonymity on creative user-generated content (CUGC) creator practices and identifies several creative benefits. Based on this anonymous creativity, the chapter develops a critique of copyright, highlighting that anonymity practices, while problematic for copyright law, are often favourable for creativity, and furthermore are beneficial for creativity in ways that copyright law often fails to be.

II. Copyright Law and Creativity

The first half of the chapter focuses on copyright law and creativity as a concept, the claims made about their relationship to one another, and the reality of this relationship. It argues that while creativity and associated concepts such as authorship and originality are viewed as central elements of justificatory and policy rhetoric for copyright law, the role that copyright law plays in creativity is in fact much narrower; copyright law benefits corporate actors more than the individual creators invoked in the rhetoric and does not fully understand the creative process, risking over-protection of works and undermining the fertile network of external influences needed for creativity to flourish. It starts with an explanation of the narratives that place creativity at the heart of copyright law, highlighting that their focus on creativity, and particularly optimising creativity, is normatively desirable. It then explores various inconsistencies in these narratives, including with the experiences of CUGC creators from Reddit and 4chan, and the implications of this for copyright policy that aims to optimise creativity.

A. Creativity at the Heart of Copyright

Creativity and related concepts such as authorship run through the heart of copyright law's jurisprudential theory and through narratives in copyright scholarship and policymaking. Creativity is described as a 'trope'[1] and the 'raison d'être'[2] of copyright law, with a 'tight linkage' between the two.[3] While the lay concept of creativity plays only a minor role in the technical day-to-day of copyright law – works need only to be creative enough in their choices to pass a very low threshold as seen in cases with football pool coupons and telephone directories in chapter two[4] – creativity plays a significant justificatory role for copyright law.

There are various theoretical approaches to justifying copyright law, with Fisher outlining the four main positions (either consequentialist or deontological).[5] In the consequentialist category, copyright acts either as a utilitarian incentive to maximise the creation of future works for social benefit[6] (incentive-based justifications)[7] or as means of achieving broader social aims, such as democratic participation ('social planning theory' justification).[8] Deontological positions include the Lockean natural rights argument that proprietary rights should be granted to creators as a reward for their labour (reward/desert justifications), and the argument that creators hold rights over their creations as they represent extensions of their personhood (personality-based justifications). Historically, there has been a divide between approaches to copyright in common law jurisdictions such as in the UK and US who favour the economic incentive model (and the natural rights position) and those in European civil law countries where moral

[1] MJ Madison, 'Beyond Creativity: Copyright as Knowledge Law' (2009) 12 *Vanderbilt Journal of Entertainment and Technology Law* 817, 820.

[2] JC Ginsburg, 'The Concept of Authorship in Comparative Copyright Law' (2002) 52 *De Paul Law Review* 1063, 1092.

[3] JE Cohen, 'Creativity and Culture in Copyright Theory' (2007) 40 *UC Davis Law Review* 1151, 1192.

[4] See: ch 2, section III.A; *Ladbroke (Football) v William Hill (Football)* [1964] 1 All ER 465; *Feist Publications, Incorporated v Rural Telephone Service Company, Incorporated* 499 US 340 (1991).

[5] WW Fisher, 'Theories of Intellectual Property' in SR Munzer (ed), *New Essays in the Legal and Political Theory of Property* (Cambridge, Cambridge University Press, 2001).

[6] The Copyright Clause found in Article 1(8)(8) of the US Constitution grants Congress the power: 'To promote the progress of science and useful arts, by securing for limited times to authors and inventors the exclusive right to their respective writings and discoveries'. In the UK, the Hargreaves Report focused on whether IP laws needed reform in order 'to promote innovation and growth in the UK economy': I Hargreaves, 'Digital Opportunity: A Review of Intellectual Property and Growth: An Independent Report' (2011).

[7] WM Landes and RA Posner, 'An Economic Analysis of Copyright Law' (1989) 18 *Journal of Legal Studies* 325.

[8] NW Netanel, 'Copyright and a Democratic Civil Society' (1996) 106 *Yale Law Journal* 283.

rights or an author's rights based on personality arguments are more prevalent.[9] While these differences still exist,[10] economic rights and their related theoretical justifications have become more widespread in civil law jurisdictions as a result of increasing supranational influence over intellectual property (IP), seen in examples such as EU IP harmonisation and the trade-focused TRIPS agreement.

The incentive theory in particular has much influence on law and policymaking. Despite vigorous ongoing debates within copyright law and scholarship, both copyright proponents and copyright sceptics accept the stance that copyright should promote creativity.[11] Alongside this, however, concepts of incentive and reward tend to be conflated;[12] Waldron argues that justificatory logic often evolves from the incentive argument into the reward theory, 'from encouragement to incentive to benefit to reward to desert'.[13] Regardless of which of the three most influential theories is relied on, creativity and related concepts are central, in some form. In the incentive justification, the aim is to maximise the production and dissemination of creative works, and in the reward and personality justifications, the inherent rights of the creator as 'author' of their works are key. This is reflected in creativity rhetoric found in policy debates which is often found in arguments for expanding or strengthening copyright law.[14] This rhetoric positions creators and creativity as the beneficiaries of copyright law, as can be most clearly seen in the rhetoric of 'fair remuneration' for artists and creators that dominates policy debates: debates in the European Parliament during the EU copyright reforms is a good example of this, where 'fair remuneration' featured heavily in supporting arguments and in the Copyright Directive that arose from them.[15]

As outlined in chapter one, what is meant and what is understood by 'creativity' is often unclear, and creativity rhetoric also falls foul of this. The theoretical arguments approach creativity in terms of the production of outputs (incentive theory and reward theory) or as a quality of an individual (personality-based justifications). However, its power as rhetoric relies on the everyday understanding

[9] In practice, the social planning theory approach has little influence on law and policymaking, being more visible in academic criticism. As such, this is not explored in detail here.

[10] As outlined in ch 2, section III.B (on moral rights in the US and UK etc).

[11] A Drassinower, 'A Note on Incentives, Rights, and the Public Domain in Copyright Law' (2011) 86 *Notre Dame Law Review* 1869, 1872; JE Cohen, *Configuring the Networked Self: Law, Code and the Play of Everyday Practice* (New Haven, CT, Yale University Press, 2012) 61–62.

[12] R Towse, 'Partly for the Money: Rewards and Incentives to Artists' (2001) 54 *Kyklos* 473, 476–77.

[13] J Waldron, 'From Authors to Copiers: Individual Rights and Social Values in Intellectual Property' (1993) 68 *Chicago-Kent Law Review* 841, 851.

[14] P Jaszi, 'Toward a Theory of Copyright: The Metamorphoses of "Authorship"' (1991) 1991 *Duke Law Journal* 455, 480; A Barron, 'Copyright Law and the Claims of Art' (2002) 4 *Intellectual Property Quarterly* 368, 368; R Towse, 'Creativity, Copyright and the Creative Industries Paradigm' (2010) 63 *Kyklos* 461, 463–464; Drassinower (n 11) 1870.

[15] See, eg, European Parliament, 'Debates – Tuesday, 11 September 2018 – Copyright in the Digital Single Market (Debate)' (European Parliament, 2018): www.europarl.europa.eu/sides/getDoc.do?type=CRE&reference=20180911&secondRef=ITEM-012&language=EN. Directive (EU) 2019/790 of the European Parliament and of the Council of 17 April 2019 on copyright and related rights in the Digital Single Market and amending Directives 96/9/EC and 2001/29/EC (Text with EEA relevance) [2019] OJ L130/92 (CDSM Directive).

of creativity that leads creators and creativity to be held in high esteem in society. Through this, creativity contributes to copyright law's ongoing development (most often its expansion or strengthening) by lending its culturally, socially and politically appealing language of artists, authors and creators to policymaking narratives around incentives and fair remuneration. In this framing, creativity does a lot of heavy lifting for copyright law, and it is the position of this book that copyright policy that centres creativity as a concept and recognises the value of the output of creators to our society is coherent and desirable. As will be explored further below, however, copyright's role for creativity is far less compelling.

B. Rhetoric vs Reality

As highlighted, creativity rhetoric and narratives are often used as a means of justifying copyright law and expansions to the law. From these narratives, it would seem we pursue copyright policy centred around optimising creativity, in the sense of creating the conditions for it to flourish, for one reason or another whether it is rewarding creators or encouraging them to create. However, it is challenging to align those narratives with how copyright law operates on a practical level. This section explores several elements of this. First, it highlights that despite the rhetoric the beneficiaries of copyright are largely corporate entities rather than creators themselves. Secondly, it explores the discrepancies between copyright law's intrinsic definitions of creativity and the reality of the creative process, both in terms of its framing of authorship and its approach to incentivising creativity. In doing so, it highlights that copyright's focus on creativity does not reflect the breadth and diversity of creative practice, prioritising one particular conception of creativity to the detriment of others.

i. The Beneficiaries of Copyright Law

One element of this is the focus on creators or authors as a focal point of arguments put forward, as seen in the 'fair remuneration' arguments described above. This focus provides a sympathetic beneficiary in the narratives,[16] tied very much into the 'Romantic' and popular notion of the artist. When the argument is more protection for poor starving artists, musicians, painters, film-makers and the like, it is understandable that the response is to support the proposition. Cohen explains, '[n]o one wants to be against creativity, and if copyright equals creativity, then no one wants to be against copyright'.[17] However, the link to creativity in copyright

[16] J Boyle, *Shamans, Software, and Spleens: Law and the Construction of the Information Society* (Cambridge MA, Harvard University Press, 1997) 142.

[17] Cohen, 'Creativity and Culture in Copyright Theory' (n 3) 1192.

law narratives is undermined to some extent by the fact that the beneficiaries of copyright law are, most often, corporate, commercial entities (who finance and distribute works rather than create them) and the law is created and amended in response to their interests.

Policymaking in copyright law is heavily influenced by corporate interests. In the past, copyright law had little impact on the day-to-day lives of ordinary people, and as such, the industries that copyright regulated were active in helping to shape the law.[18] Despite the fact that copyright law's impact is no longer limited in that way due to digital technologies, the influence of industry on law and policymaking in this area remains high. First, they are often offered a seat at the negotiating table where other stakeholders are not; Litman describes the negotiations leading up to the Digital Millennium Copyright Act and how the copyright industries were instrumental in shaping the law, while others such as public interest groups, libraries and universities were less visible or absent entirely from discussions.[19] The economic importance of the copyright industries in Western economies gives them leverage to continue leading and influencing the development of copyright law.[20] This in turn means that copyright law and policy reflects the interests of those industries, while the interests of other stakeholders can often be drowned out.[21]

Secondly, because the copyright industries have a lot to lose in the new digital creative environment and also have deep pockets, they are able to invest large amounts of money lobbying lawmakers to strengthen IP rights in their favour. The success of this lobbying is often aided by low voter interest in copyright issues,[22] which means industry can be the dominant stakeholder voice in consultations. However, even where there is significant voter interest industry retains an upper hand because it is better funded; campaigns for user rights online are usually grassroots campaigns or led by civil society organisations and as such are operating on limited budgets. This means that copyright debates are often stacked in industries' favour, and lead to laws that prioritise their needs.

That is not to say that there are not valuable reasons to provide protection for commercial interests. Exclusive rights for corporate entities may be essential for the distribution of some creative works and therefore benefit creativity in general; without copyright, intermediaries would not take on the risk of investing

[18] JD Litman, *Digital Copyright* (Amherst, NY, Prometheus Books, 2006).

[19] ibid 127, 140.

[20] P Ganley, 'The Internet, Creativity and Copyright Incentives' (2005) 10 *Journal of Intellectual Property Rights* 188, 189; Towse, 'Creativity, Copyright and the Creative Industries Paradigm' (n 14) 462.

[21] B Klein, G Moss and L Edwards, *Understanding Copyright: Intellectual Property in the Digital Age* (London, SAGE Publications, 2015) 41; DJ Gervais, *(Re)Structuring Copyright: A Comprehensive Path to International Copyright Reform* (Cheltenham, Edward Elgar Publishing, 2017) 55.

[22] B Farrand, 'Lobbying and Lawmaking in the European Union: The Development of Copyright Law and the Rejection of the Anti-Counterfeiting Trade Agreement' (2015) 35 *Oxford Journal of Legal Studies* 487.

in the marketing, publishing and distribution of works.[23] However, the correlation between corporate and creator interests may be overstated. Davis identifies that the risk being borne by intermediaries is unlikely to be as high as to justify current levels of control over works, instead arguing that it is more about maximising all possible profit.[24] Furthermore, there have been arguments that the role of intermediaries is dwindling as digital networking technologies allow individuals to distribute their creative work themselves.[25] While undoubtedly true to some extent, there remains a need for intermediaries in many cases, and Barnett argues that copyright law that preserves corporate intermediaries' ability to exist is vital so that there is an efficient creative economy, that is, the most effective form of distribution can be pursued for each creative work.[26] However, it cannot be the only priority within copyright law, otherwise the rhetoric about creators as beneficiaries is misleading.

The benefit of corporate-held copyright for individual creators is also undermined by the reality that individual creators do not tend to benefit from increases in copyright protection. Merges argues that it is acceptable to prioritise the needs of commercial entities over, for example, amateur creators, as they are the ones who pay, employ and train creators, allowing individual creators to make a living from their creative work (which he sees as the point of copyright law).[27] However, rewards from copyright for creators tend to be small except for a few very high earners, and in many cases artists' and creators' earnings are linked to royalty rates they have negotiated with a distributor.[28] Of course, without the initial copyright they hold, creators would not be able to negotiate these rates, but the balance of power in these negotiations is rarely equal[29] and so the value of the copyright to the distributor is, comparatively, greater. Furthermore, that remuneration for creative work is so disparate between the low and high earners indicates that this process is not working effectively – Davis describes it as a lottery.[30] As such, it does not seem that copyright created and expanded in response to corporate interests has much direct relation to the experience of individual creators.

This is problematic for the authenticity of copyright's creativity rhetoric. The claims it makes trade on the social value given to creators, while instead it mainly benefits corporations. That corporate actors benefit is, in itself, not a problem.

[23] JM Barnett, 'Copyright without Creators' (2014) 9 *Review of Law & Economics* 389, 390–91; G Davis, 'When Copyright is Not Enough: Deconstructing Why, as the Modern Music Industry Takes, Musicians Continue to Make' (2017) 16 *Chicago-Kent Journal of Intellectual Property* 373, 391–92.

[24] Davis (n 23) 392.

[25] Litman, *Digital Copyright* (n 18) 104–05; Y Benkler, *The Wealth of Networks: How Social Production Transforms Markets and Freedom* (New Haven, CT, Yale University Press, 2007).

[26] Barnett (n 23) 424–26.

[27] RP Merges, 'The Concept of Property in the Digital Era' (2008) 45 *Houston Law Review* 1239, 1250.

[28] R Towse, 'The Quest for Evidence on the Economic Effects of Copyright Law' (2013) 37 *Cambridge Journal of Economics* 1187, 1195–96.

[29] Towse, 'Creativity, Copyright and the Creative Industries Paradigm' (n 14) 467–68; Klein, Moss and Edwards (n 21) 29.

[30] JD Litman, 'Real Copyright Reform' (2010) 96 *Iowa Law Review* 1, 9–10; Davis (n 23).

But would calls for copyright expansion have been as successful were they framed more accurately? Large corporate entities are certainly far less compelling as beneficiaries. Furthermore, that copyright is largely corporate held and influenced is particularly of concern in relation to the public domain. Increasing corporate-held copyright may particularly stifle forms of creativity as tighter copyright controls restrict the individual creator's access and use of existing works and cultural references. Scholars have argued that a further effect of this is a reduction in cultural and creative diversity: since large corporate copyright owners create and control more cultural and creative points of reference and restrict other forms of creativity, they become the dominant creative voice, leading to a homogenous corporate creative environment.[31] The significance of the public domain is explored further below, but is an essential component of the creative process. As such, a narrow focus on corporate influence may not be adequate for creativity-focused copyright policy.

From this we can see that creators are often not the main beneficiaries of copyright law and policymaking, but that framing them as such can lead to copyright expansions that benefit the actual, mostly corporate, copyright holders.

ii. Copyright Law and the Creative Process

If copyright aims to optimise creativity, as it claims and this book argues it should, then it needs to accurately reflect the creative process. However, copyright law struggles to acknowledge the diverse reality of the creative process, both in how it defines and recognises creators through notions of authorship and originality and in how it attempts to incentivise production. On these issues, copyright law's understanding of the creative process is too narrow to be able to comprehensively and effectively regulate creativity.

The author is a key foundational concept in copyright law as its constitutional subject.[32] Its legal definition focuses largely on the Romantic, solitary creator from whom inspiration springs to make them the sole originator of a work, but this has been criticised for prioritising some forms of creativity and excluding others[33] and overlooking the influence of existing cultural and semiotic sources on creators and their works.[34] Instead, copyright's view of authorship based on individual originality has been highlighted as arising from the eighteenth century, rather than a reflection of the intrinsic nature of the creative process. Before this, the author was generally viewed as an interpreter of culture or craftsman, rather than

[31] F Macmillan, 'Cultural Diversity in an Era of Corporate Dominance: A Clash of Rights?' (2007) DIME Working Papers on Intellectual Property Rights, Working Paper No 29, 8–9.

[32] Ginsburg (n 2) 1064.

[33] P Jaszi, 'On the Author Effect: Contemporary Copyright and Collective Creativity' (1991) 10 *Cardozo Arts & Entertainment Law Journal* 293, 302; Boyle, *Shamans, Software, and Spleens* (n 16) 119.

[34] (Disputing their point) RA Spinello and M Bottis, *A Defense of Intellectual Property Rights* (Cheltenham, Edward Elgar Publishing, 2009) 121.

an individual genius.[35] This view recognises that there is a non-static and collaborative quality to creativity as works build on what has come before to code and recode meaning, even where they are not an obvious example of collective effort;[36] creativity cannot happen in a vacuum. This view also therefore calls into question the concept of originality[37] and the legal protections afforded to authors on that basis.

This critique of the concept of the author translates particularly well to the digital age, where the ability to build extensive networks easily facilitates large-scale interaction with external sources and creative processes built more explicitly on collaboration, bricolage and co-creation, seen in examples such as Wikipedia or open-source software.[38] We see parallels in the narratives here between pre-eighteenth century creativity and online creativity, with online creators similarly framed as interpreters,[39] their outputs as flows rather than static ideas,[40] and their processes as a challenge to copyright's understanding of authorship and the creative process.[41]

This flawed understanding of the creative process can be problematic as the requirement of originality sets the boundaries of what are creative works and who are creative authors. In its current form, copyright law can find it difficult to recognise multiple authors in complex interactions. While there is scope within the law to acknowledge joint works, the law can struggle with larger-scale projects or projects where contributors and contributions are difficult to define as it awards protection only to identifiable authors with identifiable inputs. In comparison to more traditional creative settings, online collaborative creative processes can be more complex, for example it is easier to identify authors and their defined contributions in an edited collection of five authors, than it is to do so for a piece of open-source computer code with thousands of contributors. This means that, in its current form, copyright law leads to a prioritisation of individual creativity over collective and collaborative production models.[42]

[35] Jaszi 'Toward a Theory of Copyright' (n 14) 455–56; M Woodmansee, *The Author, Art and the Market: Rereading the History of Aesthetics* (New York, Columbia University Press, 1996) 36–37; C Hesse, 'The Rise of Intellectual Property, 700 BC–AD 2000: An Idea in the Balance' (2002) 131 *Daedalus* 26, 32.

[36] RH Rotstein, 'Beyond Metaphor: Copyright Infringement and the Fiction of the Work' (1993) 68 *Chicago-Kent Law Review* 725; K Aoki, 'Adrift in the Intertext: Authorship and Audience Recoding Rights – Comment on Robert H Rotstein, Beyond Metaphor: Copyright Infringement and the Fiction of the Work' (1993) 68 *Chicago-Kent Law Review* 805.

[37] Waldron (n 13) 878.

[38] P Levy, *Cyberculture*, R Bononno trans (Minneapolis, MN, University of Minnesota Press, 2001) 116; M Deuze, 'Participation, Remediation, Bricolage: Considering Principal Components of a Digital Culture' (2006) 22 *The Information Society* 63; Benkler (n 25); L Lessig, *Remix: Making Art and Commerce Thrive in the Hybrid Economy* (New York, Bloomsbury Academic, 2008).

[39] Levy (n 38) 132.

[40] ibid 129–31.

[41] M Chon, 'New Wine Bursting from Old Bottles: Collaborative Internet Art, Joint Works, and Entrepreneurship' (1996) 75 *Oregon Law Review* 257, 263.

[42] M Woodmansee, 'On the Author Effect: Recovering Collectivity' (1991) 10 *Cardozo Arts & Entertainment Law Journal* 279, 291–92.

Of course, as Merges points out, individual creativity still occurs[43] and not all online creativity is overtly collaborative. Indeed, the type of CUGC that is the focus of this book is often 'individual' in the sense that it has been produced by one person, in a way that very much resembles the notion of the sole genius author being criticised here. However, on closer inspection this fails to address the much broader argument that even where creative work is undertaken by an individual rather than a collective, that individual is drawing from a broad range of sources and the work is created as interplay between its creator and his or her external network. Taken to its extreme, this argument undermines any workable notion of originality and means that attributing exclusive rights to an individual would be flawed if not unjustifiable. However, this is not the position taken here. Regardless of the breadth of external inputs into the creative process, the author still plays a significant role in that process, as the 'creative catalyst' and therefore still merits some protection.[44] However, this understanding of the creative process does mean that the way that copyright law is structured in relation to access to works and the public domain is highly important. Such a need for access to creative and cultural material is supported by neuroscience that indicates that regardless of the brilliance of an individual mind, it needs to be able to interact within a 'fertile' external network of sources, information and influences to make the necessary connections for creativity.[45] Copyright policy that does not recognise this runs the risk of getting the balance wrong and undesirably restricting the scope of this network.

Beyond its conceptions of authorship, copyright law's understanding of the creative process is also flawed in relation to its approach to incentives. As outlined above, the incentive argument is one of the key strands of creativity rhetoric underpinning copyright law. Inherent in the incentive argument for copyright are several assumptions about creativity.[46] Framing copyright as an incentive is a utilitarian approach that argues that private rights are an economically efficient way to incentivise creativity and therefore promote innovation for social benefit; exclusivity rights enable creators and distributors to exploit the market for their works, thereby providing the opportunity for them to recover the costs of expression and production, without which it is said that they would not create.[47] Copyright law, via this reasoning, views creativity as a rational, economically motivated activity whose intended output is a commodity. The problem with this is that creativity has been shown to be messier, more diverse and more complex than this in many ways.[48]

[43] Merges (n 27).

[44] Spinello and Bottis (n 34) 127; R Rosenthal Kwall, 'Originality in Context' (2007) 44 *Houston Law Review* 871, 873.

[45] E Reuveni, 'Copyright, Neuroscience and Creativity' (2013) 64 *Alabama Law Review* 735, 752.

[46] Cohen, 'Creativity and Culture in Copyright Theory' (n 3) 1151.

[47] Landes and Posner (n 7).

[48] R Tushnet, 'Economies of Desire: Fair Use and Marketplace Assumption' (2009) 51 *William & Mary Law Review* 513, 516; J Silbey, *The Eureka Myth: Creators, Innovators, and Everyday Intellectual*

First, scholars of copyright's 'negative space' have explored the flaws in considering copyright law a necessary incentive to all creativity by studying specific creative industries and communities that thrive outside the protection of copyright law, such as in the graffiti and street art subculture, or the fashion industry.[49] These studies have highlighted that even where copyright protection is either not available or is available but not enforced, creativity is not lacking, and in many cases is in fact better served by being in a 'low-IP' environment.[50] Rosenblatt sets out several reasons why this may be the case even when IP protection is available (as it often is for CUGC). She argues that sometimes it is because creators have an ideological interest in ensuring free access to creations, as they prefer to use financial resources to create rather than pursue IP protection or enforcement, or because the community relies on building on others' work (as argued above).[51] Sometimes, however, it is because there are other motivations for creativity,[52] which directly conflict with the incentive theory's narrative as it shows that creativity is not always economically motivated and copyright is not always essential.

Of course, rather than a belief that all types of creativity can be incentivised by the same measures, copyright policy may instead be merely indifferent to incentivising those creators that are not economically motivated. This may be because they are willing to create without the law stepping in, like the creators in the negative space studies, or because the law is focusing on what is most important. For example, Merges argues that the incentive argument can be considered as a quality rather than a quantity issue. For him, rather than focusing on generating the highest number of creative outputs possible, economic incentives allow more time and effort to be put into works and mean a creator can invest time developing to 'become in a true sense a creative *professional*'.[53] He also argues that copyright law is not universalised, as creators and industries or communities can and do elect to ignore or waive their rights. As such, a spectrum of protection can be chosen, whereas in the alternative approach of lowering protection, choice is denied to those who would like or need higher protection.[54]

Property (Stanford, CA, Stanford University Press, 2015); C Sprigman, 'Conclusion: Some Positive Thoughts about IP's Negative Space' in A Perzanowski and K Darling (eds), *Creativity without Law: Challenging the Assumptions of Intellectual Property* (New York, NYU Press, 2017) 257.

[49] eg, see: K Darling, 'IP without IP: A Study of the Online Adult Entertainment Industry' (2013) 17 *Stanford Technology Law Review* 709 (on the pornography industry); M Iljadica, *Copyright Beyond Law: Regulating Creativity in the Graffiti Subculture* (Oxford, Hart Publishing, 2016) (on graffiti and street art); J Loshin, 'Secrets Revealed: Protecting Magicians' Intellectual Property without Law' in CA Corcos (ed), *Law and Magic: A Collection of Essays* (Durham, NC, Carolina Academic Press, 2010) (on magicians); K Raustiala and CJ Sprigman, 'The Piracy Paradox Revisited' (2009) 61 *Stanford Law Review* 1201 (on fashion).

[50] EL Rosenblatt, 'A Theory of IP's Negative Space' (2011) 34 *Columbia Journal of Law & the Arts* 317, 322.

[51] ibid 342.

[52] ibid.

[53] Merges (n 27) 1262–63.

[54] ibid 1240.

However, this narrow approach to incentives is problematic for multiple reasons. First, even if it is accepted that focusing on economically productive creativity is desirable, the approach to incentives is not particularly economically efficient, either in terms of creativity or the economy more widely. In their empirical study, Ku, Sun and Fan found that the responses to changes in copyright law were inconsistent across different types of work, and as such they 'cast serious doubt on the idea that … one size fits all' in terms of incentives.[55] This universal approach to various types of creativity, industries and communities comes with a 'uniformity cost' as works are invariably under-protected or over-protected making the system inefficient.[56] Furthermore, earlier in this chapter it was explained that the remuneration many individual creators receive for their work is limited, with only a few becoming highly successful. This could be seen as an economic motivator, in that creators produce works as a way of playing the success lottery in the hope of winning. However, Davis highlights that it is an inefficient social system that encourages lots of people to create commercially unviable works instead of spending their time in a socially productive way, for example working a role that pays and needs filling.[57] This undermines an argument built on economic efficiency or social utility.

Secondly, the current legal approach could be counterproductive for creativity as economic incentives may be ineffective motivators, leading to below optimal creative outputs. While economic evidence to support copyright's incentive argument is lacking,[58] research into the psychology of creativity provides insights that suggest that copyright law may be ineffective at incentivising creativity because it focuses on the least effective types of motivators. There are two types of motivators for creativity: intrinsic/internal and extrinsic/external.[59] Intrinsic or internal motivators ('intrinsic motivators') emanate from within the creator, and encompass 'inherent interest, involvement, or challenge found in a given task or project'[60] as well as enjoyment and pro-social behaviour, such as an

[55] R Ku, J Sun and Y Fan, 'Does Copyright Law Promote Creativity? An Empirical Analysis of Copyright's Bounty' (2009) 62 *Vanderbilt Law Review* 1667, 1669.

[56] MW Carroll, 'One for All: The Problem of Uniformity Cost in Intellectual Property Law' (2005) 55 *American University Law Review* 845, 856; LA Heymann, 'A Tale of (at Least) Two Authors: Focusing Copyright Law on Process over Product' (2008) 34 *Journal of Corporation Law* 1009, 1011.

[57] Davis (n 23) 385–86.

[58] Conducting economic research to properly assess copyright's role in incentivising creativity is tricky and, so far, such evidence is lacking. Towse highlights that it is hard to conduct economic research into copyright law because there are lots of variables (different rights, different works, etc) and because finding the data is difficult because of registration. She argues that the research that does exist focuses on measuring the contribution to GDP of the copyright industries, but that none of this addresses the core issue of incentives (nor presumably can it due to the limitations previously mentioned): Towse, 'The Quest for Evidence on the Economic Effects of Copyright Law' (n 28) 1190–91.

[59] GN Mandel, 'To Promote the Creative Process: Intellectual Property Law and the Psychology of Creativity' (2011) 86 *Notre Dame Law Review* 1999, 2007–10; C Dent, 'Decisions Around Innovation and the Motivators that Contribute to Them: Patents, Copyright, Trade Marks and Know-How' (2016) 6 *Queen Mary Journal of Intellectual Property Law* 435, 437–38.

[60] Mandel (n 59) 2008.

action that will benefit a community.[61] Extrinsic or external motivators ('extrinsic motivators') on the other hand, are external goals and come in the form of threats or rewards, for example a salary or a prize.[62]

Research shows that intrinsic motivators are far more effective at incentivising creativity than extrinsic motivators,[63] and that extrinsic motivators can in fact have a negative impact on creativity as, while they lead to a higher number of works, these tend to be less creative.[64] This is because extrinsic motivators encourage creators to focus on the external reward rather than engaging with the task at hand, which leads to a formulaic approach to problem-solving and a reduced level of creativity in the final work.[65] This conflicts with Merges' claim that economic rights facilitate higher quality work as Merges argues. The research also shows, however, that there is scope for extrinsic motivators to have positive effects where they increase intrinsic motivators, for example where they become 'reputational', that is, where they 'relate to the role particular actions have in altering how other people react to the person concerned'.[66] Reputational motivators are extrinsic motivators that enhance intrinsic motivation, for example by confirming the creator's competence with a prize awarded by peers on the basis of their ability. When construed as an economic incentive, copyright seems to fall into the category of an extrinsic motivator, as a 'task performance reward'[67] and as it is available to all works regardless of creativity level, it is unable to offer creators the confirmation of their competence that is required for it to be a reputational motivator.

Finally, to focus narrowly on creating the conditions for only particular types of creativity to flourish is a short-sighted way of viewing the creative environment. Arguments about quality are flawed and outdated in the digital age. Litman explains how considering non-commercial creativity to be of lower quality is incorrect and argues that there is much that would be worth paying for, identifying several examples of copyrightable works provided for free online by their creators that are of higher quality than those available commercially.[68] Furthermore, as the discussion later in this chapter outlines, these non-commercial communities are seen by some as an important and more accessible element of their creative training by providing them with the opportunity to get feedback, edits and suggestions from others in the same way Merges deems necessary for creators to become professional. It seems therefore important to consider and balance the needs of all types of creativity and copyright holder, and to ensure that the way copyright law

[61] Dent (n 59) 437.
[62] Mandel (n 59) 2008; Dent (n 59) 437–38.
[63] TM Amabile, *Creativity in Context*, 2nd edn (New York, Routledge, 2018) 17.
[64] Mandel (n 59) 2007–08.
[65] ibid 2008.
[66] Dent (n 59) 438.
[67] Mandel (n 59) 2013.
[68] Litman, *Digital Copyright* (n 18) 107.

is set up to benefit economically motivated creativity does not disproportionately undermine other forms.

This links particularly with earlier points on the significance of access to a network of inspiration and the public domain, where high levels of copyright protection may negatively impact wider creative practices. Reuveni highlights that access to the 'fertile' external network of sources referred to above is a potential 'choke-point' where copyright policy could, if configured incorrectly, have a negative impact on creativity were it to restrict what is available within this network.[69] Boyle has argued that this is the case as the copyright industries react to the 'internet threat' by lobbying for increased copyright provisions to protect their business models[70] and we have seen increasing levels of copyright protection and enforcement over the past few decades. The effect of copyright in this case is therefore not merely neutral with regard to the creative process, but in fact possibly negative, and as such calls further into question the creativity rhetoric used in support of it. The wider implications of copyright's flawed understanding of the creative process and of its focus on corporate beneficiaries is that the creativity rhetoric lacks authenticity; when it evokes sympathetic narratives relating to creativity it is not clear that it means only some creativity, some of the time, and nor that its effect as an incentive is similarly limited. When it is used to influence copyright policy, rhetoric overstating copyright's link to creativity can lead to over-protection of works.

C. Creative Incentives on 4chan and Reddit

Having identified these concerns, this part of the chapter moves on to explore the extent to which the creativity rhetoric and criticisms thereof are reflected in the qualitative findings from 4chan and Reddit. In particular, it outlines what motivates CUGC creators to create and share within online communities. While previous research has identified diverse motivations for creativity, it is important to also understand what motivates the specific creators being focused on in this book. The data collected and presented here focuses on what motivates, incentivises and inspires creators in CUGC communities to create and share their work. This was collected from 12 online interviews (8 with Redditors and 4 with 4channers) and 44 relevant online thread discussion (33 from Reddit and 11 from 4chan).

A wide range and variety of themes emerged from the data, and the findings correlate with the arguments already made above in that motivators are shown to be diverse and complex, with creators often citing multiple factors. The majority of the motivators mentioned were internal or endogenous in that they were about the

[69] Reuveni (n 45) 761.

[70] J Boyle, *The Public Domain: Enclosing the Commons of the Mind* (New Haven, CT, Yale University Press, 2008).

creator's own drive, interest or enjoyment ('I love to create')[71] or about the positive effect being creative or creating something has on them. For example, the most commonly mentioned theme across the data was that creators were motivated by the happiness, fun and enjoyment they derived from the process, with a natural or innate creative drive or ability also being frequently cited. Relatedly, some creators highlighted that being creative was part of their identity, or that they had to create to express themselves.

There were several external motivators that acted as pull-factors in creativity, of which economic or professional reasons and validation ('It's a wonderful feeling when someone genuinely likes your work and takes time to say something nice')[72] were the most significant. Competition was also cited as an occasional external motivator ('sometimes when I write I want to prove to myself that I can write something a bit better [than other authors]'),[73] as was being inspired to create by something, often another creator or creative work, but also nature or other interests.

Some of the motivators focused specifically on the process, with little interest in the form or quality of the resulting creative work. For example, a theme of 'well-being' emerged, with creators finding the process therapeutic. There were also a number of creators who were motivated to create in order to process knowledge or understanding by clarifying their thoughts or to work through difficult things, or for the sense of achievement from taking on a challenge and accomplishing something. Personal self-improvement was also a theme, with creators finding working towards a goal or continued learning to be valuable to them. Improving creatively was also a motivator, with some commenters citing this creative process as an alternative to more formal creative education. Others saw the creative process as a means to an end, in that it either encourages them to explore new places or adventures, or that it more generally gives them something to do to pass the time.

Some of the motivators related to a focus on the final product. A theme of 'necessity' aligned with creators responding to a gap in the market they wish to be filled, for example by writing the specific piece of fan fiction they want to read but no one else is interested in writing. Some creators wanted to create and share work in order to have an effect on individuals by making them feel happy or on the world by leaving work as a legacy. Some wanted to create something in order to document their experiences and to capture memories.

Most of the motivators focused on the individual themselves, whether internal or external (for example, 'for myself', or professional motivations) but there were also some motivators that were community-focused. These motivators indicate where the creator sought to have a broader effect beyond themselves, for example to have an effect on individuals by entertaining other people

[71] Participant 2: DeerDecipher.
[72] Participant 2: DeerDecipher.
[73] Participant 8: Scribe576.

('I did those pieces for myself, but why not share them, if someone else might enjoy it?')[74] or to have an effect on the world by contributing to positive social change. Some creators had social motivations behind their creativity (wanting to spend time with friends, increase popularity or contribute to their community). Often descriptions of these sorts of motivators included comments that showed that this too provided some sort of reward or validation to the individual ('It's satisfying knowing they get something they enjoy';[75] 'Just the thought that something I did gave a little bit of entertainment to someone thousands of miles away makes me very happy')[76] and that these motivators were more honourable in comparison to individually focused motivators that were sometimes viewed as selfish, embarrassing or unhealthy.

Some creators explicitly did not find some of these things a motivator. For example, some stated that as they became more experienced and skilled, they became more motivated by the possibility of critique and less motivated by the validation of others. One creator felt that seeking fame is futile online due to the large size of the community ('To say you're going to create something that leaves an impression on the internet is like saying you're going to be a rockstar. Almost impossible … haha I mean your 15 seconds of Fame is more like 5 Seconds of Fame on the internet').[77] This highlights that motivations for creativity are diverse even within communities.

Economic and professional reasons for creating were highly ranked in the findings, indicating that economic incentives were a factor to some extent. 'Sometimes there will be a prompt there and I'll think "yeah I should do that". Whether I come through or not, haha, eh, no paycheck attached'.[78] It should be noted, however, that these were mostly with regard to economic and professional *aspirations*, with only a small proportion relating to actual, current economic benefit. Furthermore, where economic and professional reasons were cited as motivators, they were frequently cited alongside other, internal motivators, particularly happiness, fun and enjoyment.

These various motivators, including the conflicts between them, demonstrate the diversity of motivators for creativity and further validate concerns about copyright law's approach to incentives. They show that for these creators, the effects of an economic incentive are certainly not universal, and that they have other reasons for, or gain other rewards from, being creative. Where economic incentives do seem to be a factor, they are usually neither the sole motivator, nor an indication of actual or successful economic exploitation. Instead, creators cite economic motivators alongside internal ones, and it is economic aspiration that motivates them rather than economic reward, much like entering the lottery to be an economically

[74] Participant 7: Kanzi.
[75] Participant 7: Kanzi.
[76] Participant 2: DeerDecipher.
[77] Participant 1: Justin.
[78] Participant 5: Well-joy.

successful creator as described by Davis.[79] In this way, we can see that this aspect of the creativity rhetoric is misleading, and therefore that we should be wary of any justifications for copyright law that rely on a universal incentive narrative. We should therefore also be critical where these are used to support expansions to copyright protection, as it is likely to lead to over-protection, whose dangers are discussed in relation to the public domain above.

Furthermore, many of the non-economic motivations cited by 4chan and Reddit creators are likely to be more effective than copyright law as they are intrinsic or reputational motivators. Internal motivators such as happiness, fun, enjoyment and creative drive mirror intrinsic motivators, as do the community-focused reasons, which reflect pro-social behaviour such as sharing happiness and enjoyment. While validation, fame and attention are extrinsic, they are also reputational, and therefore enhance intrinsic motivation; Johnson explains that rewards in the 'currency of gratitude, feedback, information and social validations' are effective motivators of creativity.[80] This therefore indicates that these are more likely to be effective at incentivising creativity than copyright law. This further undermines copyright's creativity rhetoric, as well as perhaps explaining in part how these creative communities continue to thrive despite their anonymity practices interfering in the effective functioning of the copyright system.

To summarise this section, then, while creativity rhetoric is key to copyright law, the role that copyright law plays in creativity is, in reality, much less straightforward. The beneficiaries of copyright law are most often shown to be corporate actors and the copyright industries rather than the sympathetic vision of the individual artist. Copyright law's conception of authorship and originality struggles to adequately recognise the significance of sources external to the creator during the creative process, and in doing so risks undervaluing the public domain. It defines creativity indirectly by delimiting when protection is available, and in doing so, recognises only a narrow form of creativity, while ignoring others. This means that what is understood by 'creativity' in lay terms is not the same as is defined within the law, which could skew policymaking and general support for law. Finally, while it may offer an incentive for creativity in some cases, it is clear that creativity comes about for various different reasons, and that some of these may be psychologically more effective at motivating people to create. At the same time, the sort of research that could quantify copyright law's role in this process is lacking, and very difficult to conduct robustly. As such, copyright law benefits rather a lot from the concept of creativity, without fully reciprocating for either creativity in general or specifically in relation to these communities.

[79] Davis (n 23).

[80] EE Johnson, 'The Economics and Sociality of Sharing Intellectual Property Rights' (2014) 94 *Boston University Law Review* 1935, 1959.

III. Anonymity and Creativity

The last part of this chapter is focused on the relationship between anonymity and creativity and looks to provide a comparative analysis of its relationship with copyright. It argues that anonymity practices can be beneficial for creativity and sets out qualitative findings to support this. It first explores the reasons why CUGC creators on 4chan and Reddit choose to share their work anonymously. It then goes on to integrate these findings with the earlier points addressed in the chapter to identify a variety of creative benefits of anonymity and to argue that online anonymity can help to facilitate an environment conducive to the creative process in some ways that copyright law cannot.

A. Reasons for Choosing Anonymity on 4chan and Reddit

That anonymity has both potential advantages and potential disadvantages is well established in the literature. Numerous scholars have clearly set out the rationales for and against anonymity,[81] the costs and advantages of anonymity,[82] or the beneficial and harmful motivations behind anonymity.[83] Within these works there are common themes. Benefits or positive motivations for anonymity include facilitating free speech without fear of repercussions (for example, whistleblowers); allowing people to seek help without stigma (for example, for mental health problems); safety or privacy; focusing attention on the content of messages rather than on their messenger; and an ability to transcend social markers and prejudice. Costs or negative motivations for anonymity include a lack of accountability; an ability to carry out crime or immoral behaviour; difficulties building relationships or a lack of trust; more difficult law enforcement; the inability to judge reputation; and an inability to pay or receive dues. From this it is possible to see that the value and experience of anonymity will vary according to the specific context, and even then such a cost–benefit analysis is unlikely to be straightforward.

Considering the 'enduring value conflicts' in relation to the role of anonymity generally,[84] synthesising an understanding of the role anonymity plays in CUGC communities from secondary sources would be unlikely to provide a sufficiently focused explanation, so this section outlines findings from the main study on the

[81] GT Marx, 'What's in a Name? Some Reflections on the Sociology of Anonymity' (1999) 15 *The Information Society* 99, 102–07; GT Marx, 'Internet Anonymity as a Reflection of Broader Issues Involving Technology and Society' (2004) 11 *Asia-Pacific Review* 142, 147–49.

[82] AM Froomkin, 'Legal Issues in Anonymity and Pseudonymity' (1999) 15 *The Information Society* 113, 114–16.

[83] V Smith Ekstrand, 'The Many Masks of Anon: Anonymity As Cultural Practice and Reflections in Case Law' (2013) 18 *Journal of Technology Law & Policy* 1, 7–29.

[84] Marx, 'Internet Anonymity' (n 81) 149.

views of members in CUGC communities towards anonymity. This was collected from 12 online interviews (8 with Redditors and 4 with 4channers) and 80 relevant online discussion threads (37 from Reddit and 43 from 4chan). These threads were diverse in their overall focus, some being specifically about anonymity practices (for example, 'why do you use a pseudonym?') and some about other topics where anonymity discussions became a relevant subtopic.

A wide range of themes emerged from the data, with positive, neutral and negative themes identified. These are explored in more depth in subsequent parts of this chapter, but a brief outline is provided here. In terms of positive themes, creators mentioned using anonymity practices to compartmentalise different parts of their lives or for safety and privacy as it helped them avoid doxing, public shaming, stalking or invasions of privacy, particularly if wanting to cover controversial topics in their creative work. Other positive reasons for choosing anonymity include its ability to decontextualise the creator from the work by removing social divisions and judgements, such as those based on ethnicity, sex or gender; its ability to level people was also cited as a way to reduce 'drama' and attention-seeking, which were viewed negatively; and its status as a defining feature of the community chosen (particularly on 4chan). Creators used anonymity to give them the freedom to fail and make mistakes without shame or embarrassment (either now or in the future) and felt more confident to post and so shared more creative work than they would otherwise have. They also felt that when people are anonymous their feedback is more authentic, genuine and reliable (and therefore useful to them as creators) and relatedly that it facilitates their own freedom of speech and authenticity. Finally, creators highlighted the positive effect of using a unique pseudonym over their real name in terms of branding and marketing, and the fact that they found anonymity practices fun or cool.

Neutral themes included using anonymity or a pseudonym to avoid practical problems with their real name, such as it being boring, common or hard to pronounce or spell. Creators also highlighted that it is a standard part of creative practice, or a norm of being on the internet, or that only professionals use their real name, so doing so would have a commercial tang. Several themes in this classification were not specifically about the reasons for choosing anonymity practices, but broader commentaries on the issue. For example, some creators highlighted that anonymity could be both good and bad, while others flagged that anonymity is not the cause of incivility in the communities. There was also some criticism of other common themes, with some creators rejecting the idea that anonymity had cultural significance on 4chan, framing strict social enforcement of the anonymity codes as embarrassing.

There were also plenty of negative themes, including some that conflict with those identified above as positive or neutral. Some creators felt that anonymity had a negative effect on feedback as it becomes overly critical and unconstructive and it is not possible to contextualise the comments within the critics' own skills and experience. Others felt that it facilitated nastiness and trolling, and means that posters lack accountability or are too insecure to use a real name. Relatedly, some creators flagged that they felt anonymity means people share less as it attracts too much negativity. Some creators felt that identifying oneself is sometimes acceptable or useful online, that it helps to get real recognition for the work put into what is shared, and that it means you invest more of yourself into your work. It can also offer future career benefits because using your real name can help to build an audience.

The themes indicate mixed experiences of anonymity within the communities, and these, unsurprisingly, mirror many of the factors set out in the existing literature. While this is not a quantitative study, it is nonetheless helpful to note that positive comments occurred around twice as often as negative comments, indicating that there is more overall support for anonymity than against, which makes sense in places where people choose anonymity practices. While there were several very common themes which were positive about anonymity (compartmentalising, safety and privacy, community, feedback, lack of attention-seeking, social judgements, freedom of speech and freedom to fail), trolling and feedback were the only very common negative themes across the data as a whole.

When viewing the breakdown of themes by platform, 4chan responses indicated a more complex relationship with anonymity. Reddit community members provided more positive accounts of anonymity practices, while 4channers were positive, but raised more negative issues and there were many heated discussion threads debating anonymity practices and their role on 4chan. In Reddit communities, the positive focus was on compartmentalising, removing social judgements and safety, whereas in 4chan communities, the discussions focused on community, compartmentalisation, feedback, safety and lack of attention-seeking. In Reddit community discussions, there was little focus on negatives of anonymity, compared with 4chan where there were concerns about trolling and feedback.

The tendency of 4chan towards strong anonymity practices in contrast to Reddit's mostly pseudonymous practices are almost certainly the cause of this disparity; with higher levels of anonymity, both the advantages and disadvantages are enhanced. Furthermore, Reddit's karma system (where points are awarded to users based on how many up-votes or down-votes their posts receive) provide an incentive to keep discourse civil, so trolling is less likely to be an issue. There is also a focus on seeking feedback and critique in the 4chan communities, often more so than showcasing work, that may also explain the particular significance of this issue in the discussions. The Reddit data also contains responses from writing communities, where there is a long historical tradition of using pseudonyms, so are more likely to be positive. These differing relationships will provide a useful point of reference in the discussion of anonymity's relationship with creativity. Regardless of these differences, however, the findings show that on both platforms communities experience anonymity positively in many ways.

B. Creative Benefits of Anonymity

This final section of the chapter builds on the findings above to explore how the positive experiences of anonymity identified demonstrate creative benefits of online anonymity. It argues that anonymity offers some practical benefits in terms of creative improvement; that it facilitates play and experimentation, which have been identified as valuable in the creative process; and that by facilitating sharing and collaboration, anonymity contributes to the creation of a rich external network of sources. Finally, it outlines how anonymity supports and intensifies the effect of several of the intrinsic and reputational motivators identified above. As such, anonymity practices have the potential to offer creative benefits to the CUGC context more effectively than copyright law.

i. Practical Benefits

It is clear that there is some practical benefit of anonymity for the creative practices of 4chan and Reddit community members as they highlight the direct link between the two when discussing the positive effect on feedback. Critique and feedback are very important parts of how CUGC communities contribute to the wider creative environment, as they help creators to develop their skills. It was clear in the data that many aspiring and developing professional creators shared CUGC as a way to improve and in some cases access the sort of training they would otherwise be unable to access. One participant described this in detail:

> I did art school for two years and I dropped out halfway through my second year because I was no longer making progress through school and I realised that … I could just improve through self-learning because … I had all the resources I could possibly want on [4chan board] as well as feedback from people on there to kind of help me guide myself … I didn't need art school any more … [the board] was there and had an unimaginable pool of resources you could just use to learn.[85]

Anonymity can help to improve the quality of feedback. Several 4chan community members mentioned that anonymity means people give more direct and often harsh feedback, but that it is valuable as it allows them to focus on their efforts to improve:

> That anonymity lets us give each other some truly brutal criticism. Honestly, people say the most creatively hurtful things to each other there, but it's almost always constructive. People get told what they need to hear in those threads, not always what their friends and family tell them.[86]

Decontextualising the work from the creator via anonymity practices also seems to help creators get genuine feedback that will more likely help them to improve

[85] Participant 12: Anon4.
[86] Participant 11: Anon3.

in the necessary areas. A 4chan creator felt anonymity led to more reliable feedback, as when the work is anonymous it is judged on the content rather than other factors such as the identity of the creator:

> If I want to get quick feedback on my music, for example, and I'm worried that people might tell me it's good or bad based on who I am, all I need to do is post it under a throwaway account or a site that doesn't require signing up … Anonymity offers the benefit of knowing people have nothing to gain either way by replying.[87]

In contrast to this, some felt that anonymity had a negative effect on the usefulness of advice: 'If I want input on how to improve something the identity of the adviser matters a lot'.[88] This creator explained he had a network of friends who are professionals who he could turn to, which likely influences this view. For beginner creators without access to such a network, however, any feedback on how to improve would be beneficial. In this way, anonymity may help improve the quality of creative works and the creative skill found within communities.

ii. Risk-Taking and Experimentation

Research has identified that risk-taking, imagination, open-mindedness and humour are optimal characteristics for creators of artistic works, and that the 'ability to try out new ideas' is significant in promoting creativity.[89] Creators from 4chan and Reddit highlighted that anonymity facilitates this sort of behaviour by enabling them to express themselves more freely, by minimising the risks of failure, and by allowing them to manage their creative and personal image. As a result of this disinhibiting effect, choosing anonymity provides some creative benefits to the communities.

Some creators highlighted that anonymity facilitated freer expression: 'I like to think there is security in anonymity, freedom in being able to express yourself how you want and not apologise for it'.[90] The linking of anonymity practices with an environment of freedom is well established in scholarship relating to freedom of expression. It has been identified that the ability to obscure real-world identities can lead to disinhibition in speech, with both positive and negative consequences, such as trolling behaviour in comments threads (something identified as a potential negative consequence of anonymity) or the ability for whistleblowers to come forward.[91] Much discussion of anonymity on the internet focuses on its dangers, for example facilitating and making it harder to police crime and antisocial behaviour. However, it is also acknowledged that it can have

[87] Participant 9: Anon1.
[88] Participant 5: Well-joy.
[89] JC Fromer, 'A Psychology of Intellectual Property' (2010) 104 *Northwestern University Law Review* 1441, 1477.
[90] Participant 1: Justin.
[91] Smith Ekstrand (n 83).

a socially positive impact by mitigating social risks from expressing unpopular or critical viewpoints, which increase diversity in public exchange and are vital for enhancing public discourse.[92] In a creative context, this equates to an overall more diverse creative environment.

The freedom to fail and the ability to manage image and reputation were also cited as reasons for choosing anonymity and pseudonymity. The possibility of having multiple online identities or being untraceable offered multiple reputational benefits. The first of these is the freedom to fail: 'It gives you room to make mistakes and start over if you choose'.[93] Using pseudonymity and anonymity was also cited as a way to manage image and reputation across different audiences and styles ('there is a measure of having different accounts for different audiences/materials').[94] A particular use of multiple pseudonyms was to create work with adult themes without it causing damage to their reputation as a creator of other work:

> Scribe576:
>
> I also, very rarely, write 'Naughty Stories'. At one point I thought I could make money off of them but realised I wanted to write something for a general audience, not fetishists. But when I started writing my naughty stories I used an entirely different pseudonym and a completely different e-mail.
>
> …
>
> The thought that crossed my mind is whether I want my normal stories to be associated with my naughty ones and the answer was 'No'. I wanted to keep my 'Dirties' and my 'Tidies' separate because … well … I am afraid that people would consider me less of a writer for that.
>
> …
>
> You start looking at your own image and reputation, and that is why I keep these two separate accounts.

Similarly, anonymity and pseudonymity were cited as a means of compartmentalising different elements of their lives, to try new things without being judged or damaging their reputation, either on a personal level ('I can post something without worrying about what my IRL friends or family think')[95] or on a professional one:

> Sometimes I just want to experiment and not really care about polish. Someone used to the standard of polish I put in my professional work could interpret that as if I'm losing touch or awareness, as it happens with many content creators and alienates their fan bases.

[92] DG Post, 'Pooling Intellectual Capital: Thoughts on Anonymity, Pseudonymity, and Limited Liability in Cyberspace' [1996] *University of Chicago Legal Forum* 139, 142–43.
[93] Participant 1: Justin.
[94] Participant 4: Paul.
[95] Participant 2: DeerDecipher.

> When I'm Anonymous, I get to just hear that something I'm not sure about is either interesting or complete crap.
>
> No further consequences, no thinking too hard about how others will see me … it will have no effect on me as a professional.[96]

These consequences of anonymity and pseudonymity can have a positive effect on creativity on 4chan and Reddit because, as outlined above, validation is one motivation for participation in these creative communities and anonymity may offer a way to mitigate reputational risks. While acknowledging the potential harms of anonymous speech, Post describes pseudonymity as a type of 'limited liability'[97] that allows people to participate in activity and speech and build up reputational capital without fear of damaging their real-world reputation.[98] Similarly, Marx sees anonymity as encouraging experimentation, play and risk-taking because of lower risks to reputation.[99]

Some have suggested that pseudonyms also provide a way to mitigate 'context collapse', that is, the effect of digital networking removing the ability to keep different areas of one's life (for example, work, family, friends) territorially separate as they converge into one accessible, searchable place.[100] We see examples of context collapse on social networking sites where your digital profile and the things that you post are seen by multiple groups of people for whom in real life you might present things in different ways. For example, you might tell your friends that you are hungover at work, but you probably would not tell your employer. It is argued that context collapse has a lowest common denominator effect,[101] where the presentation of self you make is in response to the most sensitive recipient, a form of self-censorship. Pseudonyms bypass this problem, as they provide a way to contextualise outward identity within this space.

Heymann applies this reasoning to developing the concept of the 'authornym', which she describes as a freeing device in the context of literary works.[102] She argues that the choice of using a pseudonym instead of a real name allows an author to experiment with new ideas, genres and topics without it impacting on other areas of the author's life, for example a primary school teacher who wanted to write an erotic novel, and to experiment with 'alternative authorial identities'.[103]

[96] Participant 9: Anon1.
[97] Post (n 92) 142.
[98] ibid.
[99] Marx, 'What's in a Name?' (n 81) 102–04.
[100] AE Marwick and d boyd, 'I Tweet Honestly, I Tweet Passionately: Twitter Users, Context Collapse, and the Imagined Audience' (2011) 13 *New Media & Society* 114; AE Marwick, 'Online Identity' in J Hartley, J Burgess and A Bruns (eds), *A Companion to New Media Dynamics* (Chichester, Wiley-Blackwell, 2013) 360–61; B Hogan, 'Pseudonyms and the Rise of the Real-Name Web' in J Hartley, J Burgess and A Bruns (eds), *A Companion to New Media Dynamics* (Chichester, Wiley-Blackwell, 2013) 300–01.
[101] Hogan (n 100) 300.
[102] LA Heymann, 'The Birth of the Authornym: Authorship Pseudonymity and Trademark Law' (2005) 80 *Notre Dame Law Review* 1377, 1398.
[103] ibid 1398–1406.

Furthermore, Smith Ekstrand makes a specific link between anonymity and the generative nature of the internet, indicating that 'online spontaneity' facilitated by anonymity can be a driver of creation as it encourages unfiltered contributions from a broad range of people which can lead to the unexpected outcomes that typify generativity.[104] The disinhibition fostered by anonymity could therefore be creatively beneficial.

Scholars who have studied 4chan have already made positive links between the role of anonymity norms and disinhibition, with the result being an increase in the expression of ideas and experimentation.[105] Tushnet argues that as the internet reduces the physical costs of creativity, including distribution of creative works, to the point of being free, an economic incentive is less necessary as the creator has fewer costs to cover. As a result, creators are able to pursue ideas and activities that may have previously been too economically risky, with the result being an increase in creativity through experimentation and trying new things.[106] This reasoning can also be applied to reputational costs of creativity in the context of 4chan and Reddit, where anonymity practices reduce the reputational costs of creativity as 'namelessness makes failure cheap',[107] and this provides even further freedom to experiment. This effect could explain the prominence of 'lulz', a play-based value system focused on humour and jest that underpins much of the participation in these communities, and that can increase unpredictability[108] and therefore increases the potential for creative generativity. Reducing the social cost of experimentation therefore allows creativity to flourish.

These conditions of play and disinhibition are arguably more effective in promoting creative activity than copyright's economic incentives in the context of 4chan and Reddit's reputationally focused social space. Copyright does not facilitate freedom from the social constraints that may inhibit participation in a creative environment and instead it relies on an economic incentive to encourage participation. However, in a market based on reputation and peer esteem rather than money it may make sense to reduce social costs rather than offer financial incentives to encourage creativity.

iii. The Creative Process: Sharing and Collaboration

This chapter has already highlighted arguments that access to a rich network of sources, external to the individual mind, is an essential part of the creative process. Both Reuveni and Cohen identify the importance of 'serendipity' of access to

[104] Smith Ekstrand (n 83) 22.

[105] M Bernstein et al, '4chan and /b/: An Analysis of Anonymity and Ephemerality in a Large Online Community', *Proceedings of the Fifth International Conference on Weblogs and Social Media* (2011): eprints.soton.ac.uk/272345/.

[106] Tushnet (n 48) 535.

[107] J Dibbell, 'Radical Opacity' (2010) 113 *Technology Review* 82, 85.

[108] Tushnet (n 48) 527.

sources in this way.[109] It is clear that while on a macro level we can consider this network in terms of the broader public domain, on a micro level we should also consider that these communities in themselves act as such a network:

> **Q**: Could you expand on how you find inspiration on Reddit?
>
> **Paul**: Well, scrolling through large numbers of pictures I'll get an idea for a composition, then sketch based on that and either continue from there and finish or set it aside, that's the visual part anyway.
>
> I'll also sometimes be inspired by a poem in [subreddit] or a writing challenge.
>
> It's … well, it's filled with more thoughts, pictures and ideas than anyone could possibly see or reflect on individually – but as an amalgamation it can help create a basis for creative thought.

Furthermore, the effect of anonymity practices on this network demonstrates that such practices help to maintain and expand this network by encouraging collaboration and sharing.

Collaboration and sharing are relevant to this external network because, as Mandel explains, collaborative practices lead to higher levels of creative outputs as creators have access to a wider range of ideas and references from others.[110] Similarly, without the willingness to share works online, the network would not exist. It seems that anonymity can encourage collaboration and sharing in two ways: first, by creating an environment where people feel physically and reputationally safe in sharing their work; and secondly, by cultivating a strong group identity which could increase the desire to participate in a sharing and collaborative system. In doing so, it ensures the reliable existence and continuation of this external network.

As mentioned, anonymity is often argued to be a way to create security.[111] In the study, many community members cited safety as a motivator for obscuring their real identity in some way, even though several noted that they did not feel the risk was particularly high: 'The last [thing] I want is a stranger from the internet injecting themselves into my real life';[112] 'I know it isn't really the case but I was always a little worried I'd say something that would rub some guy the wrong way and he'd track me down and try to kill me'.[113] This and the mitigation of reputational risks that anonymity practices provide (as discussed above) work together to create a low-risk environment for sharing creative works. As one creator put it: 'If I didn't have anonymity, there's a good chance I wouldn't post creative work'.[114]

[109] Cohen, *Configuring the Networked Self* (n 11) 93–94; Reuveni (n 45) 753.
[110] Mandel (n 59) 2000–01.
[111] Marx, 'Internet Anonymity' (n 81) 148; Smith Ekstrand (n 83) 14.
[112] Participant 2: DeerDecipher.
[113] Participant 3: UseYourHead.
[114] Participant 2: DeerDecipher.

This was an area of tension within the communities, however, with some concerns about the level of hostility associated with anonymity practices and an acknowledgement that sometimes this made people less inclined to contribute. On balance, it is likely to be seen as a low-risk rather than high-risk environment for sharing by most community members as they choose to perpetuate anonymity through their own anonymity practices. However, there are further arguments to support the role of anonymity practices in sharing and collaboration.

Froomkin highlights that when people are anonymous, they are strangers and this can lead to a reduction in trust,[115] but the 4chan and Reddit community members also highlighted several ways where choosing anonymity or pseudonymity helped to build a cohesive community and group. Some Redditors said that using a pseudonym was just part of internet culture and being on Reddit means that people post under usernames as a cultural norm on these sorts of platforms ('using your real name seems weird';[116] 'on one hand it's simply what you do'),[117] or even considered using a real name as being something that has a 'commercial tang',[118] something that professional creators and celebrities did as part of their business: 'I know a lot of artists just use their own name. Those guys are the pros, though. I assume they use their real name because that's who they want businesses to contact lol'.[119] Furthermore, the cultural significance of anonymity practices on 4chan was a major theme in the data, with community members highlighting that it is a defining feature of the community and what makes it unique. Choosing anonymity or pseudonymity therefore helps to position creators as members of the community, rather than as an outsiders.

Additionally, anonymity has a positive effect on the community as it removes context from the interaction. Community members highlighted how anonymity practices allowed them to participate without their ethnicity or gender being known and how using tripcodes (unique alphanumerical identifiers attached to posts to allow them to be linked to others by the same author) are vehemently disliked 'because they make divisions between us all'.[120] For this creator, anonymity acts as a social leveller: 'as fellow anonymous posters, we're all the same'.[121] Marwick explains that identity on social media is constructed through customisation of various markers, such as names and profile pictures;[122] it could therefore be argued that when these are taken away, and the only marker is 'anonymous', the focus shifts from individual identity to membership of the group.

[115] Froomkin (n 82) 114.
[116] Participant 7: Kanzi.
[117] Participant 4: Paul; This aligns with another of Marx's rationales for anonymity: 'traditional expectations': Marx, 'Internet Anonymity' (n 81) 148.
[118] Participant 4: Paul.
[119] Participant 3: UseYourHead.
[120] Participant 9: Anon1.
[121] Participant 9: Anon1.
[122] Marwick (n 100) 358–59.

This is supported by social psychology research that, counterintuitively, shows that anonymity can increase the social influence of groups and their norms. Postmes et al and Lea et al use the Social Identity Model of Deindividuation Effects (SIDE) to show the limitations of the traditional understanding that anonymity leads to a loss of self-awareness in groups (known as 'deindividuation') and therefore causes anti-normative behaviour.[123] Instead they argue that when a person self-categorises as a member of a group, anonymity can lead to increased conformity to group norms, as it obscures personal features thereby facilitating a shift in focus from the individual to the group.[124] This can be rationalised with 4chan, for example, as even though it is argued that anonymity leads to a lack of accountability, the 4chan community values honesty and authenticity over accountability, and so anonymity has a positive effect for them. Bodle has also highlighted SIDE theory's application to 4chan, noting that de-individuation has been shown to increase a sense of group collective identity in relation to the hacktivist group Anonymous.[125]

As sharing and collaboration is normative for CUGC communities on Reddit and 4chan, anonymity practices could therefore increase the desire of individuals to comply with and participate in a collaborative or sharing system. Furthermore, anonymity practices could also work to reduce the hesitation to participate in sharing and collaborative systems. Johnson identifies that some people may have concerns that they or their work might be exploited in ways they are not happy with, for example moral, commercial or political uses, and so choose not to participate in a sharing system.[126] If anonymity practices work to increase community cohesion, however, there may be less concern regarding individual exploitation and a higher concern for the benefits to the group, thereby reducing the reluctance to share.

Anonymity can therefore be additionally beneficial for creativity as it can help support sharing and collaborative communities in ways that copyright law is unable to. Due to its focus on individualised creative processes and exclusive rights to restrict uses, copyright law fails to acknowledge the role that sharing and collaboration systems could have in creativity. But while copyright law is poorly placed to encourage the sort of large-scale sharing and collaboration that is beneficial to creativity, anonymity practices might.

[123] While this seems difficult, at least in part, to reconcile with the concept of disinhibition, the SIDE research explains that it relates to local group norms, rather than wider societal norms. As a result, it is possible that group members are conformative to norms at the group level, while experiencing wider social disinhibition: M Lea, R Spears and D de Groot, 'Knowing Me, Knowing You: Anonymity Effects on Social Identity Processes within Groups' (2001) 27 *Personality and Social Psychology Bulletin* 526, 536; T Postmes et al, 'Social Influence in Computer-Mediated Communication: The Effects of Anonymity on Group Behavior' (2001) 27 *Personality and Social Psychology Bulletin* 1243, 1252.

[124] Postmes et al (n 123) 1253; Lea, Spears and de Groot (n 123) 534–36.

[125] R Bodle, 'The Ethics of Online Anonymity or Zuckerberg vs Moot' (2013) 43 *ACM SIGCAS Computers and Society* 22, 27.

[126] Johnson (n 80) 1974–75.

iv. Anonymity and the Creative Process: Creative Motivations

This chapter has already outlined the creative motivations of community members and highlighted how these challenge the universal incentive arguments that are central in much of copyright's incentive argument. It has also highlighted that copyright law's focus on economic incentives may be ineffective in light of psychological research into the motivators of creativity. The following section argues that anonymity acts as a positive factor in a creative environment by creating the right conditions for some reputational and intrinsic motivators to flourish.

First, as has been outlined, anonymity practices facilitate collaboration and sharing, which in turn support and maintain a broad network of sources which can influence creators. Being inspired by something was one of the motivators identified in the research, with many community members recounting the creators, works, artistic styles or interests that make them want to create something. As such, it is clear that anonymity practices contribute to building a vast repository of potential inspiration for potential creators. This creative benefit is reciprocal, however, with those who share benefiting alongside those who access. Johnson argues that sharing provides rewards for creators that encourage creative production[127] because sharing itself is rewarding and the resulting social interconnectedness is an intrinsic motivator.[128] This was shown to be the case for the 4chan and Reddit creators above, where they identified wanting to have an effect on other people, often finding pleasure in sharing their ideas with other people to make them happy or entertain them. Johnson further argues that sharing is a more efficient means of promoting creativity than copyright's economic incentives in many cases, as the number of works that have commercial value is comparatively small, so sharing systems provide a way that other works can still have social benefit.[129]

Secondly, as has also been outlined above, anonymity practices facilitate freedoms to act and speak with low personal, professional, creative or social risk. The creative motivators of 'wellbeing' and 'self-expression' identified above would directly benefit from this as it not only allows creators to take risks and experiment, but also to address sensitive, personal or controversial topics. A subsection of the discussion of wellbeing as a motivator framed it within the context of mental health issues or other sensitive issues. While much of the 'wellbeing' motivator focuses on the process of creation as relaxing or meditative, being able to create and share CUGC on such sensitive topics is also beneficial.[130] This ties in with the motivation of self-expression, as anonymity practices offer the possibility of expression on a

[127] Johnson (n 80) 1945–46.
[128] ibid 1959–60.
[129] ibid 1937–38, 1994–95.
[130] That anonymity helps community members to disclose mental health issues is addressed in M De Choudhury and S De, 'Mental Health Discourse on Reddit: Self-Disclosure, Social Support, and Anonymity', *Proceedings of the Eighth International AAAI Conference on Weblogs and Social Media* (2014).

wider range of topics when the social costs are reduced. As both wellbeing and self-expression are intrinsic motivators and, according to the psychology literature are therefore effective motivators for creativity, where anonymity practices support these motivators, they support creativity.

Thirdly, a direct link can also be drawn between validation as a motivator and anonymity's positive effects on marketing, feedback and freedom of speech. Several creators who used a pseudonym saw it as a type of branding. Some used the same pseudonym across a variety of platforms in order to build an audience, while others saw the username as a more 'catchy' way to identify themselves:

> P3: I have a very common name so it would be hard to keep it easy to find.
>
> My username is far less common.
>
> If you google that, I'm probably the only thing that you'll find lol.[131]
>
> P8: I think that, perhaps, I use the pseudonym as a sort of … 'Brand'. It's the pen name I use, and I use it on a lot of sites. So when people see 'Scribe576' or 'RealScribe576' they would know it's me. It's a lot more catchy than, I dunno (just an example) JohnSmith33.[132]

Viewing pseudonyms as brands was not necessarily linked with commercial activities, and instead seemed to be more about reputational branding and being identifiable within the community: 'at this point I guess it's more of a brand, just not a valuable one LOL'.[133] From a practical perspective, therefore, pseudonyms can have benefits for the creator by facilitating social validation; the pseudonym is a way of negotiating the accumulation of reputation (an intrinsic motivator). Furthermore, the pseudonym offers this while also insulating the creator's real-life reputation by allowing the creator to separate their online activity from other realms of their life.

Anonymity practices can also serve to intensify the reputational intrinsic motivation that results from positive social validation in some cases. As described above, community members highlighted that anonymity practices meant they felt freer to provide a more honest and accurate evaluation without fear of repercussions for negative comments. If creators believe such feedback to be more likely to truly reflect the quality of their work, it is possible that validation from positive feedback will be increased. This is the case on 4chan in particular, where it is considered that anonymity practices often lead to incivility: 'when 4chan like something, because they're so cynical, you know that your stuff is usually pretty good if you're not getting any … negative feedback'.[134] Anonymity may therefore have a positive effect on creativity levels in 4chan and Reddit communities as they can facilitate and intensify their social validation mechanisms. In contrast with copyright law, which has been identified as potentially an ineffective motivator of

[131] Participant 3: UseYourHead.
[132] Participant 8: Scribe576.
[133] Participant 3: UseYourHead.
[134] Participant 12: Anon4.

creativity, social validation mechanisms are likely to be more efficient motivators and anonymity can enhance their effects.

In summary, therefore, we have seen that there are multiple experiences of anonymity within these communities, both positive and negative, and that some of these can contribute to a beneficial environment for creativity. Anonymity practices enable brutal honesty, which in turn means creators can rely on practical feedback to improve more effectively. They also give creators more freedom in what they post because it reduces the risk of damage to their reputation which can encourage the sort of experimentation, play and risk-taking vital to creative activity. By allowing community members to take part in the social custom of anonymity practices, and by removing social markers of hierarchy, anonymity practices encourage a culture of sharing and collaboration which in turn creates a rich network of inspiration to draw on. Finally, anonymity practices can facilitate and intensify the effect of intrinsic and reputational motivations such as validation. In doing so, anonymity practices may mitigate deficits in copyright law's relationship with creativity.

IV. Conclusion

This chapter has shown that while creativity rhetoric is core to the justificatory logic underpinning copyright law (and often its expansion), the actual relationship between copyright law and creativity is less clear, indicating that this rhetoric may be misleading. Copyright law does not fully reflect the realities and diversities of the creative process, and in some instances may undermine it. While creators are at the heart of copyright policymaking narratives, the largest beneficiaries of copyright law are commercial copyright holders. Furthermore, its recognition of creativity through the concepts of authorship and originality means that it fails to acknowledge the role of existing works in the creative process, and prioritises only certain types of creativity, in some cases at the expense of others. Finally, copyright's role in incentivising creativity has been shown not to be universal and perhaps ineffective.

In contrast, however, anonymity practices offer multiple creative benefits and contribute to the effective functioning of creative user-generated content (CUGC) communities and may be more effective than copyright law at doing so. Anonymity practices enable creators to remove or reduce the reputational risk of creating and sharing their works, and as such are more likely to engage in risk-taking or experimental behaviour of the type beneficial to creativity. Anonymity practices can also help to foster a closer, safer and less hierarchical community, which in turn can make the sort of sharing and collaboration that benefits creativity more likely. Furthermore, anonymity practices can facilitate or encourage some intrinsic and reputational motivators to create, and in line with the psychological findings, this is likely to be an efficient motivator and more so than copyright's economic incentive.

These findings provide a potential explanation why creators elect to perpetuate online anonymity through their anonymity practices, despite the negative implications for their ability to rely on copyright law to protect their works. Copyright law offers them and their creative practices less than anonymity. As such, it seems that copyright's relationship with creativity is currently overstated, and anonymity works to further accentuate critique in this regard. Simultaneously, the role of anonymity practices for creativity should be considered if we are to properly understand how creativity is regulated in these communities. The implications of these conclusions for reform are explored in detail in chapter six.

4

Regulating Creative User-Generated Content: Norms and Values

I. Introduction

Previous chapters have highlighted questions about the effectiveness of copyright law and its relevance to creative practices in the creative user-generated content (CUGC) environment, especially when anonymity is also a factor. As such, this is the first of two chapters presenting qualitative findings to explain how CUGC is regulated in reality. The concept of ownership and control is a fundamental question of intellectual property,[1] and as such this chapter focuses specifically on identifying and explaining ownership norms and the concepts and values underpinning them. Chapter five then explores the mechanisms through which the communities and creators articulate, police and enforce these norms.

Detailing this is important for several reasons. First, and most straightforwardly, understanding how these significant creative spaces are regulated is useful. For those who may want to use CUGC for some purpose, this knowledge will be interesting and helpful. Secondly, understanding the specifics of CUGC ownership norms in relation to copyright will help to inform the critique of copyright that is put forward in chapter six, by addressing some of the questions raised about copyright law in chapters two and three and providing an additional lens to engage with existing scholarship. In particular, the detailed and empirical nature of these findings will help to avoid some of the pitfalls of critique based on theory rather than reality. Finally, chapter six considers the appropriateness of reform and what it should look like. An understanding of the reality of the existing model of regulation and the role of copyright within it is essential for that task.

The first part of the chapter explores the relationship between pervasive anonymity and the concepts of ownership or exclusive rights over CUGC. It demonstrates that while sharing CUGC in the anonymous online environment could be interpreted as an act that is incompatible with the exclusive rights that copyright provides, it is inaccurate to view such acts as a dedication to the public domain. It therefore establishes that a broad model of individual ownership of

[1] K Raustiala and CJ Sprigman, 'The Piracy Paradox Revisited' (2009) 61 *Stanford Law Review* 1201, 1201.

CUGC exists within these communities. In addition, it is highlighted that there is no normative rejection of the copyright system in its entirety. Instead, we find that CUGC creators often view copyright as broadly valuable but irrelevant or poorly balanced to their specific creative practices.

The chapter then goes on to explore what individual ownership means in more detail. It describes the normative rules and values that regulate interactions with CUGC once it is shared online, comparing these with the regulatory framework provided by copyright law. This part of the discussion details the *what*, *when*, *who* and *why* of these ownership norms. It looks at what individual ownership means in terms of the restrictions that can be placed on uses of CUGC; when normative restrictions will apply to CUGC; who is deemed to own CUGC and therefore benefit from these restrictions; and finally the justifications for this normative approach.

Lastly, the chapter identifies significant differences between the normative system and copyright law, in particular the comparative permissiveness of the norms system. These differences present challenges to copyright as it is currently structured, but the chapter also highlights that many of the differences between the two systems are not so discordant that coherent copyright reform to narrow the gap would require radical changes.

II. Why Creative User-Generated Content does not Belong to the (Anonymous) Internet

This chapter is concerned with how CUGC communities approach issues of ownership and control of works. While the second part of the chapter looks at the specific details and mechanics of community norms in this regard, this first part looks to address the broader idea that a conception of 'ownership' of CUGC is, normatively, something that exists at all with these communities. This is necessary because, where anonymity is pervasive there are numerous credible reasons that could lead us to assume or to believe that this was not the case.

The existence of a plausible question mark over the existence of individual ownership and control in relation to UGC generally, and therefore CUGC specifically, can be demonstrated by a phrase commonly seen online: 'it belongs to the internet'.[2] The essence of this position is that once you post something online you waive the right to control what then happens to it and this was reflected in some of the interviews conducted with creators in the study: 'As far as I'm concerned, as soon as I post my stuff online it belongs to the internet'.[3] For some, this was a

[2] J Meese, '"It Belongs to the Internet": Animal Images, Attribution Norms and the Politics of Amateur Media Production' (2014) 17 *M/C Journal*: journal.media-culture.org.au/index.php/mcjournal/article/view/782.

[3] Participant 2: DeerDecipher.

positive, deliberate part of their CUGC experience: 'Once I put it out there, it's out there … the world works better when ideas are shared'.[4] However, others held this view from a more passive position: 'But really, once it's on the internet, you kind of lose control of it'.[5]

The idea of CUGC being in the public domain contradicts the legal position. In chapter two, section III, it was highlighted that CUGC creators often hold copyright in their work and so unless there has been a specific waiver or abandonment of rights, CUGC does not 'belong to the internet'. As will be seen in the second part of this chapter, to assume that sharing CUGC online should automatically constitute such an abandonment of rights, or an attempt of such, is not an accurate reflection of creator desires and about the use of their CUGC.[6] So why is it so widespread? Again, online anonymity is relevant to this question. Chapter two, section IV, already highlighted some of the practical challenges anonymity could create for copyright regulation in this context, and to some extent this explains those creators who state that 'it belongs to the internet' from a position of resignation; when creators are unable to enforce their rights, the practical result is that their CUGC can be used as if it were in the public domain, even if legally it is not and they would rather it was not.

However, beyond that negative conception the pervasive anonymity of the CUGC environment can also contribute to the assumption that creators are not interested in ownership and that they share CUGC with the deliberate intention to waive their rights in the work. First, where a creator chooses to share CUGC anonymously or within a context of wider online anonymity, it could indicate a voluntary forfeiture of ownership or control over that work; it would seem logical to reason that if you wanted to be able to assert control over how a work is used, and sharing it where anonymity is widespread reduces your ability to rely on copyright law to do so, that you would not choose to share CUGC in those circumstances.

Secondly, it could be argued that, on a conceptual level, anonymity undermines the creator's interest in copyright law as a mechanism as copyright is, fundamentally, reliant on a link between the creator – as author[7] – and the work to assign first ownership.[8] The link of 'origin', that is, that the work stems from the creator in

[4] Participant 7: Kanzi.

[5] Participant 3: UseYourHead.

[6] Whether it is legally possible to waive or abandon copyright in the UK is disputed. See, eg: P Johnson, 'Dedicating Copyright to the Public Domain' (2008) 71 *Modern Law Review* 587, 599, 601, 604–07; and E Hudson and R Burrell, 'Abandonment, Copyright and Orphaned Works: What Does It Mean to Take the Proprietary Nature of Intellectual Property Rights Seriously?' (2011) 35 *Melbourne University Law Review* 972, 1003. Later parts of the chapter render this debate moot, as it is clear there is neither a waiver of copyright nor a licence.

[7] UrhG, s 7; CDPA, s 9(1); *Burrow-Giles Lithographic Co v Sarony*, 111 US 53, 58 (1884).

[8] UrhG, ss 1 and 29(1); CDPA, s 11(1); 17 USC s 201(a) unless in the UK or US and the work was created in the course of employment: CDPA s 11(2); 17 USC s 201(b). Copyright is inalienable in Germany: UrhG, s 29(1).

some way, becomes blurred where anonymity is pervasive, as traceability reduces.[9] Furthermore, it is established that property should be understood as a way of defining relationships between people.[10] At its extreme, anonymity makes such definitions impossible, because individuals are unidentifiable. Knuttila argues that the anonymity on 4chan leads to contingency, that is, a condition that 'rebuffs and denies fixed meanings, systems of hierarchy and regiments of pattern'.[11] Such a system, where meanings are more flexible and the link between people, and between creator and work, are blurred, obscured, weakened or perhaps severed entirely does not seem compatible with an ownership that is necessarily reliant on those meanings and links.

However, this is not an accurate representation of CUGC communities on Reddit and 4chan,[12] who demonstrated no clear-cut rejection of concepts of ownership or control over works.[13] Instead, viewpoints varied. It was generally understood that creators retained 'ownership' of their CUGC when it was posted, even if the level of actual control they could retain in practice might be limited. Some creators and community members *did* feel that their works belonged to the internet, with some highlighting the contrast between the concepts of 'sharing' and 'owning', but this was certainly far from a majority view.[14] Instead, the data showed that people viewed themselves as the owners of works, even when posted online: 'My work being exposed to the world doesn't make it anyone else's property'.[15] This was seen in numerous discussions about works being misused, appropriated and 'stolen'.[16] There were also frequent discussions, particularly in writing communities, where creators worried about their ideas being 'stolen'. It is clear then that merely posting CUGC online does not mean it belongs to the internet.

Having established that individual ownership of CUGC is a broad norm within these communities, it seems valuable to note that there was also general support for a copyright system, despite some differing opinions. Themes in the discussions

[9] Ch 2, section II.C provides a detailed explanation of pervasive anonymity in the CUGC environment.

[10] CM Rose, *Property and Persuasion: Essays on the History, Theory, and Rhetoric of Ownership* (Boulder, CO, Westview Press, 1994) 27–28.

[11] L Knuttila, 'User Unknown: 4chan, Anonymity and Contingency' (2011) 16 *First Monday*: firstmonday.org/ojs/index.php/fm/article/view/3665.

[12] While the qualitative findings in this study are limited to the field sites, it is interesting to note here that Reddit and 4chan have strong cultures of anonymity relative to other UGC websites. They would therefore arguably be the online communities where the arguments against ownership would be most compelling.

[13] The qualitative analysis that follows is based on a subset of the data, comprising 12 interviews and 54 discussion threads (26 from 4chan and 28 from Reddit).

[14] As explained in ch 1, section V.E, for ethical reasons, no direct quotations from discussion threads will be included.

[15] Participant 9: Anon1.

[16] Most discussions of this sort use the language of theft to describe the situation, and so this is reflected in the language used here, despite there being significant legal differences between property theft and intellectual property infringement.

revolved around whether copyright infringement was equivalent to stealing, the morality of piracy and the appropriate scope of copyright protection. Within these debates, there were some examples of anti-copyright positions, for example those for whom piracy was an acceptable practice. Some interview participants also expressed anti-copyright sentiments: 'I just don't think people should be able to own intellectual property … because the world works better when ideas are shared'.[17] In communities of such a scale and potential geographic diversity, diverging opinions are inevitable. These views were much less frequent than positive or neutral copyright comments, and also often received numerous and harsh responses about their perceived idiocy or naivety.

At the other end of the spectrum, there were some very strong proponents of the copyright system. On 4chan in particular there were some who viewed the rights granted under copyright law to be unquestionable, accusing those who raised concerns about some aspects of the system of being communists, lazy and unimaginative, and framing their arguments against perceived wrongdoers within an uncritical view of copyright by essentially arguing that *the law's the law!* However, more widespread, and particularly within Reddit, copyright law as a concept was seen as valid or necessary but community members expressed significant criticism of copyright law as it currently exists. Most of the interviewees when asked about their views on copyright perceived an inequality in the current law that favoured corporate interests at the expense of amateur creators:

> On one hand I would be overjoyed, but on the other copyright is not a 'necessary evil', it's necessary but its laws have to be reviewed. If you would ask me what they ought to be I cannot tell you as I am no legislator, but I would want to know that my work, and that of other people is protected from theft. But I would not want people to be able to exploit copyright in the other direction, being over-protective just to ensure their profits. And by that I mean things such as trying to bend the legislation to over-extent [sic] a copyright, for as long as it is possible. I would be fine if after a few years the copyright to my work expired. A few years after its publishing, that is, not my death.[18]

Several of the interview participants felt particularly strongly about this topic, and it is likely this influenced their decision to volunteer for the study. However, the same themes were found in the observational work on discussion threads where numerous criticisms of the scope of copyright protection, its duration or the penalties associated with its enforcement were discussed. Disney were often the particular target of criticism, as they were viewed as both a key actor in lobbying efforts to increase copyright protection and a particularly harsh enforcer of rights they hold. This position does not equate to a rejection of copyright in its entirety; mostly what is wanted is a fairer balance with less corporate influence, particularly in relation to copyright exceptions, terms and penalties to allow them more flexibility to use these works in their own creative activities.

[17] Participant 7: Kanzi.
[18] Participant 8: Scribe576.

Similarly, several interviewees made it clear that for them copyright law was legitimate, either because it benefits them specifically or because it benefits artists more generally: 'It matters to me how, when, and by whom the things I make are used';[19] 'Copyright is a pretty important concept for any artist. We tend to get used pretty often'.[20] In the discussion threads, such views were often argued to be hypocritical or ironic in the wider context of arguments for more lenient copyright provisions, with criticisms that creators want to uphold their rights, but are happy to infringe on corporate-held copyright. Others, however, were less positive about copyright's effect on their creative practice, flagging that it prevents them using other works and as such stifled creativity: 'Copyright was made to promote creativity and not to stifle it and right now it's definitely being stifled'.[21] Furthermore, copyright law was seen to have little value to amateur creators, either because it was considered relevant only to monetised or commercial works or because it does not offer sufficient practical protection:

Q: So what are your thoughts about copyright's relevance to you?

SwirlHigher: From what I've seen, it doesn't give much protection to online creators.

Again, this does not indicate rejection of copyright as a concept; instead it highlights the (currently unfulfilled) potential for copyright law to play a role in the regulation of creativity in these CUGC communities. This seems logically contradictory in light of the role of identifiability in the construction of ownership under copyright law but part of this contradiction may be explained by the fact that absolute anonymity is rarely practised, and instead the identifiability of creators and other community members will be obscured to varying degrees on a spectrum, based on factors such as names and art style as discussed in chapter two, section II.C. In cases of non-absolute anonymity, the conceptual links between creator and work are merely weakened or blurred rather than removed entirely.

It is therefore clear that, despite some objections to specific elements of the copyright system, these CUGC communities should not be assumed to reject the concept of individual control of works, or even of copyright specifically.

III. The Specifics of Ownership Norms

As it is not the case that control over CUGC is undesired, waived or forfeited, nor that CUGC creators and communities reject the concept of copyright, the rest of this chapter is spent exploring the specifics of 'ownership' norms in relation to CUGC, outlining the *what*, *when*, *who* and *why* of these norms in comparison to core elements of copyright law. While copyright scholarship has often

[19] Participant 4: Paul.
[20] Participant 11: Anon3.
[21] Participant 12: Anon4.

highlighted the differences between community norms and copyright as a basis of critique,[22] the aim here is to go further in this analysis in order to build a more detailed understanding of the construction of these norms and of the differences and commonalities with copyright law. Doing so leads us to see that while some aspects of community ownership norms clearly diverge from copyright in numerous ways, there are also many commonalities. This influences the arguments that can be made about the need for reform, and what form that should take, as explored in more detail in chapter six.

A. What: Restrictions on Using Creative UGC

Our starting point for exploring ownership norms in more detail is the issue of what 'ownership' means in terms of the rights that derive from it. The potential benefit copyright law offers to creators is because it provides the owner with the exclusive right to control how the work is used and distributed. This is true regardless of which philosophical tradition underpins a particular jurisdiction's laws. For those focused on economic rights, copyright law allows the owner of a work to exploit it within a marketplace (with the aim of incentivising production of creative works, or ensuring creators are justly rewarded for their efforts), while for those focused on authors or moral rights, copyright law allows the owner of a work to restrict unwanted uses of it by others (with the aim of protecting the creator's dignity and personhood).[23] Copyright law grants the rights-holder certain rights over a creative work, and the form and function of these rights shows us how we should interpret ownership in the legal context. By looking at the law, we can see that owning copyright in a work equates to having a high level of control over what other people can do with the work and some of the relevant rights granted by copyright law were outlined in chapter two, section III.B. To briefly summarise again, these generally include exclusive rights to control reproduction, distribution, public performance, communication to the public and adaptation.[24] In addition, copyright law also provides some moral rights, such as attribution and integrity.[25]

Chapter two, section III.B, has already demonstrated that these rights are very restrictive and would regulate many of the ways that someone can interact

[22] See, eg: L Lessig, *Free Culture: The Nature and Future of Creativity* (New York, Penguin Books, 2005); LJ Murray, ST Piper and K Robertson, *Putting Intellectual Property in its Place: Rights Discourses, Creative Labor, and the Everyday* (Oxford, Oxford University Press, 2013); K Darling and A Perzanowski (eds), *Creativity without Law: Challenging the Assumptions of Intellectual Property* (New York, NYU Press, 2017).

[23] WM Landes and RA Posner, 'An Economic Analysis of Copyright Law' (1989) 18 *Journal of Legal Studies* 325; WW Fisher, 'Theories of Intellectual Property' in SR Munzer (ed), *New Essays in the Legal and Political Theory of Property* (Cambridge, Cambridge University Press, 2001).

[24] CDPA, ss 16(1) and 20(2)(b); UrhG, ss 15 and 19a; 17 USC s 106(1)–(3).

[25] CDPA, s 77(1) and s 80(1); UrhG, ss 13 and 14; 17 USC s 106(a)(1)(A) (in relation to visual art only) and s 106(a)(3)(A).

with CUGC, including reposting it either within the community or on another platform (reproduction, communication to the public); reposting it, or part thereof, without attribution (attribution); remixing it (adaptation, reproduction, integrity); sharing those remixes (distribution, communication to the public); or using CUGC for private purposes such as a phone wallpaper (reproduction). Chapter two, sections III.B and IV.B, also highlighted that the options available to avoid needing express permission to use CUGC, such as limitations and exceptions and implied licences, do not provide a comprehensive solution in relation to CUGC, reinforcing copyright's restrictiveness in this context. Where interactions with CUGC happen without the creator's permission, the law would view them as infringements of copyright except in a few limited scenarios. One of these is that the interaction with CUGC is the use of the idea underpinning it, rather than the expression of it, as only the latter is protected by copyright law.[26] Another is where an insubstantial part of the CUGC has been used: in order to be infringing, copied elements must often be a substantial part of the work it derives from.[27] Another potential outlier is the scraping of CUGC for use in training datasets for generative AI models, where relevant exceptions or limitations in some jurisdictions seem to be permissive, or where creators have seemingly given permission for platforms to allow such scraping through the acceptance of broad terms of service. As such we see that legal rights over CUGC are highly restrictive.

Ownership norms in CUGC communities deviate from this highly restrictive approach, although individual viewpoints varied, as to be expected in communities of this scale where unanimity is impossible.[28] The quotes on the legitimacy of copyright law earlier in this chapter demonstrate some of these variations. The type of control that individual creators wanted varied along a spectrum. For some creators, 'anything goes'; several of the creators I interviewed wanted or expected little to no control over what people did with their work: 'They can post it anywhere, edit it, rip-off the idea, show it on TV, put it on a t-shirt and sell it, anything.'[29]

[26] See, eg, *Baigent v Random House Group Ltd* [2007] EWCA Civ 247; [2008] EMLR 7, where the court dismissed the appellants' argument that Dan Brown's bestselling novel, *The Da Vinci Code*, copied the 'central theme' of their own book about the holy grail and the bloodline of Jesus. The court held that the central theme was too general and abstract to warrant protection.

[27] In the UK, this is set out in s 16(3) CDPA 1988. In the US, this is part of the four-factor approach to fair use under 17 USC s 107. In Germany, UrhG, s 57 exempts de minimis uses from infringement. There is some concern about the lack of clarity on what constitutes a substantial part, but European case law that suggests a relatively low bar for substantiality; in the *Infopaq* ruling, the court held that just eleven words could constitute infringement (Case 5/08 *Infopaq Int'l A/S v Danske Dagblades Forening* ECLI:EU:C:2009:465, [2009] ECR I-6569).

[28] The qualitative discussion that follows here is based on a subset of data from the main study comprising 12 interviews and 104 discussion threads (38 from 4chan and 66 from Reddit). Discussion threads were either threads specifically set up to complain about an 'unacceptable' use, eg, someone complaining that their creative work had been posted elsewhere; where someone posted creative work that was then later used by someone else in the thread, eg, set up as their phone wallpaper, or remixed and reposted in the thread; or where people were discussing how works had been used in other contexts. It also includes data from the AI study, with 73 discussion threads (29 from 4chan and 44 from Reddit). All of these threads discussed the relationship between creativity and AI in some way.

[29] Participant 2: DeerDecipher.

Q: So when you post stuff you don't really mind what happens to it?

Anon4: No, not really. I post it with the awareness that it might get spread and that's fine.

A common theme in the comments of those with strongly permissive attitudes was that of being flattered by people using their work. Most often this was in relation to non-commercial uses, but sometimes also extended to commercial activity too: 'During the summer I serendipitous came across prints of one of my [photoshops] being sold and found it flattering! It made my day, honestly'.[30]

At the other end of the spectrum were creators who wanted to retain control over everything, even their ideas. This expectation is not widely sustained and that also applies to the 'anything goes' approach. As such, it is possible to identify the more widely held views that better represent ownership and control norms that fall somewhere in the middle.

In a non-commercial context, there are generally permissive attitudes towards the utilisation, distribution and remix of CUGC.[31] Making a copy for personal use, for example setting an image as the wallpaper on a mobile phone, and even in some cases, printing a copy, is generally acceptable: '"My new background" even "I'm going to make prints or t shirts of this" a tattoo? Sure'.[32] Credit is usually irrelevant in this context.

In terms of copying, publishing and reproducing a CUGC work without express permission, it is generally viewed to be acceptable to distribute the work within the wider community (for example, within Reddit). Credit is usually expected, or at least desired: 'Of course they're free to share it as well I just hope they give me credit LOL … I mean I'd certainly be peeved if they didn't give me credit'.[33]

Cross-community posting is seen as marginally more controversial but is still widely accepted: 'cross-posting to a new platform can get a little dicier, but as long as the link is still there, credit is still there'.[34] There was some divergence from this norm, however. In 4chan's photography community, there were several instances of community members collating shared photographs into digital photobooks for the community to enjoy. In one example, the organiser stated openly that they created the document without permission (and their hope that this was okay). In another, the organiser requested submissions, rejecting arguments that he or she could simply take the images from the board without permission.

There were also examples of creators being unhappy that a particular creative work had been shared, although not necessarily because they wanted control over all of their creative content. In some cases, writers needed to restrict other distribution so as not to jeopardise any future publishing deal. In others, creators were unhappy or embarrassed because the work that got shared was old, poor quality or lewd and they wanted control over who saw it.

[30] Participant 2: DeerDecipher.
[31] Ch 2, section II.B provides detailed definitions of these terms.
[32] Participant 1: Justin.
[33] Participant 3: UseYourHead.
[34] Participant 5: Well-joy.

Remixing and transforming an image into a new, non-commercial work is also usually acceptable, although the new work must be sufficiently original. If not, or if the creator's work is still a substantial element of the new work, they will also usually expect proper attribution:

> P8: I would be fine with people using my work in a non-commercial manner, as long as, somewhere, they cited who the original author is.[35]
>
> P4: I think the general rule as it is now is 'everything non-commercial is allowed as long as you give credit'.[36]

However, if any utilisation, distribution or remix activity was for commercial purposes, this would contravene the communities' and creators' expectations. Commercial purposes include obvious examples of prints or t-shirts being sold, but also if someone reposts a work on monetised accounts: 'I'd have no problem with my work being used for something personal, but I would have a problem if someone was benefiting from my work monetarily and I didn't get anything from it'.[37] 'Any commercial use needs to pay'.[38] This aligns with the findings in the AI study, where there were frequent discussions about how their content was being used to train commercial generative AI models. Some creators expressed that they were not troubled by this, largely because the scale of the datasets being created means that their individual work is unlikely to be visible in the outputs generated, and this reflects the natural, human process of creation that draws on a huge range of source material. However, more often it was viewed in a highly negative way by creators who often framed it through the language of theft or stealing. That their work was being used for commercial purposes was a particular source of annoyance.

While there are some who do not have an expectation or preference for credit in relation to non-commercial distribution and remix, there were much stronger feelings about someone actively claiming the work as their own. Again, some were flattered by this, but for most creators, even those with very permissive attitudes, this was one of the most clear-cut examples of wanting control. Lack of credit was also raised occasionally as a complaint about their work being used by generative AI models:

> **Q:** When you post your work, what do you view as acceptable use of that by others?
>
> **DeerDecipher**: Anything and everything. They can post it anywhere, edit it, rip-off the idea, show it on TV, put it on a t-shirt and sell it, anything. I don't need credit, either. As far as I'm concerned, as soon as I post my stuff online it belongs to the internet. Although I'd probably get upset if someone tried to claim the work as their own.
>
> P1: The worst thing you can do is claim someone's work as your own.[39]

[35] Participant 8: Scribe576.
[36] Participant 4: Paul.
[37] Participant 11: Anon3.
[38] Participant 4: Paul.
[39] Participant 1: Justin.

Furthermore, some creators talked about wanting control over works to prevent them being used in ways that were in conflict with their political or moral views:

> P9: There might come a day when someone whose rhetoric or actions might go against everything I believe in could use my work as a way to make their message more palatable in spite of the fact I would never agree to such a thing.[40]
>
> P8: I feel like people can post other's creative work or alter if they give the original creator credit and not disrespect his or her work and ethics … sometimes people would want to use that content to use it to push for a political agenda or an ideology that clashes with the morals or the principals of the creator.[41]

From this we can see that the types of control that creators expect over their works reflect some of the restrictions set out in copyright law but are often much more permissive. Where copyright law restricts most interactions with CUGC, whether commercial or non-commercial, these online communities do not seek to widely restrict non-commercial uses of works shared within them. They do, however, want to retain control over commercial uses in most cases. It is interesting, and perhaps ironic, that one of the few areas where CUGC creators would like more control (use by generative AI) is one where the law currently provides the least ability to do so, either because copyright law is more permissive or because broad terms of service have circumvented the need to get permission from them. Similarly, moral rights issues seem to be more significant, with the most agreement being found over the issue of taking credit for someone else's work, and additional concerns about upholding the integrity of works. In the case of the US and the UK, attribution and integrity rights are rather weak, and as such, these communities expect a higher protection than the law on this issue.

This approach to norms is not limited to 4chan and Reddit communities; studies into other online amateur creative communities outline similar findings. A study into online video creators found that 74 per cent of those surveyed agreed that they felt owning copyright was important, and several highlighted that someone else making money from their videos would be upsetting, even if they did not view their own work as commercial.[42] Fiesler et al's content analysis of several remix and fandom communities found 'frustration' from creators that they were limited in how much they could restrict how their work was used, implying a desire to retain control over it. They also found strong norms against plagiarism, in the sense of others claiming work as their own.[43] In a later work, Fiesler and Bruckman conducted interviews with fan creators, identifying 'highly consistent copyright-related norms' linked to attribution, plagiarism and commerciality,

[40] Participant 9: Anon1.

[41] Participant 8: Scribe576.

[42] P Aufderheide and P Jaszi, *Reclaiming Fair Use: How to Put Balance Back in Copyright*, 2nd edn (Chicago, IL, University of Chicago Press, 2018) 7.

[43] C Fiesler, JL Feuston and AS Bruckman, 'Understanding Copyright Law in Online Creative Communities', *Proceedings of the 18th ACM Conference on Computer Supported Cooperative Work and Social Computing* (New York, ACM Press, 2015) 116, 122–23.

similar to those found here.[44] An ethnography into the online art community, DeviantArt, identified similar themes in relation to requiring permission, expecting credit and making a profit, with even very permissive users having issues with the latter.[45] Meese and Hagedorn's exploration of norms in relation to UGC outside specifically creative communities identified different expectations about circulation and sharing depending on platform, but respondents were consistent in their view that commercial exploitation of UGC was unacceptable, and there were positive views about attribution.[46]

As such, while ownership norms align with copyright law in the sense that the types of uses that are to be restricted (commercial exploitation and others claiming the work as their own) could be dealt with by the law, the scope of the law far exceeds those norms, in fact restricting a lot of what is deemed acceptable appropriation. As has been shown, copyright law operates from a position that all unlicensed uses are an infringement unless they fall into one of the few categories where this is not the case. In contrast to this 'infringement unless' approach, ownership norms are more easily understood as 'permitted unless'.

B. When: Originality Criteria

The next step is to examine community norms and values in relation to concepts that underpin 'ownership' in copyright by asking how these concepts are understood by the communities and whether they play the same role in underpinning their norms. The first of these concepts is that of originality and the approach to determining *when* the community ownership norms outlined above are deemed to apply to a CUGC work. The detailed discussion of originality that follows is particularly essential to this book's task of evaluating copyright law in the CUGC context. Questions of when works and elements of works can and cannot be 'owned' are central to all creative environments, but they are particularly relevant in online creative spheres where the fact that creative works build on one another becomes particularly evident. We see this in specific examples of remix and collaborative communities, such as fan fiction or memes, but also more generally in all forms of creativity, even those that resemble a more 'traditional' individual form of creation. In the latter, the internet facilitates exposure to a wider range of sources which allows creators to draw from a wider pool of inspiration.

[44] C Fiesler and AS Bruckman, 'Creativity, Copyright, and Close-Knit Communities: A Case Study of Social Norm Formation and Enforcement' (2019) 3 *Proceedings of the ACM on Human-Computer Interaction* 241: 1, 2.

[45] D Perkel, 'Share Wars: Sharing, Theft, and the Everyday Production of Web 2.0 on Deviant Art' [2016] *First Monday*: firstmonday.org/ojs/index.php/fm/article/view/6795.

[46] J Meese and J Hagedorn, 'Mundane Content on Social Media: Creation, Circulation, and the Copyright Problem' (2019) 5 *Social Media + Society* 1, 4–7.

Alongside this, the internet acts as a form of register (albeit a relatively unreliable one) where sources of inspiration are visible, perhaps dated and attributed, and most likely searchable, so those who view creative works online are themselves more likely to have been exposed to the same sources of inspiration, or are able to identify them and use the technology to more closely compare them. As such, understanding first when elements of a work are 'owned' under copyright law, and secondly when derivative works can themselves be protected, are central issues in understanding when copyright will apply to CUGC. Beyond this, much existing copyright scholarship focusing on UGC has identified originality as a key sticking point,[47] as discussed in chapter three, section II.B.ii – it is therefore an essential element of engaging with those critiques, as will be undertaken in chapter six.

In copyright law a right arises when the subsistence criteria are met: subject matter, fixation and originality. The discussion in chapter two, section III.A, highlighted that the first two of those criteria are largely uncontroversial in relation to CUGC, with most examples meeting those requirements. Instead, it is originality that will most often act as a threshold between subsistence of copyright or not, with particular issues relating to the use of existing works as originality determines when works (or parts thereof) are protected by copyright law. It also plays a key role in defining the boundaries of the public domain; allegedly infringing elements of a work must themselves be original in order for such a claim to stand, otherwise they may be considered part of the public domain and therefore free for others to use.

We know already from chapter two, section III.A, that there are jurisdictional variations towards the concept of originality. There, we highlighted that the varying approaches can be understood as 'constellations' rather than 'silos'.[48] In his analysis of existing case law from a wide range of jurisdictions, Fisher states that generally within law originality is understood as 'not copied' plus 'something extra' contributed by the author.[49] He then sets out six distinct but not mutually exclusive conceptions of originality:[50] independent creation (ie, the work is not copied); the amount of labour required to create the work (either as time or as intensity of effort); the skill required to create the work; creative choices or creative freedom reflected in the work (ie, the creator was able to choose how to express the elements of a work); the personality of the author is reflected in the work, as a form

[47] See, eg: P Levy, *Cyberculture*, R Bononno trans (Minneapolis, MN, University of Minnesota Press, 2001) 116; M Deuze, 'Participation, Remediation, Bricolage: Considering Principal Components of a Digital Culture' (2006) 22 *The Information Society* 63; R Tushnet, 'User-Generated Discontent: Transformation in Practice' (2007) 31 *Columbia Journal of Law & Arts* 497; L Lessig, *Remix: Making Art and Commerce Thrive in the Hybrid Economy* (New York, Bloomsbury Academic, 2008).

[48] EF Judge and DJ Gervais, 'Of Silos and Constellations: Comparing Notions of Originality in Copyright Law' (2009) 27 *Cardozo Arts & Entertainment Law Journal* 375, 403.

[49] WW Fisher, 'Recalibrating Originality' (2016) 54 *Houston Law Review* 437, 438.

[50] The US, Canada, India, the Netherlands, Belgium, France, the UK, Japan, China, South Africa, New Zealand, and Switzerland.

of self-expression; and finally, novelty.[51] He identifies that each of the countries considered in his assessment require independent creation to establish originality, alongside different combinations of the others. Nine out of 12 of the jurisdictions use creative choices as a measure of originality, seven use self-expression, five use skill, three use labour, and only one (Switzerland) uses novelty.[52] Fisher also identifies that value is *not* used as a way of defining originality, that is, the quality of the work as a piece of creativity is not considered. In line with this, chapter two, section III.A highlighted that conceptions of originality in the UK, the US and Germany focus on independent creation (in the sense of no slavish copying) and creative choices.[53] It also highlighted that for derivative (user-derived) CUGC to be protected, it would need to meet the same criteria: *Infopaq*'s standard of 'the author's own intellectual creation'[54] or *Feist*'s non-trivial 'creative spark'.[55]

In the CUGC communities, the understanding of originality followed some similar themes and there were several recurring discussion contexts: the merit of hyper-realistic or photo-realistic art; the merit of photography as an art form; the validity of using references in art; and the relevance of new ideas in writing.[56] There was plenty of debate on these issues, and again, unanimity on this issue is impossible, but several possible criteria to assess the originality or value of CUGC works were identified.

There was reasonable consensus on some of these criteria, but considerable debate about others. That creative content needed to be independently created was not controversial, but what was understood by independent creation varied, encompassing one or more of the subsequent criteria. Requiring creative content to be built on original ideas was not widely seen in the data. There were numerous threads and posts discussing concerns that ideas would be stolen if shared or worries that their own ideas were not original enough. Significantly, these were most often found in the Reddit writing communities. In these discussions, other community members usually clarified that originality is not about ideas but about what the creator does with those ideas in their work (in line with copyright law's distinction between idea and expression). Significantly, it seemed that those most concerned about originality in ideas were less experienced creators, with those explaining the other perspective often responding in a way that seeks to reassure them. As such, it would not be accurate to describe novel ideas as a normative criterion for originality in these communities.

[51] Fisher, 'Recalibrating Originality' (n 49) 448–49.

[52] ibid 450.

[53] *Feist Publications, Incorporated v Rural Telephone Service Company, Incorporated* 499 US 340 (1991); *Infopaq v Danske Dagblades Forening* (n 27).

[54] *Infopaq v Danske Dagblades Forening* (n 27).

[55] *Feist Publications* (n 53) 359.

[56] The qualitative discussion that follows here is based on a subset of data comprising 12 interviews and 134 discussion threads (57 from 4chan and 77 from Reddit). Discussion threads were selected because they focused on 'originality'.

Similarly, there were mixed views on whether skill or labour are required or sufficient criteria. In art and photography communities on both platforms, there were divergent views on this point. In art communities, there was debate about the merit of photo-realistic art, where creators had used a single photograph as a reference point and translated it, often exactly, into a different medium. For some, this displayed a lack of effort (or laziness), for others it demonstrated significant effort (or patience) or skill. Some felt that such processes required labour and/or skill, but that level was less than for works less reliant on one reference source. All of these positions seem to indicate labour or skill as valid criteria, but there were also some comments arguing that regardless of the amount of skill or labour put in, it does not mean the CUGC has merit as an original work.

In photography communities, the discussions followed a similar pattern, this time discussing photographs as artistic works. Here the debates centred on whether photography could be considered an artistic work when the process is, to some extent, automated and/or mediated by the camera equipment. Some argued that photography can be just luck; someone might take a good picture despite little effort or skill if they happen to press the shutter at the right time and in the right direction. Others argued that there is more to photography than pressing a button, whether in preparation or editing, and reject the likelihood of a lucky shot, instead arguing skill and technical knowledge are the reliable means of achieving good photography. There was also discussion of the 'monkey selfie' dispute, which focused on the copyright ownership of a self-portrait photograph taken by a macaque monkey using photographer David Slater's camera equipment. The photograph is variously argued to be in the public domain, under copyright held by Slater, or under copyright held by the monkey.[57] The discussions here flagged similar arguments in relation to labour; several commenters argued that Slater had put the time in with the monkeys, and this is what meant he held the copyright. As such, we can see that skill and effort are viewed by some – although not all – art and photography community members as valid criteria for originality, although there is less agreement around what constitutes skill or labour.

More agreement was to be found in relation to the significance of creative choices and self-expression. In art communities, the discussions often focused on heavy use of references in drawing and painting, and the line between copying and referencing. While it was argued and accepted that referencing is part of creating art, this was not widely accepted as meaning direct copies were original. Such heavy reliance on single references was seen as lacking creative choices. One commenter explains why referencing a source almost exactly is wrong: the original creator spent lots of time setting up a photograph or working on the composition of an artwork, and the second creator then gets to benefit from those choices. Where arguments were made that artists' studies have a long history, this is dismissed

[57] A Guadamuz, 'The Monkey Selfie: Copyright Lessons for Originality in Photographs and Internet Jurisdiction' (2016) 5 *Internet Policy Review* 1.

by the critics, however, as a flawed comparison: the Old Masters painted from live models positioned by them in order to execute their vision, which is fundamentally different from drawing heavily from a photograph or artwork created by someone else. Furthermore, such a process, without creative choices, could be beneficial for learning and perhaps demonstrate skill, but could not be said to be original and should not be shared as such. Suggestions of suitable creative choices included visual or aesthetic changes, using a different style, adding further context, developing it, or selectively combining multiple influences or sources to 'make it their own':

> P5: If someone uses a low-res image from Reddit and materially changes it in a way that it is now one element of their own creative work I think it's fine.[58]
>
> P12: If I post something, the original one would obviously be mine but if someone [wanted] to make fanart of stuff or just added something that's mine and try to put their spin on it, that edit I would obviously not say is mine but what I would say is obviously theirs.[59]

Again, photography communities argued over whether there are sufficient creative choices to be made in photography and arguments followed the same lines as for skill and labour: there are creative choices to be made in the set-up and the edit, or that there are fewer but still some creative choices to be made. To avoid copying, photographers could add their own vision, combine influences, use a different style, or express a different sentiment or view. In writing communities, choosing things such as pace, setting, characters or plot in a story were all things argued to elevate works to originality, as was using their own style or voice, or making a new work sufficiently divergent from the source material.

From this we can see that there are various criteria for assessing originality in these communities, and that there is sometimes a lack of consensus on what specifically is needed. This conflict and variation in approaches can be framed through practical issues related to creativity and the creative work. It seems that the type of work may have an impact, for example, concerns over ideas being unoriginal were often expressed in writing communities (although certainly were not the consensus). Writing offers the creator almost infinite choices in their expression of an idea and therefore is likely to be seen as a highly creative activity, offering more possibility of high levels of originality. Inversely, this was less visible in photography communities where creative choices are more limited. Based on the discussions it is clear, however, that novel ideas are not required, skill and effort may be sufficient, and that creative choices will be. These positions fit within Fisher's broader conceptions of originality, with themes relating to novelty, skill, labour, self-expression and creative choices all present in their discussion, suggesting that there is not an insurmountable conflict between copyright law and the community's conception of originality assessment.

[58] Participant 5: Well-joy.
[59] Participant 12: Anon4.

Discussions about the outputs of generative AI from the AI study also provide insights that support this. In particular, there was a widespread attempt to distinguish these outputs from other types of creative work. While a few individuals saw AI outputs as no different from other forms of creative work, AI outputs were mainly framed as 'other'. Some argued that they could not be considered art or creative work in the true sense; AI outputs were described as merely imitative of human creativity and requiring too little from the user in terms of choices. Sometimes it was highlighted that the outputs were too abstracted from real creative processes in that they might look like art, but the people who made them could not be deemed artists. A very common theme was to highlight that the things AI produces are generic and derivative. It was particularly raised that they lack an essential human 'something', often 'soul', meaning or emotion, but sometimes also skill and effort (with those who use AI branded as lazy). This links closely to themes from the main study about originality in terms of creative choices, skill and labour and self-expression. Even where creators thought AI outputs to be equal to other creativity, they used similar themes to justify this, particularly in relation to the skill needed to generate an output of any reasonable quality.

There was also a distinction made between two ways of using generative AI: as a tool within wider creative effort, or as the main element of the creative process. The former was largely deemed to be more acceptable. For example, using generative AI to brainstorm or research, or using editing tools that include generative AI features, seemed to be tolerable practice as it still required the creator to provide their own creative input. Photographers in particular found this acceptable as it is widely available in standard editing software and sometimes cameras themselves. It was slightly more controversial in writing communities, where the use of AI-assisted grammar checking tools was sometimes questioned. Often concerns were raised about the potential negative impact of such tools on the learning and improvement of creative skills.

Normative expectations of originality therefore broadly reflect legal originality criteria, but is originality as significant to community norms as it is to copyright law? It was clear that there was some divergence within the communities about the standards of originality required for ownership norms to apply to a CUGC work. This divergence can be distilled into three distinct approaches on a spectrum from low to high originality standards. These can be described via common refrains found in the communities: 'you're a hack'; 'good artists borrow, great artists steal'; and 'no rules, just tools'. The majority position is that of 'good artists borrow, great artists steal'.

'You're a hack' represents the extreme, and ideological, originality stance taken by some creators. Sometimes bitingly referred to as the 'trace police', these community members (mostly from 4chan's art community) expected high levels of autonomous creative expression, and in many cases, a high level of unique inspiration, expression and ideas. Those who do not meet the required standard in their eyes are 'hacks'. Community members ascribing to this view may also take time to seek out (and publicise) the source material used by other creators they consider to be 'copying'. An interviewee described this approach:

> The passion for their own work makes them draw a very distinct line between memetics and ownership.
>
> If anything, there were people who were very mad at a developer who used drawings from an old book that had entered public domain as sprites on a commercial project because they felt the developer was not advertising the fact the art was not drawn by him from scratch enough.[60]

The second phrase – 'good artists borrow, great artists steal' – represents a more moderate middle ground, where it is accepted that creators draw on previous works and incorporate elements of these into their own works as usual creative practice:

> [Everything] you make is built on the shoulders of giants, it just, you know, we're a collective in that sense where no idea is from one person, it has to come from somewhere else.[61]

However, this acceptance comes with some caveats; despite this phrasing sounding as if it supports 'theft' from other works, instead it actually means that creators need to 'make it their own' when taking inspiration from others. In essence, using elements and ideas from other works is acceptable as long as the creator uses it in their own way rather than a direct copy.

The third approach described by 'no rules, just tools' is a pragmatic stance taken by those who prioritise getting creative work done rather than ensuring it meets strict originality standards. In their eyes, referencing heavily, for example when it comes to body positioning or facial features, is an efficient way to create. Often this approach is justified as a normal part of professional creative practices. For these creators, the fact they use tactics such as tracing does not detract from the fact that they are the originator of a work and that it is therefore theirs. This was reflected in the AI study too, with a minority of people arguing that all forms of generative AI are merely tools, equivalent to a camera or other previous technological development.

The divergence on the standard of originality needed for ownership to vest tended to link to how functionally the creator themselves viewed creativity. Those who held the concept of creativity up in an idealistic light and saw their creative process as an end in itself, often had high originality standards. Those with weaker originality standards often viewed creativity as having different or multiple functions in their life, for example professional creators often talked about the reality of the creative process and getting the job done, such as needing to meet client expectations or deadlines, meaning that high originality standards were unfeasible. This aligns with the earlier findings that many CUGC creators viewed

[60] Participant 9: Anon1.
[61] Participant 12: Anon4.

copyright as something to protect professional and monetised works, with little value to amateurs, as those who are viewed to be more likely to benefit from copyright often have the more lenient approach to originality standards and so are less strict about when works should be protected.

Similar findings have been found in other studies. In his study of blogging communities, Singh highlights what he describes as a form of 'militancy' towards plagiarism; despite blogging practices relying heavily on linking to other works and the fact that, in many cases, blogs are collages of other works, the community polices its expectations relating to copying harshly. Credit to the original authors must be given, and Singh gives examples of community members dedicating large amounts of time to identify plagiarists (ie, those who fail to credit adequately).[62] Fiesler finds a similar situation in her paper on fan fiction communities, where plagiarism within the community is socially taboo despite the works freely drawing from outside sources,[63] and this is also seen in online knitting communities, where it is seen as acceptable to use licensed characters in their work (for example, printed on fabric), but not to copy patterns within the community.[64]

Therefore, despite the diverging viewpoints on standards of originality the moderate view was the most influential across communities. While like the law this approach recognises the importance of an individual's creative choices, it gives more recognition to the cumulative creative process. Those with high originality standards, however, expect more than the law requires. As such, it can be seen that the normative concept of originality within these communities does not diverge too greatly from that of the law, but its role as the arbiter of ownership does not align so neatly.

C. Who: Asserting Ownership and Creatorship

Like originality, authorship is a fundamental concept in copyright law. The author is usually the first owner of copyright in a work (usually with the exception of works created in the course of employment) as he or she is viewed as the originator of the work.[65] The role of the author is therefore closely linked with the conception of originality. As explored in chapter three, section II.B.ii, there is an established body of scholarship that is critical of the way that authorship is constructed in copyright law. This argues that where creativity is cumulative and collaborative, with creative works building on one another, the individualistic role

[62] A Singh, 'Anonymity, Authorship, and Blogger Ethics' (2009) 16 *symploke* 21, 31–32.

[63] C Fiesler, 'Everything I Need to Know I Learned from Fandom: How Existing Social Norms Can Help Shape the Next Generation of User-Generated Content' (2007) 10 *Vanderbilt Journal of Entertainment and Technology Law* 729, 753–54.

[64] K Robertson, 'No One Would Murder for a Pattern: Crafting IP in Online Knitting Communities' in LJ Murray, ST Piper and K Robertson (eds), *Putting Intellectual Property in its Place: Rights Discourses, Creative Labor, and the Everyday* (Oxford, Oxford University Press, 2013) 55.

[65] See above (n 8) for legal authorities.

of the Romantic author under copyright is inaccurate. Instead, creators should be viewed as interpreters of culture, or craftspeople, rather than creative geniuses. In this view of authorship, there can be no original flash of inspiration at an individual level, and therefore giving the creator extensive control over how a work is used is unjustifiable.[66]

Under this view, we would expect a move away from the individualism at the centre of copyright's view of authorship in community norms as it has already been highlighted that cumulative creativity flourishes, whether by explicit remix practices or by more subtle developments of works from exposure to inspiration and sources. The element of anonymity would further seem to add to this rejection of creativity as individual as it functions to remove hierarchy and individual traits. On 4chan particularly, anonymity is seen as a social leveller and using identifiers is frowned on: 'There are of course, tripcodes, which are abhorred because they make divisions between us all and should really only be used in specific situations'.[67] In this sense, anonymity as well as the cumulative forms of creativity online seem at odds with the individualism seen in copyright's conception of the author.

However, the communities' views of authorship were more nuanced than an outright rejection of individual creativity and individual control. On both 4chan and Reddit, creatorship is discussed in solemn terms. Creators often take their work seriously, even when they are beginners, hobbyists or creating something humorous, such as a piece for r/photoshopbattles, where creators alter an image using photoshop, trying to outdo the other posters:

> Just to expand a bit more on the work being 'throwaway': I do not say that with disdain, or to imply that I don't take pride in crafting my work. I really try to produce as high quality content as possible.[68]

Some of this does align with narratives of the creator as either interpreter or craftsman, with many discussions about the requisite diligence to become a good artist or writer; daily dedicated practice is often cited as necessary. Additionally, as set out in the discussion of originality above, many community members follow the approach of 'good artists borrow, great artists steal', which does support a view of the author as not 100 per cent original and individualistic. However, as discussed, approaches to originality are varied and there is a small minority (in the 'you're a hack' camp) whose viewpoints strongly support the idea of the genius author.

[66] See, eg: P Jaszi, 'Toward a Theory of Copyright: The Metamorphoses of "Authorship"' [1991] *Duke Law Journal* 455, 455–56; M Woodmansee, *The Author, Art and the Market: Rereading the History of Aesthetics* (New York, Columbia University Press, 1996) 36–37; C Hesse, 'The Rise of Intellectual Property, 700 BC–AD 2000: An Idea in the Balance' (2002) 131 *Daedalus* 26, 32.

[67] Participant 9: Anon1; Tripcodes are unique series of letters, numbers and symbols that can be added to posts as a way of proving that a sequence of posts comes from the same person, in the way that a username might work elsewhere. On 4chan, a mere username can be typed in by anyone, and therefore replicated, but the tripcode is created from a code that the poster enters with each post, and therefore cannot be appropriated by others.

[68] Participant 2: DeerDecipher.

As was explained above, community norms support exclusive rights to control how CUGC is used, and position the creator as the legitimate controller, even if these rights are more permissive than copyright and approaches to originality recognise the cumulative aspect of creative practice. This indicates that authorship is still a valid issue for these communities, despite their anonymity.

D. Why: Justifications for Conceptions of Ownership

The last aspect to consider is how these norms are justified. There are numerous possible reasons for giving creators exclusive rights to control their works. These were explored in detail in chapter three, section II.A, but most often copyright law is justified as an economic incentive to create, particularly in common law jurisdictions, but increasingly in civil law jurisdictions. Other theories used to justify copyright law include the Lockean argument that the author deserves such rights as a reward for their labour, as well as personality-based arguments that works are manifestations of the creator's personality.[69]

A key question, then, is how the views outlined in this chapter are justified by the communities. As with the other elements discussed in this chapter, there was mixed rhetoric about why creators should or should not be given control over the works they create. Much of this can be interpreted within existing copyright justificatory narratives. It was often framed as an issue of justice and desert, that creators should be rewarded for their efforts, neatly falling into a Lockean labour narrative. Community members framed CUGC works as resulting from 'hard work',[70] and argued that CUGC creators had spent time learning their skills and paying for equipment, all of which made it unfair for others to benefit from that. Often, benefit was framed in terms of attention, with community members expressing concern that the correct person should receive the appropriate recognition, and inversely, that it was not fair that people got recognition they did not deserve, for example if they inaccurately claimed a work was their own. This theme arose on multiple occasions in relation to generative AI, either because the inclusion of creative work in the training data was deemed to be exploitative of the efforts of human creators, or because someone was receiving (in their view, undeserving) praise for content that was created by AI.

There was also some support for personality-based arguments. Community members viewed following the normative expectations around use of works to be a matter of respect to artists and creators, with transgression framed as disrespectful, insulting, hurtful, rude and offensive. Some creators themselves described the personal impact that their work being used in an unacceptable way had on them and their feelings, with one creator explaining that it caused

[69] Fisher, 'Theories of Intellectual Property' (n 23).
[70] Participant 1: Justin.

genuinely depressive feelings. Themes relating to disrespect, despair, heartbreak and disgust arose when creators were discussing the rise of generative AI outputs in creative spheres. These perspectives align with a notion of creative works as somehow part of the creator.

Significantly, there was little to no indication that control is seen as an incentive to creators, which is logical considering the non-commercial nature of the communities, and mirrors the findings on incentives in chapter three, section II.C. There was some acknowledgement that there were economic reasons for respecting ownership in some cases, but these were not reflections on the creator's own perspectives:

Kanzi:	I know some artists, they post on fb all the time about art theft.
Q:	Why do you think they feel so differently to you?
Kanzi:	Because their livelihoods depend on it.

Therefore, while copyright law is concerned with protecting works in order to maximise return, community norms seem to uphold different standards.

Most often, control over works was considered to be a moral issue: 'It's just a really evil thing to do, take credit for others hard work'.[71] Community members often viewed the misuse of works as fraudulent, dishonest and unethical in both studies. Morality extended, however, to upholding a certain level of creative and artistic integrity, most notably in art communities. Here, creators themselves saw it as shameful or cheating to transgress expectations, particularly expectations in relation to originality, and to do so undermined their standing not just as community members but as artists. This helps to explain the discord between the high originality standards of the 'you're a hack' position and nonetheless permissive levels of control – if you uphold high originality standards, it would be logical to expect more control. What became clear in the research is that these conceptions of originality and authorship are not merely issues of copyright law and individual ownership. While they clearly do play a role in this (something underpinned by the frequent occurrence of copyright discussions) the protection and enforcement of the individual rights of creators is not their sole focus. Tied in with these is a strong moral stance that upholds artistic and creative integrity, that is to say, that standards of originality are enforced as a means of protecting art and creativity itself.

As such, we can see that the narratives behind ownership norms within these communities reflect some of the justificatory narratives found in copyright law, including the reward and personality theories. There is, however, little reflection of ownership as an incentive. Justificatory narratives here diverge from those in copyright law in the value they place on morality, and particularly on the maintenance of artistic integrity.

[71] Participant 1: Justin.

IV. Conclusion

This chapter has demonstrated that control over creative user-generated content (CUGC), and therefore the concept of 'ownership', plays a significant role in online communities, often in conflict with what would be expected. The first part highlighted that while sharing CUGC anonymously, or where anonymity is pervasive, could be viewed as a deliberate forfeiture of ownership or fundamentally incompatible with copyright, in reality, CUGC works do not 'belong to the internet'. It was found that a model of individual ownership of rights over CUGC existed and that creators and communities are not generally hostile to copyright law as a concept. Instead, there was general support for a copyright system, with some exceptions. Mostly, it was recognised that copyright was beneficial for professionals, but that there are concerns about its current set-up and perceived prioritising of corporate interests.

The second part explored the substance of ownership norms in more detail. It found normative systems diverged significantly from copyright law in certain respects but that there were also commonalities. A key difference was that community ownership norms operate on a system of permission, and restrict only in limited circumstances (*permitted unless*) – in comparison with copyright law which would restrict many of these uses deemed acceptable within the community (*infringement unless*). The strongest normative positions within the community were that commercial appropriation (including by generative AI models) and false attribution of CUGC were unacceptable. As such, ownership norms provide creators with the right to control such uses, even if the creator was not interested in exploiting the CUGC commercially themselves, or was happy for it to be used without credit otherwise. Conversely, permissive approaches to CUGC mean that it could be reposted by others without permission (with some variation on whether credit was required or not) or utilised for private uses such as phone wallpapers. Ownership norms therefore do not provide the right to control non-commercial sharing or private uses. Remixing was generally also deemed acceptable, subject to meeting originality requirements, and often providing proper attribution.

Ownership of CUGC arises when it is sufficiently original. There were strong variations on the level of originality required to meet the threshold, making this a more complex element to navigate. Most commonly, originality was framed in terms of creative choices and labour or skill, aligning with the conceptions of originality in the UK, US and Germany. Other viewpoints were also found, but even these fell within Fisher's broader taxonomy of originality. Expectations about the standard of originality required sometimes exceeded those of copyright law, particularly where community members felt strongly about artistic integrity. Most commonly, the cumulative creative process was recognised (good artists borrow, great artists steal) but with the caveat that creators needed to 'make it their own'. Despite anonymity, there remained a strong sense of individual authorship, with CUGC creators being viewed as the legitimate controllers of their works. Finally, the narratives that underpin these norms reflected some aspects of the personality and desert theories of intellectual property, but an economic incentive justification was notably absent. Key themes related to respect, morality and artistic integrity.

Therefore, although there are significant differences between ownership norms and copyright law, the two systems also mirror each other in several ways. These similarities indicate that suitable changes to copyright might be possible through compromise rather than a radical overthrow of the system. Chapter six will consider this possibility in more detail.

5

Regulating Creative User-Generated Content: The Communication, Enforcement and Efficiency of Norms

I. Introduction

The previous chapter explored community norms in relation to the ownership and control of creative user-generated content (CUGC). This chapter looks to explain how these values translate into practice, to understand how communities and the individuals within them attempt to enforce their norms and expectations. With the help of qualitative findings,[1] it explains and evaluates four steps of this process: communication and interpretation of norms; deterrence of transgression; detection of transgression; and remedies or sanctions for transgression. In this regard, it considers whether the system that exists is able to fill the gaps left by copyright law. To do this, it should respond flexibly to the differing levels of control desired by creators and communities in differing circumstances; it should be clear and coherent to provide certainty both within and external to the community; it should not have high barriers to access (either cost, or legal knowledge); and it should contribute positively to the creative process by maximising the sharing of creative works online.

The role of anonymity within these processes is also explained, finding that it causes some practical problems for individuals but may offer some benefit to community-level approaches. The chapter also evaluates the efficiency of the norms system as a regulator of the use of CUGC in place of copyright. It highlights that the system is not flawless as it lacks clarity and certainty, and this could undermine the CUGC sharing community. It also argues that the norms system is incapable of fully superseding the copyright system, and so problems of clarity are further entrenched by the confusion caused by the simultaneous applicability of different rules under copyright law.

[1] The qualitative findings here are drawn from 12 interviews with individual creators (8 from Reddit and 4 from 4chan) and 92 online discussion threads (60 from Reddit and 32 from 4chan). The discussion threads' focus varied; some were generic discussions about fear of misuse or of how to prevent or deal with misuse, others were more specific discussions of an identified example of misuse.

It seems important first to note the risk of misuse of CUGC is unquantified. Chapter four, section II showed that creators recognise the inevitability of their work being used, and therefore misused. Sometimes, for example where a popular or high-quality work was shared, it was seen as almost inevitable that the work would be 'stolen'. Comments were also seen that praise the quality of the work and then add something along the lines of 'shame it is going to get ripped off'. In other instances, people argued (sometimes in reference to their own work) that it is so trivial or poor quality, or the community is so small, that no one is going to steal it. The reality is, however, that works do end up being used by others without the permission of the creator. Several of the creators interviewed in the main study had personally experienced it, and numerous discussion threads detailed the misuse of community members' works.[2] Examples of CUGC being misused after being posted online somewhere range from low-level reposting without credit through to numerous examples of work having been taken for significant commercial uses, including t-shirts sold by a major international retailer, advertising posters in a major city, and promotional materials for a world famous band. Regardless of frequency, this is problematic if the creator wants to retain any form of control over the work. Furthermore, the issue of CUGC misuse has arguably become more widespread, if not ubiquitous, now that generative AI businesses scrape such content from online platforms and websites in order to train their models.

II. Communicating and Negotiating Norms

Chapter four provided a detailed description of community norms relating to ownership, originality and control of works that guide, generally, what is acceptable within creative communities online. In his esteemed theory of norms, McAdam argues that in order to become a norm, consensus on an issue needs to be teamed with the risk of detection of transgression and sufficient knowledge of the consensus and of the risk of detection.[3] Essentially, people need to be able to know what the norms are, and that they might be caught if they behave unacceptably. The first part of this section therefore looks to outline how those norms are communicated to and come to be understood by individuals. It flags that there are two key ways that social norms are communicated within these communities: actively (through explicit, written rules); and passively (through dialogue and time spent within communities). It also highlights some of the limitations to understanding norms, including transient community participation and clashes between individual and

[2] A further example can be seen here: JB Kris, 'Things I Learned After My Photo Hit #1 on Reddit, and Why I Probably Shouldn't Have Posted It' (*Petapixel*, 25 July 2014): petapixel.com/2014/07/25/things-learned-photo-hit-1-spot-reddit-probably-shouldnt-posted/.

[3] RH McAdams, 'The Origin, Development, and Regulation of Norms' (1997) 96 *Michigan Law Review* 338.

community values. The second part of this section then considers how norms are complied with, specifically in relation to the issue of getting permission to use CUGC works.

A. Communicating Norms

Communities can actively communicate their norms to individuals through express, written rules. In the CUGC context, this might be seen with specific community rules if there are defined online spaces for the communities, as on Reddit and 4chan. On Reddit, some subreddits have written rules set out in the sidebar, and these sometimes include rules relating to copyright or attribution. For example, on *r/Art*, *Rule 1* requires the author to be named in the title of the post,[4] and on *r/Photographs*, *Rule 2* requires images shared to be the original work of the person posting.[5] Some 4chan boards also have specific rules, for example on /ic/ rule 2 states that posters must not claim authorship of works they did not create, with /p/ only permitting the sharing of photographs taken by the individual posting.[6] These are useful as they provide clear statements, accessible to community members and outsiders equally. However, subreddit rules are not always provided[7] and are not comprehensive. As such they are not a reliable means of fully communicating what normative values the community has regarding using works.

Where communities arise from less structured formats (for example, through hashtags on Instagram or Tiktok), explicit communication of rules will be at a more general, site-wide level, and often through terms of service and content policies. These often address legal obligations, including copyright law, rather than specifically reflecting the norms of the communities necessarily. Reddit and 4chan also have these site-wide rules. Reddit also has something called 'Reddiquette' which articulates the broad values of the Reddit community and includes prompts such as looking for and linking to the original source of content.[8]

Norms are also communicated passively, with individuals learning the rules through observing and participating in dialogue with the community. Generally, individuals gain understanding of norms gradually through being a community member, by being corrected when they accidentally transgress these norms, by seeing others being corrected, or by seeing the normative values expressed by others in other ways. For example, Trammell highlights the importance of 'lurking' on 4chan for a long period of time before participating to properly understand

[4] 'R/Art' (*Reddit*): www.reddit.com/r/Art/.

[5] 'R/Photographs' (*Reddit*): www.reddit.com/r/photographs/.

[6] 'Rules – 4chan' (4chan): www.4chan.org/rules.

[7] C Fiesler et al, 'Reddit Rules! Characterizing an Ecosystem of Governance' [2018] *Proceedings of the Twelfth International AAAI Conference on Web and Social Media* 72.

[8] 'Reddiquette' (*Reddit*): reddit.zendesk.com/hc/en-us/articles/205926439.

the parameters of the community and to correctly present oneself as a community member[9] and this is backed up in the data:

> We have no big expectancies within the community, but also some degree of understanding of its unspoken rules.
>
> Which I and others try desperately to turn into very outspoken rules whenever someone new shows up and asks questions that imply they don't really understand. Fair Use or anything similar.
>
> It's this cycle of learning and sharing information, even if in the form of memes and rude remarks that allows us to maintain the overall shape of a community that while anonymous and composed of people all around the world, moderates and teaches itself its own values.
>
> Not by one person deciding anything, but arguing endlessly until what is obvious stands out from any preposterous proposals.[10]

We can also see here how strong anonymity enhances the development and communication of norms within the community as it leads to what could politely be called 'robust' debate of all issues. Anonymity allows people to talk openly without fear of retribution[11] and the effect of this is that discussions are often rude, aggressive and offensive, and as Anon1 describes, it means that community members can efficiently learn what is expected of them as it is made very clear to them.

In contrast with the explicit rules, this inductive approach is more comprehensive in its representation of the nuances of community norms. It does face some issues, however. The first of these is that community membership is transient and learning rules in this way takes time and willingness.[12] There is a large body of literature that highlights the success of normative systems as an alternative to copyright law,[13] but the vast majority of these can only be effective due to their composition as close-knit, bounded communities, where outsiders are unlikely to get involved in matters relating to appropriating members' intellectual property. Examples include performances in the Israeli drag scene,[14] and nicknames in female roller-derby leagues.[15] CUGC communities, however, are easily

[9] M Trammell, 'User Investment and Behavior Policing on 4chan' (2014) 19 *First Monday*: firstmonday.org/ojs/index.php/fm/article/view/4819.

[10] Participant 9: Anon1.

[11] See discussion in ch 3, section III.

[12] R Maguire, '"It Doesn't Belong to the Internet': Copyright Reform for User-Generated Content' [2022] *Intellectual Property Quarterly* 141, 156–57.

[13] D Oliar and CJ Sprigman, 'There's No Free Laugh (Anymore): The Emergence of Intellectual Property Norms and the Transformation of Stand-Up Comedy' (2008) 94 *Virginia Law Review* 1787; K Raustiala and CJ Sprigman, 'The Piracy Paradox Revisited' (2009) 61 *Stanford Law Review* 1201; J Loshin, 'Secrets Revealed: Protecting Magicians' Intellectual Property without Law' in CA Corcos (ed), *Law and Magic: A Collection of Essays* (Durham, NC, Carolina Academic Press, 2010); D Fagundes, 'Talk Derby to Me: Intellectual Property Norms Governing Roller Derby Pseudonyms' (2011) 90 *Texas Law Review* 1093.

[14] E Sarid, 'Don't Be a Drag, Just Be a Queen – How Drag Queens Protect Their Intellectual Property Without Law' (2014) 10 *FIU Law Review* 133.

[15] Fagundes (n 13).

accessible to outsiders and their content easily appropriable.[16] You do not need to be inducted into Reddit and 4chan communities to be able to access what is posted there. In fact, you do not even need an account. This means that non-community members who have little knowledge or interest in the norms can access the CUGC shared online.

Furthermore, unlike many of the other examples covered in the literature, a wide range of people could have reason to appropriate CUGC. The people who could likely make use of the stylistic choices in a drag performance is mainly limited to other performers, but CUGC has many potential uses because it can be applied to anything that art, photography or writing can be useful for. CUGC communities are also very large, and this means that it can be more challenging to communicate norms clearly. As was seen in chapter four, there were always some dissenting voices in relation to the norms identified. In communities of this scale that is to be expected, but it does mean that even a small proportion of dissenting voices can make it more challenging to learn what is expected.[17]

Even if community norms are clearly communicated, if those norms then come into conflict with the values of a CUGC creator, the potential user of CUGC is left with a confusing choice. This is particularly an issue where the individual's position in relation to acceptable uses of their work is more restrictive than the community norms, as the restrictive view would be supported by copyright law. This clash of the law ('infringing unless') and of norms ('permitted unless') leads to the potential for confusion. It was clear that some community members themselves also found it difficult to navigate this issue:

> **Q**: So how do people know what they are allowed to do with works that are posted?
>
> **DeerDecipher**: The short answer is nobody really knows.

To navigate this uncertainty, potential users can make a decision on whether their intended use is acceptable based on their understanding of the community's norms, their understanding of the creator's wishes, or their own views. This is problematic, however, as they may not know the creator's wishes, and the norms or the user's views may perhaps not reflect them. One creator explained that he or she had experience of their work being sold by someone else on the print-on-demand art marketplace, Redbubble, and they had to contact them to ask them to remove it: 'I sent him a DM asking him to take it down and he did but I don't know if it ever registered to him as something that could upset me'.[18] Relying on the user's values for a judgement call on acceptability could therefore lead to misunderstandings or conflict:

> Treat others as you'd want to be treated (of course that's trickier when 'others' are corporations and not people lol) everyone has a different perspective on what's OK.[19]

[16] Maguire (n 12) 156.
[17] ibid.
[18] Participant 3: UseYourHead.
[19] Participant 3: UseYourHead.

As such, even though community norms exist in CUGC communities, there are aspects of the community that add layers of complexity for those trying to navigate them, particularly when it comes to interacting with CUGC in some way. It is also the case that this analysis has operated on the assumption that norms are being communicated to and interpreted by a human. The AI study highlighted that scraping of CUGC for generative AI training was considered beyond the expectations of CUGC creators. However, this comes into conflict with the legal position where this seems in many cases to be legal.[20] Scraping tools do not understand the language of norms. Instead, they recognise code, and unless the code tells them not to include specific content, they will collect it. In some cases, it is possible for websites to opt out of web crawling tools, but this is left in the hands of the website holder rather than the community members themselves. In this context, therefore, communication of norms is immaterial.

B. Negotiating Use

Despite CUGC community norms taking a 'permitted unless' approach to uses of works, it was clear in chapter four that these works are not in the public domain. Instead, there were consistent expectations around getting permission for commercial uses, and relatively widespread expectations around credit. In order to comply with getting permission, the user would be expected to contact the creator to arrange an informal licence. Such negotiations can take place through comments threads on posted works, or through private contact using a direct messaging service or other private contact channels where available. It is difficult to know how well this is complied with in practice. Certainly, the CUGC creators interviewed took this approach:

> P3: I like to keep everything I do as original for my own reason of wanting it to be all me. But if I REALLY wanted to do a remix or something, I would definitely get permission from the artist if they are contactable (and if it isn't something ubiquitous).[21]
>
> P7: If I'm going to make money off it, I'd talk to them first if not, I don't feel like I need to ask.[22]
>
> P4: I would never use someone's work without asking.[23]

Most of the creators interviewed explained that they would not use a work without permission if they were planning to monetise the work in any way, and that they expected others to similarly ask permission from them. One creator had personal experience of being approached for permission for the use of one of their works in

[20] The legal position of generative AI datasets was explored in more detail in ch 2, section III.
[21] Participant 3: UseYourHead.
[22] Participant 7: Kanzi.
[23] Participant 4: Paul.

the background of a television programme. There was also some limited evidence of permission being sought beyond normative expectation, with comments in discussion threads asking to utilise, distribute or remix a work non-commercially, for example asking permission to print a copy of a photograph to hang in their home. While it was possible to identify certain instances and practices in relation to asking permission in this way, it is not possible to assess whether compliance is routine as the examples where permission was *not* sought, or was done through private channels, are invisible in the data.

Seeking permission is only one half of the equation, however. It is also necessary to get a response from the creator. In the cases where permission was seen to be requested, responses by the creators were inconsistent. Some requests in discussion threads were met with prompt responses, where others did not receive a reply from the original poster (OP).[24] In some cases, separate requests on the same thread to the same creator were not dealt with consistently, that is, the OP responded to some requests but ignored others. This confirms some of the potential difficulties of getting permission from creators in a fast-paced and anonymous environment identified in chapter two, section IV.B.

Informal licensing seems therefore to be a limited practice in reality, particularly with regard to non-commercial use, as there is difficulty in communicating expectations and getting permission can be an unreliable and inefficient process. If there is less clarity regarding the acceptability of a use at both the community level (as a norm) and at the individual level, this creates a system whereby creators may see their works used in unacceptable ways despite the good faith of the user.

III. Deterring Transgression

Transgression of community norms or of the expectations of creators can be deterred in several ways. This part of the chapter sets out the ex-ante effects of the threat of community sanction, and of strong community culture of anonymity on 4chan, both of which encourage conforming behaviour and compliance. It then outlines some of the defensive measures taken by individuals to prevent or discourage misuse of their works and the CUGC they share.

Encouraging compliance with norms is an effective way to deter transgression. McAdams identifies that people feel obligated to follow norms either because there is a threat of some sort of sanction, or because they feel a sense of obligation or duty.[25] We see that the threat of community shaming or ostracism, or the desire to avoid the internal sense of shame and guilt that accompanies breaking the rules, act as incentives to conform to community norms. Where community

[24] 'Original poster', ie, the person who started the thread.
[25] McAdams (n 3) 340.

norms are transgressed, shaming and ostracism are the predominant sanctions, as will be explored later in this chapter. This is unsurprising as existing scholarship has identified the use of such measures in communities generally, and in specific cases.[26] We also know from existing scholarship that such ex-post measures can lead to behaviour that conforms with norms, as people aim to avoid the negative sanctions that follow from transgressing.[27] As such, the threat of future possible community sanctions can thereby prevent or deter uses of CUGC that conflict with community expectations.

It should be noted that although copyright law itself provides the threat of sanction if its rules are not followed, it is unclear that this would have a similar ex-ante effect on users. In reality, we know that people regularly ignore the law's expectations of behaviour. There are two main reasons for this: first, because they do not think the law can or will be enforced against them; or secondly, because the expectations of the law do not correspond with their own social norms. Copyright law struggles to act as a regulator in online communities as it lacks a bite to its bark. Reed identifies that while copyright can, sometimes, be enforced online at the individual level despite the myriad difficulties of this (for example, identifying and locating infringers and negotiating territorial copyright laws in an international context), for the law to control behaviour ex ante, it requires consistent enforcement at the macro level, something it finds difficult.[28]

While Svantesson argues that copyright's bark, even if it lacks the bite of being enforceable, is under-appreciated and can still play a role in guiding behaviour as it articulates society's values,[29] this can only be the case where the values it is advancing mirror those of the communities themselves. Where law and social norms conflict, the law tends to lose.[30] Some studies of online creative communities have identified that social norms regarding uses of creative works either track copyright law[31] or are stricter than copyright law,[32] and from the norms described

[26] C Reed, *Making Laws for Cyberspace* (Oxford, Oxford University Press, 2012) 121; TM Gates, 'Providing Adequate Protection for Comedians' Intellectual Creations: Examining Intellectual Property Norms and Negative Spaces' (2014) 93 *Oregon Law Review* 801; Sarid (n 14); E Nelson, 'Unacknowledged Legislators: The Contemporary Poetry Community's Quasi-Regime of Intellectual Property' (2015) 91 *North Dakota Law Review* 633; C Fiesler and AS Bruckman, 'Creativity, Copyright, and Close-Knit Communities: A Case Study of Social Norm Formation and Enforcement' (2019) 3 *Proceedings of the ACM on Human–Computer Interaction* 241, 256–58.

[27] EL Rosenblatt, 'Fear and Loathing: Shame, Shaming, and Intellectual Property' (2013) 63 *DePaul Law Review* 1, 5, 9, 21.

[28] Reed (n 26) 54.

[29] DJB Svantesson, *Private International Law and the Internet*, 3rd edn (Alphen aan den Rijn, Kluwer Law International, 2016) 12–14.

[30] See, eg: DM Kahan, 'Gentle Nudges vs Hard Shoves: Solving the Sticky Norms Problem' (2000) 67 *University of Chicago Law Review* 607; McAdams (n 3).

[31] J Meese, '"It Belongs to the Internet": Animal Images, Attribution Norms and the Politics of Amateur Media Production' (2014) 17 *M/C Journal*: journal.media-culture.org.au/index.php/mcjournal/article/view/782.

[32] C Fiesler, 'Everything I Need to Know I Learned from Fandom: How Existing Social Norms Can Help Shape the Next Generation of User-Generated Content' (2007) 10 *Vanderbilt Journal of Entertainment and Technology Law* 729.

in chapter four, we can see that in some ways this is also true of the communities studied here, for example preventing commercial exploitation and false attribution, or dealing with non-original derivative works. But even if this is the case, that does not mean that copyright law is influencing behaviour; it is just coincidence. If the social norms were different, then so too would be the behaviour.[33] It is therefore the potential bite of social shaming, rather than legal sanctions, which likely drives community members to conform.

Anonymity also raises some questions about how effective this ex-ante mechanism can be. Rosenblatt argues that increased anonymity lowers the effectiveness of shaming as a social sanction.[34] In his work on online avatars, Castronova explains that for norms to be effective they need to be enforceable against an individual, but where identity is obscured and you can effectively re-set by creating a new persona, this could be problematic. Norms can only be useful where a user has made such a high investment in their online identity that deleting the identity has a negative effect on the user.[35] While Reddit, with its system of awarding karma points to good community contributors, likely avoids this trap, the anonymity on 4chan would be expected to render the bite of social sanctions rather blunt. How do you shame 'anonymous'? However, while the threat of external shaming may be less effective, strong anonymity may facilitate the internalisation of group norms, leading to similarly normative behaviour as is explored further below. Furthermore, the bark of community norms is a loud one, and threatens a nasty bite, as anonymity means that issues are discussed in a brutal manner, and sanctions can also be fierce, with the effect of enhancing normative behaviour.

Rosenblatt also identifies that '[s]hame is the natural response of psychologically healthy individuals when they fail to conform to their own values or to the prevailing values of their family or social community'[36] and that the desire to avoid this feeling leads users to behave in ways consistent with those values.[37] This process is reliant on community members internalising those community values, which is facilitated both by clear articulation of those values and a process of teaching community members what those values are, and by a strong sense of group identity.[38] Anonymity again plays a role in this through its impact on communicating normative values, but also by supporting conformity with social norms out of a sense of duty to the community. Anonymity can, counterintuitively,

[33] The commonly found preference for socially created norms over externally imposed law is discussed in, for example: RC Ellickson, *Order Without Law: How Neighbours Settle Disputes* (Cambridge MA, Harvard University Press, 1991); E Ostrom, 'Collective Action and the Evolution of Social Norms' (2000) 14 *Journal of Economic Perspectives* 137.

[34] Rosenblatt, 'Fear and Loathing' (n 27) 36.

[35] E Castronova, 'Theory of the Avatar' (2003) No 863 CESifo Working Paper 31: www.CESifo.de.

[36] Rosenblatt, 'Fear and Loathing' (n 27) 5.

[37] ibid 21.

[38] ibid 24, 10–11.

increase pro-social behaviour as it repositions the focus from the individual to the group.[39] Fiesler and Bruckman similarly discuss how the Social Identity Model of Deindividuation Effects (SIDE) theory supports a positive effect of anonymity on the internalisation of norms.[40] One of the interviewees recognised this effect in practice:

> And the interesting thing is, even without threats to one's livelihood or reputation, human decency works.
>
> It might be because as fellow anonymous posters, we're all the same.
>
> There's no class other than what you contribute at that exact moment.[41]

Where community members view themselves as part of the whole group, they are more likely to conform to the social norms relating to acceptable and unacceptable uses of creative works. This leaves us with the situation where anonymity facilitates free speech in a way that means community norms about artistic integrity, originality and ownership can be robustly expressed, debated and communicated within the community, and transgressions are dealt with in a similarly forceful way. Simultaneously, anonymity encourages community members to conform to those norms with the expected effect that within communities (and particularly within 4chan communities with stronger levels of anonymity) the occurrence of uses that conflict with the communities' ideas of acceptable uses should be reduced. We see that this is the case, even where community members themselves do not agree with the community standpoint. Here, Anon4 describes the effect of extreme standards of originality on 4chan to which he does not subscribe:

> So it motivates me to … try to make it more original, to put more of myself into it than other people's … influence into it, you know. So that's the silver lining. It does make me very self-conscious of that.[42]

While there are clear benefits to preventing misuse through threats of sanction or through shame, most obviously the flexibility it grants communities to avoid the one-size-fits-all approach of the law, and its cost-effectiveness,[43] there are also drawbacks to a system built on shame and shaming. First, Anon4's quote above demonstrates how this process might be problematic, as the loudest voices may not represent the majority viewpoint but may nevertheless influence behaviour. Rosenblatt highlights that those shouting the loudest may also be the least

[39] See, eg: T Postmes et al, 'Social Influence in Computer-Mediated Communication: The Effects of Anonymity on Group Behavior' (2001) 27 *Personality and Social Psychology Bulletin* 1243; T Postmes et al, 'Individuality and Social Influence in Groups: Inductive and Deductive Routes to Group Identity.' (2005) 89 *Journal of Personality and Social Psychology* 747.

[40] Fiesler and Bruckman (n 26) 255–56.

[41] Participant 9: Anon1.

[42] Participant 12: Anon4.

[43] Oliar and Sprigman (n 13) 1836; Rosenblatt, 'Fear and Loathing' (n 27) 25, 32–33.

reasonable.[44] As such, and especially where expectations are going beyond the law, this could lead to negative effects of over-regulating behaviour.

The risk of over-regulation of behaviour is further seen in the lack of limits on community shaming and norm enforcement, as it is not subject to the same limitations or exceptions as the law. For example, it is perpetual and is not required to consider whether users have fair use defences or similar.[45] It is also 'unpredictable',[46] 'indeterminate'[47] and lacking due process, as there is no external or independent adjudicator meaning it can go too far.[48] This has further potential negative effects as the line between effective shaming and harassment, vigilantism or mob justice is easily breached,[49] and the psychological impact of shaming on an individual can be significant.[50] Therefore, where shaming sanctions are insufficiently tempered, it can deter individuals from sharing CUGC at all, for example where they fear they risk being accused of being insufficiently original.

The threat of shame and shaming as a system of regulation is also limited in its reach. Shaming only works when someone hears it, which is increasingly difficult online.[51] Users can delete or ignore shaming comments, meaning it cannot be consistently applied. Furthermore, Pham highlights that community norms do a bad job of regulating the behaviour of outsiders, particularly in situations relating to social media, and in situations where users do not share the community's values or do not care about transgressing them or being shamed.[52] It is also only possible to shame humans, and so generative AI's scraping tools will continue unaffected. Additionally, the wishes of individual creators may diverge from the community norms, and this provides no protection for those cases. This means that while the system of shame and shaming is likely to provide ex-ante protection against misuse in line with community norms, there are some fundamental problems with it as a mechanism.

Beyond the ex-ante threat of sanction, 4chan's strong culture of anonymity affords it two additional protections to misuse. The first protects against misuse within the community, in particular claiming a work as one's own. The second protects against misuse by outsiders. The 4chan communities benefit from internal protection against someone claiming their work as their own because its

[44] Rosenblatt, 'Fear and Loathing' (n 27) 39–40.

[45] Oliar and Sprigman (n 13) 1836–38.

[46] Rosenblatt, 'Fear and Loathing' (n 27) 35.

[47] K Klonick, 'Re-Shaming the Debate: Social Norms, Shame, and Regulation in an Internet Age' (2016) 75 *Maryland Law Review* 1029, 1045.

[48] Sarid (n 14) 176.

[49] Oliar and Sprigman (n 13) 1836–38; Klonick (n 47) 1045; Fiesler and Bruckman (n 26) 257–58.

[50] Rosenblatt, 'Fear and Loathing' (n 27) 34.

[51] ibid 35–36.

[52] H Pham, 'Standing Up for Stand-Up Comedy: Joke Theft and the Relevance of Copyright Law and Social Norms in the Social Media Age' (2019) 30 *Fordham Intellectual Property, Media & Entertainment Law Journal* 55.

anonymous identity norms remove any incentive to do so – there is no reputational gain. Some of the interview participants from 4chan highlighted this issue:

> P9: I mean, when a community is anonymous by nature and encourages fresh content, it makes the whole idea of trying to take credit for something you didn't do preposterous. Who would you be trying to impress, really?[53]
>
> P4: [O]n a page like reddit, karma becomes something of a secondary social currency as well, which means successfully lying about something can give you some measurable social currency.[54]

In Reddit communities by contrast, individuals are rewarded for posting popular content with upvotes and karma points and therefore there can be incentives to repost content without crediting the original creator. There may also be an incentive in the potential for increasing social capital more generally, as other community members are impressed by the content that user has posted and think it is their own. Where there is no system for reward or validation, even informally, because posts are anonymous, there is therefore no incentive to post someone else's work as your own as there are no rewards.

Secondly, it can be argued from existing scholarship that anonymity makes a significant contribution to the particularly brutal and confusing culture within its boards and communities. Outsiders can find navigating 4chan's culture difficult. Both Trammell and Manivannan highlight that aggressive discourse and trolling (by way of anonymity) are a way of policing community boundaries and excluding others.[55] Knuttila argues that the contingency caused by anonymity positions 4chan outside 'an increasingly dominant Internet economy'[56] and it is clear that 4chan is far less of a mainstream, accessible and commercial online space than most. As such, it reduces the possibility that works will be taken by those external to the community, particularly for commercial purposes, as they are able to insulate themselves from outsiders to some degree. Essentially, people are less likely to venture onto 4chan. Strong anonymity therefore provides some effective protection both within and outside the community.

Beyond the community level, individuals can take a range of steps to protect their works before misuse occurs, and examples of defensive measures to prevent or discourage misuse were found in both studies. Regardless of community norms, individual creators, even when anonymous, can choose to exercise a certain level of control over the works they post online. They can do so through a range of non-legal processes before, and after, they share the work, but before any

[53] Participant 9: Anon1.

[54] Participant 4: Paul.

[55] V Manivannan, 'Attaining the Ninth Square: Cybertextuality, Gamification, and Institutional Memory on 4chan' [2012] *Enculturation*: www.enculturation.net/attaining-the-ninth-square; Trammell (n 9).

[56] L Knuttila, 'User Unknown: 4chan, Anonymity and Contingency' (2011) 16 *First Monday*: firstmonday.org/ojs/index.php/fm/article/view/3665.

undesired uses have taken place. This control takes the form of various defensive mechanisms, all of which can be employed while remaining anonymous to some degree.

The first of these mechanisms is a selective approach towards what creators post online. The most extreme of these is, of course, choosing not to share work at all. Less extremely, it can also take the form of only sharing CUGC that they do not hope to exploit commercially to avoid jeopardising it (this is particularly the case for writers). Those who were particularly concerned sometimes chose not to even share their creative *ideas*, for fear that they may be used by someone else, particularly within writing communities. Some creators also chose not to share particularly significant pieces that they felt an investment in and where undesired use would have an emotional impact on them, such as those created for loved ones or those that had taken a particularly large amount of time and effort. DeerDecipher explained:

> If I spent real time and effort on something intended to have a long life, then I'd be more attached. For example: I have spent (I think) hundreds of hours creating a font, and haven't shared it online.

Relatedly, some creators in the AI study mentioned moving away from digital methods to more traditional ones, such as oil painting. It was viewed that this, paired with caution about sharing work online, would help to reduce the amount of their content available for generative AI model training. Another, more significant strategy was to consider not just what, but where, creators chose to share CUGC. There was much discussion about alternative platforms such as Cara, which offer artists reassurances that their content will not be mined by AI, and this was seen as an alternative to platforms such as Instagram which were deemed riskier. There was also some discussion of opt-out options offered by some platforms but only within the EU, where the text and data mining (TDM) exception requires it. Some creators who had gone through the opt-out process highlighted that it was not a particularly user-friendly process.

By undertaking a risk–benefit analysis and choosing only works where the impact of potential undesired uses would be lower than the potential value of sharing the work, creators can mitigate the risks of sharing their work online. This was relatively widespread as a practice, with community members often commenting on threads about 'stolen' works and that they do not share their works online for this reason. As a practice, it offers high levels of control to the individual over what happens to their work, but it can also lead to undesirable overcautious behaviour; several creators mentioned that in communities about finding creative collaborators, for example comic book scriptwriters looking for comic book artists, some creators are reluctant to share their ideas for fear that they will be stolen. This undermines the ability of the community to function effectively. Furthermore, reluctance to share reduces contributions to the community which could restrict the creative value of the community; chapter three, sections II.B.ii and III.B.iii, highlighted the value of an external network of sources for the creative process, the role of these communities as such networks, as well as the value of sharing for creativity, all of which would be restricted where fewer works are posted.[57]

The second defensive mechanism is manipulating the quality, size or format of the version shared to reduce the ability of others to use the work in ways that would be undesirable. Thus images of artworks may be taken to include elements that would reduce their value to others, such as art tools or hands, or be taken from an angle. Such formatting would not reduce the ability of others to post it again, but it would make remixes or commercial uses, such as printing on t-shirts, more difficult. Photographs might be shared in low resolution or cropped so that the image could not be used in commercial quality projects such as prints or websites. Chapters of novels may be shared when still in draft, but whole, finished stories would not be, as the work required to make a partial draft valuable protects it from being taken by others. Furthermore, where creators do not take these steps it was sometimes seen as implicit permission to use the work: 'if someone posted a print-resolution piece to reddit, then whelp, they're choosing to give any [viewer] the ability (and implied right) to print that image'.[58] Again, this was also an approach considered by creators looking to avoid scraping for AI training. Discussion threads suggested several tools, such as Nightshade and Glaze, which claim to make images difficult for AI models to read, although the effectiveness and longevity of this approach was questioned.

These strategies allow creators to lower the potential value of the work to nefarious users, while still allowing them to enjoy the benefits of sharing, such as increased exposure, validation and the ability to experiment and test new ideas. It was flagged, however, that with sufficient skill, low-resolution images can be made suitable for commercial uses, so it is clear that they are not a perfect guarantee of control.

The third defensive mechanism is closely linked with the second in that it too reduces the work's value to users, but it also positively asserts the creator's ownership over the work. This takes the form of adding signatures and watermarks. Again, this potentially limits uses, but it also ensures that if their work is used in any way that they are still credited, something that is important to many creators. These measures are, however, limited in effectiveness, as many other community members pointed out; signatures and watermarks can be removed and replaced easily using Photoshop. It was highlighted on multiple occasions in the AI study that watermarks will have very little impact on whether CUGC is used by generative AI, despite it being suggested relatively regularly as a solution. Watermarks were also often derided by those who feel they indicate an

[57] See, eg: E Reuveni, 'Copyright, Neuroscience and Creativity' (2013) 64 *Alabama Law Review* 735; EE Johnson, 'The Economics and Sociality of Sharing Intellectual Property Rights' (2014) 94 *Boston University Law Review* 1935.

[58] Participant 4: Paul.

unwarranted seriousness regarding ownership and the significance of the work, and so creators may be deterred from using them by this social pressure.

IV. Detecting Transgression

Where CUGC is used in ways that conflict with the individual creator's wishes or community norms about acceptable uses, the first hurdle that creators and communities meet in enforcing the expected standards is finding out that the misuse has taken place. Chapter two, section IV.A, outlined the difficulties of locating infringers in an anonymous online environment that is so vast but there are various approaches, individual and community-based, used to undertake this difficult task. These include relying on the wider community to identify misuse and notify the relevant creator, the use of search tools, and third-party detection services.

While some creators did identify those difficulties ('I will just say this briefly, people's work is stolen constantly, be it written or art. An artist rarely has the chance to discover his work is stolen unless he himself discovers that or somebody tells him'),[59] others felt more optimistic about locating misuse, in particular someone claiming work as their own ('they will get caught in the lie eventually').[60] A significant amount of the data reflected here comes from photography communities, rather than art or writing communities. Photographs possibly have a broader range of uses by others, including commercial uses such as being put on websites or printed on t-shirts, or creators are more likely to undertake some paid or professional work (or aim to) and therefore have greater concerns, or more risk, or more experience of this happening to them and their fellow community members.

The community was shown to provide a partial solution to the problem of locating misuse, in that the wider creative community operates a neighbourhood watch like system of flagging the misuse of works to the original creator. This was highlighted by interview participants:

> P9: If anyone that isn't the author finds content stolen from one of us anywhere on the internet, they'll try to bring it up in boards the author frequents.[61]
>
> P12: I made a specific comic a long time ago and it really went viral. It got millions of hits and somebody – it was on imgur[62] actually – somebody reposted it for the likes and stuff and people were calling him out on it and they were pointing out to me 'hey, this guy's doing this or that'.[63]

[59] Participant 8: Scribe576.
[60] Participant 12: Anon4.
[61] Participant 9: Anon1.
[62] An online image sharing community.
[63] Participant 12: Anon4.

Creators from both Reddit and 4chan gave examples of being informed of a misuse of their work by someone else, and others mentioned having themselves seen misuses of others' work during their online activity. However, the efficacy of this system may be undermined by anonymity. Without a reliable system to contact individuals in the anonymous online environment, either because of their anonymity practices or because of the difficulties in tracing them, the CUGC creator may never find out even if someone does notice and want to inform them. From Anon1's quote above, however, we see that even within anonymous communities, attempts can be made to notify creators, and that this approach can be successful.

Individuals can themselves also take steps to locate misuse. The first method that individuals use to locate examples of their works being used is through the use of search engine tools. For artists and photographers, Google's reverse image search function offers the possibility to find out if their works are posted elsewhere on the internet and was a common suggestion. Similar services that were popular also included Tineye,[64] and the Who Stole My Pictures? browser plug-in. For writers, the Google search function allows them to search sections of their text in a similar way, and Google Alerts allow writers to be notified if their author name is used online, which could identify if pirated copies of their works are uploaded. While for artists and photographers this offers a quick and free means of approaching this problem, it will only reliably identify uses of the work where it is simply copied without any transformative element. The reverse image search or Google Lens function does provide results of visually similar images so may identify remixed or otherwise altered works (for example, cropped images) but this is not guaranteed. For writers, it is even less helpful, as sections of any length of a written work may be used, and so using a Google search of phrases would be time-consuming if it were to be comprehensive enough to cover the entirety of the work. Again, it will also be less reliable where the work is not copied exactly, for example where some words are changed.

The second method available to and used by individuals to locate uses and misuses of their works is using third-party detection services, such as Pixsy,[65] Lenstag[66] or Plaghunter.[67] These allow photographers to upload their images and the service then conducts an initial search for other uses of the work on the internet (similar to the reverse image search process described above) while continuing to monitor for new uses, notifying the photographer if any are found. Some services, including Pixsy, provide support in responding if the use is unauthorised. These services offer some benefits in that creators do not have to manually monitor uses themselves, and the process to upload work in batches is simplified, but they so far apply only to photography.

[64] 'TinEye Reverse Image Search': tineye.com.

[65] 'Pixsy – Find and Fight Image Theft' (*Pixsy*): www.pixsy.com.

[66] 'Lenstag' (*Lenstag*): www.lenstag.com.

[67] 'Plaghunter: Reverse Image Search & Plagiarism Checker' (*Bilderklau im Internet finden mit Plaghunter*): www.plaghunter.com/en/.

We see, therefore, that despite it being very challenging – like finding a needle in a haystack – there are some community and individual processes to help locate misuse of CUGC. However, unsurprisingly it is impossible to reliably locate all misuses, especially for writers. Again, the generative AI issue causes particular issues in that while it was widely viewed that if CUGC was shared online then it was being used to train AI models, it was also recognised that being able to prove the specifics of that was impossible. Where misuse goes undetected, no remedy or sanction is possible, and this has implications for the effectiveness of norms to *prevent* misuse. As explored above, there is not only a need for people to know what the rules are but also that they are at risk of being detected and sanctioned if they transgress.

V. Remedies and Sanctions

A variety of approaches are used to sanction or remedy misuses of CUGC. As has already been highlighted, community shaming and ostracism is a common consequence of misuse when it is detected. Relatedly, individuals can decide to publicly address misuse themselves. There are also options that rely, either directly or indirectly, on the legal system such as suing or using notice and take-down tools, or direct negotiation. An additional approach that was popular was inaction. Several creators expressed feelings of resignation to unacceptable uses, or reluctance to take action. Sometimes this was because they felt it was futile to try to control uses once a work was shared and had no desire to, but sometimes even when they did want to restrict certain uses. This is certainly accessible to all creators but is clearly not ideal.

Shaming and ostracism are used relatively widely where norms relating to CUGC content are transgressed. Across all of the communities, there was a general sense that if there is a use that offends the communities' norms, for example CUGC copies heavily from another, lacks sufficient creativity, fails to credit the creator, or is mis-attributed, then this will be called out by someone. This may be the creator themself or the wider community. These individual and community responses are linked, as the other community members may bring the issues to the attention of the creator and vice versa. The effect of such action can be to flag the rightful creator or to shame the person who did it. While such responses can comprise a comment or two on the bottom of a post, it can also scale up to bigger, more intense reactions, although such behaviour is often banned in community or platform rules. This can include coordinated downvoting, large numbers of comments about the unacceptable use, aggressive comments, brigading,[68] or even doxing.[69]

[68] Where members of one subreddit invade another to purposely downvote its content.
[69] The publishing of personal details such as real name, address, etc online as punishment.

What is interesting about these processes when they stem from the community is that they are often uninterested in the ownership rights and wishes of the individual. Whether community sanctions are issued depends on whether the community feels that its norms and values have been breached:

> I'm assuming you're familiar with the concept of 'not your personal army'.
>
> Asking for action doesn't get you anything.
>
> ...
>
> People have to feel that whatever it is that you're out to do or achieve aligns with their own interests.
>
> Luckily, there are some things that universally appeal to imageboard users.
>
> Their own getting ripped off is one of them.
>
> As such, you don't really need to ask. They know what to do when they see something wrong.
>
> That's what's really tricky about this.
>
> There's no one person who gets to say it.
>
> It's a decentralised thing, and it makes for a very hard to deal with hivemind.[70]

So, while creators may flag an unacceptable use to the community, this does not guarantee that any social sanction will be made;[71] conversely, the community may choose to take action even where the creator does not view the use as unacceptable. This makes sense as the social norms that govern these uses are sometimes more interested in sustaining an ethical or moral viewpoint of what it is to be an honourable creator, that is, one that strives for originality, rather than private ownership. From this, it seems that the enforcement of these social norms through shaming sometimes more closely mirrors a public system of justice rather than a private one, and as such prioritises the interests of the group rather than the individual. This reflects the artistic integrity and morality justification for restricting some uses of creative content that were identified in chapter four, section III.D.

Furthermore, while approaches built on shaming can be responsive to the nuances of the norms of the community and are accessible even to those without legal knowledge, they have multiple limitations and negative effects. Many of these were outlined earlier in the chapter, but include being indeterminate and unpredictable, as well as the potential for inefficient over-protection and harassment. Another possible drawback is that in shaming individuals for misuse, that person is alienated and therefore is more likely to transgress again.[72] Shaming is therefore not an ideal means of sanction, particularly in a system where the rule may not always be fully clear.

[70] Participant 9: Anon1.

[71] An alternative community solution is to report misuse to community moderators where it violates community rules.

[72] Rosenblatt, 'Fear and Loathing' (n 27) 15, 37–38.

The alternative to shaming and calling out misuse is for CUGC creators to try to navigate their rights under copyright law. Discussions of unauthorised uses in the data often referred to the formal use of copyright law as an appropriate response. As this book has argued, copyright will often subsist in CUGC and so legal action is technically a valid response to misuse. It is not surprising this was considered in some circumstances; any serious suggestion or explanation of the use of lawyers or the courts was in relation to significant commercial misuses of works, and in cases of commercial misuse, the individual expectations and community norms reflect those of copyright law. When faced with a scenario of misuse, the main advice given or approaches available included seeking legal representation and/or suing (or threatening to) or using copyright infringement reporting tools on platforms.

The data shows some suggestions and examples of creators seeking legal advice, instructing lawyers to send cease and desist letters, or bringing an infringement claim in the courts. While clearly within the rights of the creator as the copyright owner, in reality this approach does not seem particularly widespread. Those who were clear that this would be their route tended to be those with more experience in the creative sector, such as professionals who already had knowledge about the law or access to legal support. In other cases, it was mainly suggested only where such action was against large commercial entities where the compensation would be likely to be high enough to justify it. While there is the option of using 'no-win-no-fee' lawyers, there was some indication of similar risk-aversion on their part, with some creators explaining they had not been able to find someone willing to help with their case in this way. One of the flaws of this approach as a mechanism is that most of the time, online creators are not professionals, do not have access to legal support, cannot afford lawyers' fees and do not have sufficient knowledge of the law for this route to be considered.[73] Additional challenges arise from pervasive online anonymity, which may make it more difficult to identify the individual to be sued, or the relevant jurisdiction.

Dealing with misuse using copyright law in this way does, however, offer some benefits to creators, such as being flexible enough for the creator to choose the outcome they want (for example, being credited, or getting paid). It also provides a certain amount of certainty to all parties involved as the law sets out the rules and people can therefore choose their behaviour accordingly, and it is mediated (and enforced) by a third party (the courts) rather than being reliant on the interpretations and expectations of individuals in the way that an informal discussion or social shaming is.

For creators for whom the costs of seeking legal advice or pursuing legal action through a lawyer are too great, or disproportionate to the misuse of their work, or whose work was being misused non-commercially, the option of using

[73] Maguire (n 12) 153–55.

copyright reporting tools on platforms or takedown notices was a common alternative suggestion. Most large sharing platforms and social media websites have automated processes through which copyright owners can report instances of infringement of their works, and if the claim is accepted by the website they will remove the content. This offers the individual creator some benefits in comparison to the first route of copyright infringement: it is quick, it is free and it is accessible without in-depth legal knowledge.

However, there are some flaws in the notice and takedown system, as it raises concerns for wider internet culture, is reliant on third-party processes, and is inflexible. On the first point, as notice and takedown systems have become increasingly automated, it can negatively affect online creators, with the copyright industries using them to enforce their rights more extensively. In particular, there has been criticism of the effect of this on remix culture as the automatic nature of the processes leaves little room for the discretion required to assess whether a use could be considered fair, and therefore non-infringing, under the law.[74] But it has also caused problems for those whose works are not based on other works in any way when the automated detection systems produce false positives. Outside the communities studied here, there have been reports of these processes bringing claims against completely original or non-infringing work.[75] While accessible, notice and takedown processes are not a perfect solution for online creators as they cause problems for the wider online creative environment.

Furthermore, for notice and takedown systems to provide an adequate solution to creators they need to be universally available and fairly administrated. This puts creators at the mercy of third-party processes. If a work is used in an unacceptable way on a website that does not offer such a system, this leaves the creator with no means of rectifying the situation. Creators cited finding their works being misused in foreign countries such as Russia and being unable to do anything. Additionally, if the system is poorly administrated, for example by appeals against claims being incorrectly dealt with, then creators cannot rely on this at all. This works in the opposite direction too, with some community members highlighting the possible danger of over-protection where creators have little knowledge of the law but feel they have a legitimate takedown claim:

> The people who've issued takedown requests have done so in accordance with the policies of whatever site they're requesting on. In other words, they might feel entitled to requesting removal (without knowing if it's legally justified), and trust is put on the

[74] See, eg, *Lenz v Universal Music Corp*, 801 F 3d 1126 (9th Cir 2015). See also JD Matteson, 'Unfair Misuse: How Section 512 of the DMCA Allows Abuse of the Copyright Fair Use Doctrine and How to Fix It' (2018) 35 *Santa Clara High Technology Law Journal* 1.

[75] eg, one YouTuber lost out on the monetisation from his original song after it was remixed by someone else and they then put in a claim against him: 'YouTube Stars Say Unfair Copyright Claims Are Making Their Lives Hell' (*The Daily Dot*, 18 December 2018): www.dailydot.com/upstream/youtube-copyright-claims-thefatrat/; Similarly, a video of white noise received 5 claims of infringement: 'YouTube Video Containing Static Receives 5 Different Copyright Violations' (*Digital Music News*, 5 January 2018): www.digitalmusicnews.com/2018/01/05/white-noise-static-youtube-copyright.

> website hosting their content that the request is handled fairly. Some users believe their work is protected legally, but I don't know.[76]

Additionally, these processes only provide online creators with an all-or-nothing approach, which may not reflect the outcome they want. For example, a creator may be happy for the post to stay up but just want to be credited. However, often the only option within these systems is to request removal.

The final approach described by community members was employing informal strategies that they do not explicitly frame as copyright-based, but that are reliant on an understanding of the creator as having a legitimate claim to control what happens to the work. These involve contacting the person who has misused the work in order to resolve the situation and this can be successful:

> I made this nice design (in my opinion lol).
>
> It was based on a show, but the imagery was original.
>
> I saw a dude on redbubble.
>
> Literally all he did was remove the text and add it back in with a different font.
>
> I was very unhappy since I was still selling at the time.
>
> I sent him a DM asking him to take it down and he did.
>
> But I don't know if it ever registered to him as something that could upset me.[77]

The difference between these processes and the legal ones is that the creator negotiates with the (mis)user directly without clear, or reliable, reference to copyright law. In this case, creators will contact the user directly (for example, through a direct messaging function on a sharing platform) to make clear their displeasure with the situation and to negotiate the outcome they want, for example to be credited or paid, or for the unacceptable use to be removed. This seems to be a more popular or discussed response to unacceptable use and this is probably because it is quick, cheap, requires no particular legal knowledge, and allows for sufficient flexibility in the outcomes of the complaint.

It is limited in its value, however, as it relies on being able to contact the user. Not all platforms have a direct messaging function, and where users are posting with high levels of anonymity, it may be very difficult to identify a recipient at all, or the contact may be too late to be useful (several comments highlighted that requesting credit on a social media repost is time sensitive; after a few hours, the content will not be as prominent on the platform). Where the user can be contacted promptly, this may nonetheless be complicated by the fact that the issue will be negotiated using reference to legal points but often between individuals with incomplete or inaccurate knowledge of the law. Furthermore, as a system operating informally outside formal legal framing, if the user chooses to ignore the request, or has a different conception of what level of control the creator's claimed

[76] Participant 2: DeerDecipher.
[77] Participant 3: UseYourHead.

'ownership' legitimises, then the creator has no means of making the user acquiesce to his or her wishes as the system is founded entirely on goodwill.

VI. The Inefficiencies of Norms in the Creative User-Generated Content Context

This chapter has therefore demonstrated that the communication and enforcement of CUGC norms is a rather complicated system that combines elements directed by the communities and those driven by individuals. The discussion so far has already taken steps to highlight the strengths and weaknesses of the strategies available. This final part looks to summarise these to evaluate the functioning of the system as a whole, and particularly its ability to effectively replace the copyright system or to mitigate its weaknesses.

The literature on 'negative space' in intellectual property (IP) draws attention to the fact that there are many creative industries and communities that flourish outside the copyright system, either because copyright does not subsist in their creative outputs, or because the rights copyright provides over their work are insufficiently flexible, with a one-size-fits-all approach.[78] The normative systems that evolve in these settings are often shown to be superior to copyright law as they better suit the needs of the specific community. However, it is the argument of this book that although the CUGC context has some overlaps with the negative space narratives in terms of their critique of copyright incentives, it cannot be considered to be another example of norms successfully supplanting copyright law because many of the flaws with copyright law remain or are replicated, and indeed copyright remains an element of the overall regulatory system.

While there is certainly an issue with the inflexibility or inappropriateness of copyright law's provisions for the CUGC context, it would be an oversimplification to reduce the issues between the two to just this issue. Certainly, copyright law's 'infringement unless' approach conflicts with CUGC's 'permitted unless', but this book has highlighted several other challenges and issues that mean that copyright law struggles to be an effective regulator of CUGC. These include the limited access CUGC community members have to legal services due to minimal funds, a lack of accurate legal knowledge which leads to confusion, and the problems caused by pervasive online anonymity that it is not equipped to respond to. The book has also highlighted that copyright does not seem to fully reflect the sort of creative processes found in CUGC communities (and beyond). As a result, it seems that copyright law does not seem to provide much of a solution for CUGC creators. Of course, this is where a normative system has the opportunity to step in.

[78] See, eg: EL Rosenblatt, 'A Theory of IP's Negative Space' (2011) 34 *Columbia Journal of Law & the Arts* 317; K Raustiala and CJ Sprigman, 'When Are IP Rights Necessary? Evidence from Innovation in IP's Negative Space' in B Depoorter, P Menell and D Schwartz (eds), *Research Handbook on the Economics of Intellectual Property Law, Vol 1: Theory* (Cheltenham, Edward Elgar Publishing, 2016).

To some extent, the system of norms relating to CUGC offers some improvement on that offered by copyright law. In particular, the wide range of approaches and strategies highlighted in this chapter provide creators and communities with significant flexibility in framing acceptable uses and applying sanctions where appropriate. Those who want stronger or weaker protection can the choose mechanisms that suit them best. Furthermore, there are many options within the system that are accessible to those without the time or resources to pursue copyright remedies formally, or where investing such time and resources is not worth it, for example social shaming sanctions are broadly accessible as an option to anyone. Some of the same issues as copyright arise in relation to the traceability of creators and users in anonymous online spaces, but online anonymity simultaneously brings some benefits to the functioning of the normative system.

Where the normative system struggles, however, is in relation to the creative process, detection and clarity. In relation to the first of these, normative permissibility in relation to non-commercial uses is likely beneficial for facilitating access to works and therefore the creative process. However, there was also evidence that community sanctions run the risk of being unpredictable and disproportionate as they are left to the discretion of community members. In a system like this, responses to minor infractions can be excessive. This can lead to community members being more hesitant to share CUGC online, or to interact with it, and the effects of this over-regulation can even extend to the threat of being the target of such shaming. It was also demonstrated that there are significant gaps in the ability to detect misuse, and as such any system that exists is going to be more heavily reliant on socially induced compliance with norms, rather than ex-post sanction.

This means that the more significant problem for this system is the issue of clarity. It is clear that CUGC community members are often – understandably – lacking in the legal knowledge required to adequately navigate the copyright system. The system that the CUGC community uses currently does not seem much of an improvement on this. First, despite community norms existing there are still issues with clarity and the ability of individuals being able to successfully understand what is expected of them. This is because dissenting voices can become quite loud in large communities, and this can mean inducting normative values takes longer. Additionally, community values can be diluted or further obscured by the fact that the communities have open boundaries to outsiders. Non-community members can access community content without knowing or ascribing to community values and caring little about potential social sanctions.[79] It is unlikely in these circumstances that a normative system could ever be comprehensively effective.

Furthermore, because of the scale and diversity of access to the communities it means that the normative system has not been able to fully supersede the

[79] Maguire (n 12) 156–57.

copyright system. This means that individuals, whether community members or otherwise, can still attempt to navigate sharing and interacting with CUGC with the legal rules as their reference point, rather than the normative ones. With some people talking the language of law and others the language of norms, it becomes even more challenging. Without a community system capable of fully superseding copyright law, it means that we are left with two flawed and often conflicting systems of regulation applying simultaneously.

The problem of uncertainty is exacerbated and entrenched by the simultaneous applicability of both permissive community norms and restrictive copyright law. This makes it even harder to assess what is permissible and what is not, and a user who draws this line too generously risks sanction by a creator who can in law restrict nearly all uses of a work, or by a community or individual who can use the powerful tool of shaming to arbitrarily impose an unpredictable or disproportionate response (for example, to creative work deemed derivative). While it is clear that many people are able to work through the challenges and confusions in the system as there are still large volumes of people sharing and interacting with creative works, this cannot be the most efficient or effective means of regulating creativity in this context. It seems that some elements of the system are beneficial to the CUGC context, but CUGC creators and users have to navigate round other elements. In these cases, the fact their creative practices continue seems to be despite the regulatory system available to them rather than because of it.

VII. Conclusion

This chapter has described and evaluated the system of norm enforcement in creative user-generated content (CUGC) communities and has demonstrated that there are a range of community and individual mechanisms and approaches to understanding the rules and negotiating use, and deterring, detecting and sanctioning transgression. The key argument is that these mechanisms do not form a coherent system of regulation, with both copyright and norms being simultaneously applicable to any use. There is an inadequate level of certainty about what uses are permitted, problems detecting misuse and an unreliable range of responses to misuse. Certainly, there are high levels of creativity and sharing in the communities, suggesting that things work well, but it seems that the creativity that thrives here will sometimes, if not often, be in spite of the system rather than because of it. The following chapter considers whether legal reform is an appropriate response to these problems, and if so, what form it should take.

6

Copyright Reform for Creative User-Generated Content

I. Introduction

Copyright scholarship has expended much energy on the question of reform, particularly what copyright law should look like in the digital age.[1] This final substantive chapter of the book looks to contribute to this discussion by interrogating the need for copyright reform in the context of creative user-generated content (CUGC). Pulling together the findings from previous chapters, it begins by detailing an argument for reform, linked to the needs of the CUGC environment specifically, and also to broader critiques of copyright. The chapter then goes on to consider what copyright reform should look like. It explores the potential of existing user-generated content (UGC) reform narratives to address the flaws identified in the existing system. The chapter argues that a generally more permissive copyright system would be supported by the findings in this book, but that existing UGC reform proposals largely overlook the role of CUGC creator as copyright owner and thereby risk entrenching the problems reform seeks to address. As such, this chapter suggests supplementary provisions to fill this gap.

II. An Argument for Copyright Reform

To argue that copyright needs reform, we need to be able to articulate what is wrong with it. That analysis will be underpinned by the stance taken throughout this book that a coherent copyright law system is one that is focused on responding to the reality of creativity and facilitating the conditions required for creativity to thrive, rather than getting in its way. In exploring copyright's relationship with creativity in an anonymous online environment, the aim of this book has been to consider both whether copyright law adequately serves the CUGC context

[1] See eg: C Sprigman, 'Reform(Aliz)Ing Copyright' (2004) 57 *Stanford Law Review* 485; J Litman, 'Real Copyright Reform' (2010) 96 *Iowa Law Review* 1; CS Brown, 'Copyleft, the Disguised Copyright: Why Legislative Copyright Reform is Superior to Copyleft Licenses' (2010) 78 *UMKC Law Review* 749; W Patry, *How to Fix Copyright* (Oxford, Oxford University Press, 2011); MA Pallante, 'The Next Great Copyright Act' (2013) 36 *Columbia Journal of Law & the Arts* 315.

and what insights that can provide into wider critiques about copyright law and creativity. What follows in this section draws together the findings from earlier chapters to consider the limits of copyright law in relation to creativity. It argues that copyright law does not work for the CUGC environment for a number of reasons. It also argues that these provide support for much of the existing critique of copyright and creativity.

This book has provided detailed insight into the way that CUGC is regulated, and this has highlighted a number of problems in the relationship between copyright law and the CUGC environment. The most fundamental of these is that copyright law does not recognise CUGC creators as copyright holders in practice. The analysis in chapter two explains that copyright law can, doctrinally, subsist in CUGC, but in practice the law cannot respond fully to the specific CUGC environment, and particularly anonymity. Anonymity online is a pervasive environmental factor but is one that copyright law struggles to overcome, particularly as it complicates licensing and enforcement efforts. That this is an indication of copyright's disregard for CUGC creators, rather than merely an unfortunate consequence of the environment itself, can be seen by its failure to adapt to these complications in ways similar to those it has taken elsewhere. The orphan works problem is one that has attracted concern about potential chilling effects and finding a balance with access, and the law has deemed it to be sufficiently important to develop specific provisions to address the issue. Chapter two, section IV.B, highlighted that where it is not possible to trace and contact the creator of a CUGC work this is by definition an orphan work. However, the legal provisions developed to circumvent the problem do not apply to CUGC orphan works, even though there is an EU Directive on orphan works as recently as 2012,[2] and these are likely to be one of the largest cohorts of orphan works that exist due to the scale of online creativity.

Furthermore, it reflects poorly on copyright law that CUGC creators themselves do not recognise that copyright law can be relevant to their creative outputs. In chapter four, creators highlighted that copyright law seemed to be for commercial creative contexts rather than their own activity. This is even though there were some overlaps between their own values and expectations and those that copyright could offer. There is little fundamental incompatibility between the two, although community norms are more permissive than copyright law as currently structured, and there are many areas where CUGC creators feel strongly about retaining control, but copyright law is either difficult to enforce or just does not prioritise these rights. For example, creators felt strongly about restricting commercial uses of their CUGC but face a range of difficulties including limited access to the legal system due to a lack of accurate legal knowledge or funds to pay for legal advice. They also felt strongly about attribution rights and credit, but the

[2] Directive 2012/28/EU of the European Parliament and of the Council of 25 October 2012 on certain permitted uses of orphan works [2012] OJ L299/5.

moral rights that protect this are weaker and less well-known provisions in many jurisdictions (including the US).

Similarly, previous chapters have highlighted that copyright law does not focus on the right things to help CUGC creativity to thrive. Chapter three, sections II.B and II.C, highlighted copyright law's heavy reliance on the incentive argument which does not reflect the creative processes of CUGC creators. Rather than needing an economic incentive, it was clear that for the most part their creativity was motivated by more diverse and complex factors. This was further supported by findings in chapter four, section III.D, which demonstrated that justificatory narratives around CUGC norms focused more heavily on desert and morality than incentives. That the heavy focus of copyright law on the role of the single author as originator means that it cannot easily recognise the cumulative and collaborative nature of creativity is another part of the puzzle. Fundamentally, copyright law is not structured to reflect the creative process in CUGC.

The final reason that copyright law does not work for the CUGC environment is that it undermines the system of regulation there by adding an additional layer of confusion. Instead of responding to the values of the CUGC environment, the law undermines their enforcement. As explained, the use of copyright law is rather haphazard, with it being one small, and unreliable, part of the system of regulation used by these communities. Chapter 5, section VI, highlighted how community norms and copyright law jointly underpin the system of regulation used by the communities studied, and that this system comprises both individual and community measures. However, in large-scale communities with open borders such as these, copyright law can therefore actually undermine the effective regulation of creativity as it contributes to uncertainty about how creative content can be used and makes it more complicated to negotiate ex post. This demonstrates a practical flaw in the copyright system as, rather than supporting CUGC creativity, it creates barriers to it.

This translates into particular risks for both creators and potential users of CUGC that interfere with an optimised creative environment. For CUGC creators, the combination of locating misuse is difficult, and even more so due to anonymity, to the extent that creators accept that they will most likely not be aware of misuse of their work, particularly when it occurs outside the community.[3] Despite several legal and non-legal mechanisms available to enforce the rules ex post, there were some issues with accessibility, flexibility, certainty and responsiveness. Legal solutions either required an often unfeasible or unjustifiable input of time, money or effort, or could be inflexible as to outcome (such as notice and takedown procedures). Non-legal solutions based on direct negotiation with those misusing CUGC lacked enforceability and so could not ensure reliable outcomes for creators. Anonymity further complicated matters as responsiveness could also not be guaranteed.

[3] See ch 5, section IV.

As a result, creators wishing to retain control of their CUGC were best served by ex-ante protection measures. However, the ex-ante effect of community norms was limited due to a lack of clarity about what was expected. This arises due to the challenges of regulating large communities with no borders, as well has having another conflicting system of regulation – copyright law – applying simultaneously. This meant that selective sharing was the most effective approach, and invariably means that the best way to minimise the risk of sharing CUGC is for creators to limit what they share. In some cases this will mean creators do not share content at all. This problem is now heightened because of concerns about generative AI training, as creators felt there are particularly few solutions to this beyond not sharing. In light of the findings in chapter three, sections II.B.ii and III.B.iii regarding the importance of a fertile external network of sources for the creative process, selective sharing is therefore not ideal for a system looking to facilitate creativity.

Potential users of CUGC face the risk of being sanctioned for good faith misuse of CUGC. As there is a conflict between the restrictiveness of copyright law and the permissiveness of community norms in relation to the non-commercial use of CUGC, the fact that these systems can be used to interpret whether the use of CUGC is allowed causes confusion. There is wide discretion for individual approaches to CUGC to diverge from each other and from community norms, and where more restrictive individual rights are supported by law, this leads to the possibility that a creator can expect and enforce more restrictive rules than are found within the community norms, leading to sanction even though the user acted in good faith. This risk is also exacerbated by the open borders of these communities, which mean that non-community members can access and interact with CUGC without sharing the same normative values, and by the large size of the communities, which mean that dissenting voices can have more impact. Both of these issues contribute to diluting clarity and certainty as communicating normative expectations takes longer and users have to work out the creator's expectations regardless of community norms. As such, users may misunderstand what those expectations are, and then face sanction.

This risk also arises where users cannot identify CUGC creators to ask permission or clarify expectations due to online anonymity. Where potential users are unsure if their intended use of CUGC is acceptable, they then have two options: to use the CUGC as intended but risk sanction; or to not use the CUGC. This latter choice equates to a possible chilling effect. There is also further uncertainty that adds to the risk in using content, in that community norm enforcement is centred on shaming and ostracism and these sanctions are unpredictable and can be disproportionate.[4] Where users are unsure of the rules and of the possible sanctions this is an unjust system. Community rules are most often underpinned by concepts of morality or integrity and seek to uphold community values rather than

[4] See ch 5, sections III and V.

individual rights[5] and this can also lead to excessive responses, as detailed by some community members. In both cases, this can mean that users experience harsh shaming treatment, or that the threat of such treatment causes hesitancy to use CUGC as they cannot be sure if they are acting appropriately.

It is clear then that there are a range of deficiencies in the relationship between copyright law and CUGC creativity, but the question is whether the problems that arise as a result are extensive enough to warrant legal intervention. The problems faced by the CUGC environment in regulating use of creative works are not catastrophic. This is still a functioning creative environment where large amounts of CUGC are shared. Leaving the law as it is would allow things to carry on in their current manner, so would legal reform not be disproportionate? Linked to this is the question of why copyright law should change to accommodate the CUGC environment and communities like 4chan and Reddit. There are many creative communities and industries that would like their specific interests better represented in the law. In relation to stand-up comedy, Gates highlights that law reform with a single industry in mind could be 'difficult and inefficient'.[6] As such, there needs to be a compelling reason behind changes to the law. At first sight, this seems difficult to justify in this context as a qualitative study such as this does not provide generalisable results, so the findings should be narrowly interpreted.

However, there are both specific aspects of the CUGC context that support consideration of such reform and also a wider argument about creativity. First, the issues facing the environment outlined above – the risks to users and the risks to creators – may themselves warrant a solution on their own merits. While community members rarely explicitly mentioned the need for copyright reform, narratives of problems were frequently woven through their discussions.[7] This indicates that the issues identified have a noticeable impact on the community members, even if they do not articulate them in the same terms as identified in this book.

Secondly, it is also nothing new for this book to argue that the CUGC environment is a significant creative space where a large volume of works is shared and interacted with, where creators can find easy exposure to a wide range of inspiration and influences and develop skills and get feedback to help them improve.[8] We can distinguish this from other creative industries or communities as the CUGC environment is one that is increasingly the focus of creative activity and attention, and therefore it is legitimate and essential to consider how well the current legal system supports it. This is further reinforced by the fact that there has been significant consideration of copyright reform for UGC generally, as will be explored below.

[5] See ch 4, section III.D.

[6] TM Gates, 'Providing Adequate Protection for Comedians' Intellectual Creations: Examining Intellectual Property Norms and Negative Spaces' (2014) 93 *Oregon Law Review* 801, 827.

[7] See the discussions in ch 5.

[8] See ch 2, section II; and ch 3, section II.C.

It is also far from a minor or niche issue because of the size and scale of the CUGC environment. Reddit is in the top 10 most visited websites in the US.[9] Many of its creative communities have over one million subscribed members; r/Art has over 18 million subscribed members.[10] Similarly, posts on creative 4chan boards can number in the thousands per day.[11] This means there is also some argument that anonymous online communities like 4chan and Reddit warrant legal reform to their benefit in ways that other communities may not. These communities are certainly larger than many of the communities considered in other empirical studies, such as stand-up comedy, magic or drag.[12] Their size means that even if the rate of negative incidents as a result of these problems is low, this still translates into a large number of incidents.

This in turn leads to an argument for reform for this specific context on the basis of legal legitimacy. As it stands, large numbers of people in these communities use copyrighted works in ways that constitute infringement if the copyright holder has not given authorisation, and that mostly have not been given authorisation. While such uses are generally tolerated by creators/copyright holders, a coherent law should not define widespread, tolerated, everyday practice as infringing: 'If everyone is breaking the law, then maybe there is something wrong with the law in the first place'.[13] As argued above, even within 4chan and Reddit alone the numbers are vast, but considered as a wider problem, this behaviour undermines the law on a huge scale.

The question then arises: why is this copyright law's problem? It could be suggested that focusing on other aspects of the regulatory system would be more appropriate. For example, rather than focus on copyright law's limitations it might be better to tackle the issue of anonymity. Online anonymity practices undeniably cause problems that make it challenging for any system – legal or normative – to be effective. However, trying to improve the regulatory system by restricting anonymity is not an appropriate solution. Largely, this is because the problems arising from anonymity can only partly be attributed to the anonymity practices of individuals and as chapter two, section II.C explained, anonymity status is far more complex. The pervasive anonymity found online and that causes problems for enforcement would remain to some extent even if anonymity practices were less widespread. Furthermore, anonymity practices provide significant social,

[9] 'Alexa – Top Sites in United States – Alexa': www.alexa.com/topsites/countries/US.

[10] 'R/Art' (*Reddit*): www.reddit.com/r/Art/.

[11] '4stats.Io – Live 4chan Board & Thread Statistics': 4stats.io/.

[12] D Oliar and CJ Sprigman, 'There's No Free Laugh (Anymore): The Emergence of Intellectual Property Norms and the Transformation of Stand-Up Comedy' (2008) 94 *Virginia Law Review* 1787; J Loshin, 'Secrets Revealed: Protecting Magicians' Intellectual Property without Law' in CA Corcos (ed), *Law and Magic: A Collection of Essays* (Durham, NC, Carolina Academic Press, 2010); E Sarid, 'Don't Be a Drag, Just Be a Queen – How Drag Queens Protect Their Intellectual Property Without Law' (2014) 10 *FIU Law Review* 133.

[13] A Guadamuz, 'Living in a Remixed World: Comparative Analysis of Transformative Uses in Copyright Law' in L Edwards, B Schafer and E Harbinja (eds), *Future Law: Emerging Technology, Regulation and Ethics* (Edinburgh, Edinburgh University Press, 2020) 359.

creative and community benefits, without which the creative environment would suffer.[14] It is also the case that anonymity plays a positive role in some aspects of the normative system of regulation.[15] As such, the solutions here need to function within the anonymous online environment, rather than seek to undermine or reduce anonymity.

Similarly, much of what is described is the result of flaws in a wider normative system. However, there are two justifications for this being something copyright law could be expected to address. First, the reliance on a normative system is necessary because of the gaps in the copyright system when applied to CUGC. We know from previous chapters that copyright will subsist in much CUGC, but that the practicalities of enforcing those rights is limited and that creators are often dismissive of copyright's use for them outside commercial activities.[16] In particular, copyright law is poorly set up to function in the anonymous CUGC environment and there are conflicts between the permissiveness of non-commercial use.

Secondly, we also know that it is common for normative systems to successfully supplant intellectual property systems in such circumstances;[17] however this is not the case in the CUGC context, where copyright law continues to apply and to interfere with regulation as described above. The critique of copyright in the CUGC system, therefore, comes from the fact that it fails to provide an adequate system of protection itself but also plays an active part in undermining the normative system. By creating confusion and conflict as it coexists with norms it positively contributes to the problems the regulatory system poses. Copyright law is therefore not a passive element in this creative environment and the problems that arise for creators and users conflict with the facilitation of thriving creativity.

Finally, we can see that the findings in previous chapters demonstrate issues not only for this particular creative context but support more general and fundamental critiques of copyright law's relationship with creativity. This means that the argument for reform put forward here goes further than just responding to the specific needs of the CUGC environment. Chapter three, section II.B, outlined extensively that there is widespread existing critique of copyright's claimed relationship with creativity. Copyright law narratives use creativity rhetoric to justify the existence of copyright and to support law and policymaking arguments (most often in favour of expansion to the law). This rhetoric includes inaccuracies about the beneficiaries of copyright and how the creative process happens. In particular, it often claims that copyright is a universal and essential incentive to creativity and recognises the author as the sole originator of a work. There are numerous existing critiques of this creativity rhetoric and these argue

[14] See ch 3, section III.B.

[15] See ch 5.

[16] See ch 2, section IV; and ch 4, section II.

[17] See, eg, EL Rosenblatt, 'A Theory of IP's Negative Space' (2011) 34 *Columbia Journal of Law & the Arts* 317.

that copyright law's relationship with creativity is much more limited than it claims, in that it does not reflect the creative process in terms of its conception of authorship or of incentives, and that a universalised system that treats all types of creativity the same means that only certain types of creativity are served by copyright law as it stands.

Chapter three also explored aspects of the creative process on 4chan and Reddit and used this to interrogate both the rhetoric and the critique, with the findings supporting the latter. As highlighted above, the creators identified a broad range of incentives and motivations behind their creativity and while some highlighted economic factors, these tended to be in relation to potential future economic gain. Furthermore, these communities were found to enforce and consider copyright protection only haphazardly or partially, if at all, and despite this are nonetheless sufficiently motivated to create. Understanding how the communities experienced the creative process demonstrated therefore that copyright law fails to reflect the way anonymous creators create.

These findings challenge the arguments that underpin copyright's existence, in that they undermine the law's links with the notion of creativity. In this way, the findings support and contribute to the wider body of critical literature on this issue, particularly the 'negative space' scholarship, which is reliant on cumulative studies of individual communities and industries to build a more compelling argument about the law's limits.[18] Much of this literature uses similar findings to argue there are inherent flaws in the law; if creativity can exist without the use of copyright, then the law cannot be considered a universal incentive, and therefore an effective law would not and should not treat all creativity in the same way.[19] Furthermore, if the law only acknowledges or functions adequately for certain types of creativity, or does not accurately represent the creative process, then its narratives are further limited. For the law to be coherent, therefore, it needs either to provide a more accurate justificatory framework or undergo reform to better reflect the reality of the creative process and to balance the needs of a wider range of creators.

The argument here is not limited only to restating and reaffirming previous critique of the law, it also looks to develop this critique by providing additional supporting arguments and a new perspective by considering anonymity. First, the complex role of copyright law in the regulation of creativity within these communities can contribute to a creativity-based critique of the law. Copyright has the potential to regulate these communities; it has already been explained above that their values in relation to permissibility of uses diverge from copyright law as

[18] See, eg, K Raustiala and CJ Sprigman, 'When Are IP Rights Necessary? Evidence from Innovation in IP's Negative Space' in B Depoorter, P Menell and D Schwartz (eds), *Research Handbook on the Economics of Intellectual Property Law, Vol 1: Theory* (Cheltenham, Edward Elgar Publishing, 2016).

[19] See, eg: Loshin (n 12); K Darling, 'IP without IP: A Study of the Online Adult Entertainment Industry' (2013) 17 *Stanford Technology Law Review* 709; M Iljadica, *Copyright Beyond Law: Regulating Creativity in the Graffiti Subculture* (Oxford, Hart Publishing, 2016).

currently structured, but its wider values are not incompatible with those of the law. For example, the criteria for assessing originality and the reasons justifying author control of works are compatible with the themes found in copyright law. However, instead of responding to these values and desires the law undermines the function of the normative system designed to fill the gaps that copyright law has left by confusing matters. This goes beyond the critique of copyright that arises from the negative space literature. The problem here with copyright's relationship with creativity is not just that it passively over-prioritises the idea of universalised incentives and a one-size-fits-all approach, but also that it actively interferes with and undermines some aspects of the CUGC environment. This then further supports an argument for reform as copyright law becomes a disruptive factor for creativity.

Secondly, the understanding of the role of anonymity in regulating creativity in the CUGC environment shines a brighter light on the weaknesses in the law's relationship with creativity. The fact that creators in this environment choose to perpetuate anonymity through their own identity practices demonstrates the practical insignificance and low value placed on copyright protection and regulation by community members. For example:

Q: Do you feel that copyright offers you any benefits as a creator?

Anon2: I can't think of very many, can you?

Furthermore, the findings in chapter three, particularly sections II.B and III, also accentuate the inaccuracies in copyright's understanding of creativity. While copyright law's efficacy in terms of creativity is questioned, the communities' experiences of anonymity indicated that it plays a beneficial role in fostering the type of environment where creativity can thrive and is encouraged. Where creative communities can benefit more from being anonymous (a characteristic that specifically makes it hard for copyright to function) than from copyright law (whose existence is, or should be, configured around creativity) then this undermines copyright law's claims to facilitate creativity. Again, if creativity can benefit more without than with the law, this seems problematic. The difficulties in reconciling the two cannot and should not be dismissed as inevitable or an unfortunate outcome that we must put up with. Instead, this incompatibility further demonstrates that copyright law is flawed. Given the creative benefits of anonymity, a law with creativity at its heart would need to adapt to the needs of an anonymous environment and anonymous creativity as well as attempt to mitigate the difficulties anonymity causes for enforcement.

As such, this research shows us numerous flaws in copyright law's claimed relationship with creativity, whether general or specific. Exploring the interrelationship between copyright, creativity and anonymity has given further perspectives through which to build this critique. Creativity critique as a whole raises fundamental questions about copyright law. Does it need a new justificatory framework or new narratives? Or would law reform to enable copyright to meet its stated purpose be more appropriate? The argument here is that the creativity rhetoric at the heart of copyright law should not be discarded, and instead the law should aim to turn rhetoric into reality. That creativity is valued so highly by society can be seen in the success of the law's narratives, and it is a valid and desirable aim that law seeks to protect, encourage or reward the things that we value. The problem here is not that the rhetoric is undesirable, but that the law is misleading; it is the law, not its rationale, that therefore needs to be fixed.

III. Copyright Reform for Creative User-Generated Content

The chapter now moves on to consider what copyright can and should look like. To do this, it explores the potential of existing UGC reform narratives to address the flaws identified in the existing system. It starts by outlining broad themes from copyright reform scholarship, before looking at proposals targeting the digital age, and then more closely at those specifically focused on user-generated content. It also looks at copyright reform where there have been legal changes made in practice. For the more general reform points, the discussion acknowledges that CUGC is just one of many spheres of creativity on which it would impact. Therefore, it does not seek to argue whether or not these proposals should be adopted more generally and instead considers only whether they might be potentially beneficial to the CUGC environment. Where themes in reform discussions focus specifically on UGC, then a more comprehensive analysis can be undertaken as CUGC creators and users are the only stakeholders. It argues that the findings of this book would support the most mainstream suggestion of a UGC exception. However, it also highlights numerous gaps in the focus of these UGC-centric proposals.

After this, the chapter then moves on to suggest three guidelines for copyright reform proposals to address these gaps, providing additional justification for such measures.

A. Gaps in Current Debates

i. Copyright Reform

Copyright scholarship and policymaking has long taken an interest in reform debates, with a wide range of views, suggestions and positions visible. These include suggestions that, while they do not specifically target the digital age, online creativity or UGC, may have some relevance to them. For example, it is suggested that the law could be improved by reframing rights to better reflect the environment and acts they apply to. This includes Gervais who argues that the right should be reformulated away from a confusing and time-consuming bundle of fragmented rights over specific types of use (for example, reproduction or distribution) and instead should focus on the restriction of uses that conflict with commercial exploitation of the work.[20] Another approach is to suggest that instead of focusing on rights of reproduction, infringement should be assessed by whether a use interferes with the legitimate interests of the copyright holder[21] or should frame the right not as one of exclusion and preventing others from using works, but as one of a right to attribution.[22]

They also include suggestions to address difficulties in accessing the law, such as rewriting the legal provisions and simplifying them to help individuals to understand,[23] or through the removal of some of the financial hurdles to pursuing a claim.[24] These scholars highlight the fact that the law is so complex that the people who need to understand it are unable to or they identify the law's inaccessibility in terms of enforcement measures.[25] The most widespread theme in copyright reform scholarship is making copyright less restrictive in some way, with many arguing that the law needs to be limited or rebalanced. Some suggestions include reducing the duration or scope of the law.[26] Others suggest reintroducing formalities.[27] It is argued that reintroducing formalities would provide greater flexibility within the scope of copyright protection, as it would ensure that access to works is only restricted as far as necessary; creators or potential copyright holders will only protect works when they want the relevant controls over works and it is worth the effort of meeting the formalities.[28] Formalities could take the form of opt-in systems, such as mandatory registration, registration for access to enhanced rights and remedies,[29] or periodic registration to renew protection.[30]

[20] DJ Gervais, *(Re)Structuring Copyright: A Comprehensive Path to International Copyright Reform* (Cheltenham, Edward Elgar Publishing, 2017) ch 9.

[21] T Pihlajarinne, 'Should We Bury the Concept of Reproduction – Towards Principle-Based Assessment in Copyright Law?' (2017) 48 *IIC-International Review of Intellectual Property and Competition Law* 953.

[22] B Depoorter, A Holland and E Somerstein, 'Copyright Abolition and Attribution' (2009) 5 *Review of Law & Economics* 1063.

[23] Litman (n 1) 33–34; Pallante (n 1) 323; R Arnold, 'The Need for a New Copyright Act: A Case Study in Law Reform' (2015) 5 *Queen Mary Journal of Intellectual Property* 110, 126; P Samuelson, 'Preliminary Thoughts on Copyright Reform' [2007] *Utah Law Review* 551, 551.

[24] KK Olson, 'The Copyright Claims Board and the Individual Creator: Is Real Reform Possible?' (2020) 25 *Communication Law and Policy* 1.

[25] Pallante (n 1) 323; Litman (n 1) 3.

[26] eg, taking certain categories of work outside copyright protection, such as for academic works (S Shavell, 'Should Copyright of Academic Works be Abolished?' (2010) 2 *Journal of Legal Analysis* 301) or digital music (RSR Ku, 'The Creative Destruction of Copyright: Napster and the New Economics of Digital Technology' [2002] *University of Chicago Law Review* 263); or providing shorter terms of protection dependent on the needs of each different type of work (Patry (n 1) 198–201).

[27] See, eg: Patry (n 1) 180; Sprigman (n 1); Samuelson (n 23); WM Landes and RA Posner, 'Indefinitely Renewable Copyright' (2003) 70 *University of Chicago Law Review* 471.

[28] Patry (n 1) 180; S van Gompel, 'Copyright Formalities in the Internet Age: Filters of Protection or Facilitators of Licensing' (2013) 28 *Berkeley Technology Law Journal* 1425, 1432.

[29] Sprigman (n 1); Samuelson (n 23); Gervais (n 20).

[30] Landes and Posner (n 27).

It has also been suggested that the law should offer differing levels of protection in different contexts.[31] Gervais, for example, argues that different types of author should be treated differently within the system, with commercial rights-holders not being the default position.[32] Furthermore, there are arguments either to raise the originality threshold[33] or to provide higher protection to more original works.[34] There are also general arguments for reforms to the exceptions and limitations to copyright law. For example, Patry also suggests a more positive role for fair use provisions in the law, including opening up any closed list provisions.[35] Geiger suggests merging wider limitations for creative uses with a system of remuneration, in an example of using compulsory licence schemes to move the right under copyright away from a right to prohibit use towards a right to remuneration.[36]

Other suggestions include reforms to US fair use provisions,[37] including considering attribution as a factor.[38] The final area of reform debate is in relation to moral rights, with some argument for the expansion of such provisions in order to serve the public interest or protect human dignity[39] and some for their restriction or removal, most often due to a lack of faith in the deontological justifications underpinning it.[40]

Some of these reform themes are also suggested as a solution to specific problems in the digital ages. For example, the use of formalities has been suggested by some to address copyright issues in the context of digital creativity.[41] These include suggestions for notice requirements[42] and opt-out systems.[43] The discussion of strengthening or widening exceptions and limitations is also one that is common

[31] Gervais (n 20); G Parchomovsky and A Stein, 'Originality' (2009) 95 *Virginia Law Review* 1505.

[32] Gervais (n 20).

[33] DA Simon, 'Culture, Creativity and Copyright' (2011) 29 *Cardozo Arts & Entertainment Law Journal* 97.

[34] Parchomovsky and Stein (n 31).

[35] Patry (n 1) 216–29.

[36] C Geiger, 'Promoting Creativity through Copyright Limitations: Reflections on the Concept of Exclusivity in Copyright Law' (2009) 12 *Vanderbilt Journal of Entertainment and Technology Law* 515, 532–33.

[37] MJ Madison, 'Rewriting Fair Use and the Future of Copyright Reform' (2005) 23 *Cardozo Arts & Entertainment Law Journal* 391.

[38] G Lastowka, 'Digital Attribution: Copyright and the Right To Credit' (2007) 87 *Boston University Law Review* 41.

[39] HL MacQueen, 'Copyright Law Reform: Some Achievable Goals?' in F Macmillan (ed), *New Directions in Copyright Law*, Vol 4 (Cheltenham, Edward Elgar Publishing, 2007).

[40] J Smiers, 'The Abolition of Copyright: Better for Artists, Third World Countries and the Public Domain' (2000) 62 *Gazette* 379, 402–03; R Rosenthal Kwall, 'Originality in Context' (2007) 44 *Houston Law Review* 871.

[41] van Gompel (n 28) 1432.

[42] eg, Wu argues that works should only become infringing when the copyright holder provides notice to the user: T Wu, 'Tolerated Use' (2007) 31 *Columbia Journal of Law & the Arts* 617.

[43] Brown (n 1) 779–80; S Dusollier, '(Re)Introducing Formalities in Copyright as a Strategy for the Public Domain' in L Guibault and C Angelopoulos (eds), *Open Content Licensing: From Theory to Practice* (Amsterdam, Amsterdam University Press, 2011); Rosenblatt (n 17) 362.

in this context.[44] Gervais in particular argues for a clearer system of exceptions and limitations to respond to the social and cultural reality of remix and similar practices, either through extensions to existing exceptions and limitations, or by introducing one similar to fair use in the US.[45] There are also arguments about reframing copyright to focus on the right to remuneration (through compulsory licensing) rather than exclusion, through the creation of a right to remix.[46]

In terms of UGC-specific reform discussions, the focus is largely on the development of a UGC exception, and examples of these are outlined below.[47] Numerous committees and scholars have argued for a UGC exception. While their proposals vary in specific formulation, there are themes within the drafting of the exceptions. UGC exceptions can be categorised as to whether they permit any use, or permit only specific types of use, or only sufficiently transformative uses. They can also be categorised as to whether they permit commercial uses or non-commercial uses, whether they require equitable remuneration or not, and whether they require adequate attribution or not. The suggestions largely focus on addressing online creative practices by creating legal routes to enable the use of copyright-protected work in UGC, often focusing on remix practices. Examples of proposals are detailed below.

Senftleben, for example, suggests a copyright exemption for the purposes of 'entertainment, illustration, or pastiche' to fill any gaps left in the existing parody and quotation exemptions for CUGC that uses existing works, as long as the use is 'in accordance with fair practice when considering the creative effort made by the user'.[48] Frosio's proposed exception permits 'private non-commercial uses of lawfully made available content … for the purpose of creating UGC content' as long as it does not impair commercial use of the first work.[49] Angelopoulos and Quintais also suggest an exception for individual users that would permit any non-commercial user activity.[50] There are also suggestions for a more generic,

[44] eg: making exceptions and limitations better respond to remix practices (Gervais (n 20) 216–19; Rosenblatt (n 17) 360–61; B Justin, 'The EU's Trouble with Mashups' (2014) 5 *Journal of Intellectual Property, Information Technology and E-Commerce* 172; A Bertoni and ML Montagnani, 'Foodporn: Experience-Sharing Platforms and UGC: How to Make Copyright Fit for the Sharing Economy' (2017) 39 *European Intellectual Property Review* 399; Guadamuz (n 13) 361–62); a more positive role for fair use provisions (Patry (n 1) 216–29); creating wider limitations alongside a system of remuneration (Geiger (n 36) 532–33); or the creation of a system of user rights (Y Li, 'The Age of Remix and Copyright Law Reform' (2020) 12 *Law, Innovation and Technology* 113).

[45] Gervais (n 20) 216–19.

[46] In opposition to compulsory licences: RP Merges, 'The Concept of Property in the Digital Era' (2008) 45 *Houston Law Review* 1239; On a right to remix based on compulsory licensing: Li (n 44).

[47] The author has also outlined this briefly elsewhere: R Maguire, '"It Doesn't Belong to the Internet": Copyright Reform for User-Generated Content' [2022] *Intellectual Property Quarterly* 141, 164–65.

[48] M Senftleben, 'User Generated Content: Towards a New Use Privilege in EU Copyright Law' in T Aplin (ed), *Research Handbook on Intellectual Property and Digital Technologies* (Cheltenham, Edward Elgar Publishing, 2020) 160.

[49] G Frosio, 'Reforming the C-DSM Reform: A User-Based Copyright Theory for Commonplace Creativity' (2020) 51 *IIC – International Review of Intellectual Property and Competition Law* 709, 740.

[50] C Angelopoulos and P Quintais, 'A Better Solution to Online Infringement' (2019) 10 *Journal of Intellectual Property, Information Technology and E-Commerce* 147.

open exception to circumvent the closed list of exceptions currently available under EU law, with these being viewed as offering particular benefit in terms of being able to respond to future technological developments.[51]

Many of these exemptions are proposed to operate alongside some form of compensatory system. Senftleben's proposal would be combined with equitable remuneration for the rights-holder, with the responsibility for this falling on platforms.[52] Frosio suggests similar for his exception, but also makes an additional proposal for (compulsory) licensing schemes to make the copyright system less exclusive.[53] Angelopoulos and Quintais suggest administrating fair compensation for the rights-holder through collective management schemes, and again funded by the platforms.[54]

Having briefly summarised the key themes in copyright reform discussions, it is now useful to consider what copyright reform has looked like in practice. Over recent history, it is clear that the general trend has been for copyright expansion, despite most of the literature arguing for a less restrictive approach, or at least a neutral one. Extensions to the duration of protection,[55] to subject matter and forms of work protected,[56] or to the scope of rights[57] has been joined by increasing penalties and legal repercussions for individuals who infringe copyright[58] and introducing auxiliary measures to facilitate the enforcement and policing of the law.[59] Where copyright law has seen some relevant reform can be seen in the addition to EU law of an exception to cover parody.

There has been a long-standing policy interest in the potential of a specific UGC exception,[60] but copyright reform at national and EU levels has largely rejected such proposals,[61] with the notable exception of Canada, which introduced a specific 'user-generated content exception' to its Copyright Act in 2012. This exception permits the use of copyrighted work to create a new work as long as it is not for commercial purposes, the original source is credited, the remixer

[51] M Lambrecht and J Cabay, 'Remix Allowed: Avenues for Copyright Reform Inspired by Canada' (2016) 11 *Journal of Intellectual Property Law & Practice* 21, 35; Frosio (n 49) 740.

[52] Senftleben (n 48).

[53] Frosio (n 49) 740.

[54] Angelopoulos and Quintais (n 50).

[55] In the UK, from 14 or 21 years in the Statute of Anne 1710 to life plus 70 years today under CDPA, s 12. In the US, extended protection terms were introduced in the Copyright Act 1976 and the Copyright Terms Extension Act 1998.

[56] eg, the expansion to cover computer programs under CDPA, s 3(1)(b).

[57] Art 8 of the WIPO Copyright Treaty 1996 includes 'making available to the public' in the right of communication to the public, and in doing so covers works communicated over the internet.

[58] eg, the UK's Digital Economy Act 2017 increased the potential prison sentence for online copyright infringement from 2 to 10 years, while in the US, the Digital Millenium Copyright Act (DMCA) also increased criminal and civil penalties.

[59] Such as the DMCA's provisions to criminalise the removal of digital rights management technology.

[60] HM Treasury, *The Gowers Review of Intellectual Property* (2006), Recommendation 11, paras 4.85–4.88, 66–68; European Commission, Green Paper – Copyright in the Knowledge Economy (Publications Office of the European Union, 2008) COM/2008/0466.

[61] eg, despite several proposals for a UGC exception, such a provision was not included in the EU's Directive on Copyright in the Digital Single Market.

has reasonable grounds to believe the original source was not itself infringing copyright and the new work 'does not have a substantial adverse effect' on the exploitation or market for the original source.[62]

There are some other major policy developments in copyright law that merit mention. The CDSM Directive brought in new provisions in relation to UGC in Article 17.[63] Some of this provision's underlying principles mirror elements of suggestions outlined above, albeit without directly creating such an exception and not without controversy in relation to its impact on online creative culture.[64] Article 17 brought in new rules that make content-sharing platforms directly liable for copyright infringing content shared on their services by users and therefore obligate them to make best efforts to obtain licences from rights-holders to enable non-profit-making uses by their users and to not display content if rightsholders have registered it with the platform or it has been previously taken down. The aim of this is to reduce the value gap of works being shared on online platforms by ensuring fair remuneration for rightsholders.

Germany, for example, has transposed this into national law in the Urheberrechts-Diensteanbieter-Gesetz (Act on the Copyright Liability of Online Content Sharing Service Providers, known as UrhDaG). This creates an obligation on sharing platforms to seek licences, and they are deemed to have fulfilled this obligation where they acquire such usage rights when they are either offered to them, available through representative rights-holders known to them or can be acquired through collecting societies or rights management organisations in Germany.[65] There has been some concern because the Act contains provisions that can only be fulfilled by content upload filters, but the Act attempts to balance this with provisions creating 'uses presumably authorised by law'.[66] This creates a rebuttable presumption that UGC that contains less than half a work or several works by third parties, combines this with other content and uses third-party works to only a minor extent is authorised by law.[67] The aim of this is to balance the freedom of expression of users within the new system.

The final major area of recent copyright reform and policy consideration in practice is in relation to generative AI technology. As mentioned in earlier chapters of the book, the EU's CDSM Directive included the requirement for Member States to extend text and data mining (TDM) exceptions and limitations

[62] Copyright Act (Canada) s 29.21.

[63] Directive (EU) 2019/790 of the European Parliament and of the Council of 17 April 2019 on copyright and related rights in the Digital Single Market and amending Directives 96/9/EC and 2001/29/EC (Text with EEA relevance) [2019] OJ L130/92 (CDSM Directive).

[64] A petition against the provision (named 'Stop the censorship-machinery! Save the Internet!') raised over 5 million signatures: 'Stop the Censorship-Machinery Petition' (change.org): www.change.org/p/european-parliament-stop-the-censorship-machinery-save-the-internet.

[65] UrhDaG, s 4(1).

[66] UrhDaG, s 9.

[67] UrhDaG, s 9(2).

to include TDM for commercial purposes,[68] with the condition that the rights-holder has not expressly reserved their right, that is opted out, in an 'appropriate manner'.[69] This has been further supported by the EU's AI Act, which places obligations on generative AI service providers to have policies in place to identify and comply with opt-outs.[70] It also requires such providers to make publicly available a sufficiently detailed summary of the content used for training data.[71] The UK's Intellectual Property Office carried out a consultation about copyright in the context of generative AI, and as a result the government announced it planned to introduce a wider TDM exception that would cover commercial uses, with no opt out.[72] These plans were then abandoned after an outcry in relation to the impact on creators.[73]

ii. Evaluating Copyright Reform

We can therefore see that there are a range of relevant copyright reform proposals and implemented provisions, and the discussion that follows looks to evaluate these in the context of the CUGC environment and the issues identified throughout this book and earlier in this chapter. It argues that many of these would broadly align with CUGC interests, few are practical suggestions. We see in the scholarship and policy developments that the most likely reform for CUGC would be an exception or limitation, but that the suggestions that exist currently focus only on one side of the CUGC creative experience and further entrench the omission of CUGC creators as copyright holders in policy discussion. It also highlights that wider copyright reform developments, such as the CDSM and the AI Act, also contribute to this.

Prima facie, many of the reforms that are non-specific to CUGC could offer benefits to the CUGC environment, either directly to creators and users, or to concepts of creativity more generally. First, many of the suggestions would help to better align copyright law with CUGC norms. For example, any change to the substance of the right under copyright law that switched the focus to commercial activities would pull the law further in line with the expectations and norms of these communities. Such measures would benefit the communities, not only

[68] CDSM Directive, Art 4(1).

[69] CDSM Directive, Art 4(3).

[70] Regulation 2024/1689 of the European Parliament and of the Councilof 13 June 2024 laying down harmonised rules on artificial intelligence and amending Regulations (EC) No 300/2008, (EU) No 167/2013, (EU) No 168/2013, (EU) 2018/858, (EU) 2018/1139 and (EU) 2019/2144 and Directives 2014/90/EU, (EU) 2016/797 and (EU) 2020/1828 (Artificial Intelligence Act) [2024] OJ L2024/1689, reg 106.

[71] EU AI Act, reg 107.

[72] 'Artificial Intelligence and Intellectual Property: Copyright and Patents: Government Response to Consultation' (GOV.UK): www.gov.uk/government/consultations/artificial-intelligence-and-ip-copyright-and-patents/outcome/artificial-intelligence-and-intellectual-property-copyright-and-patents-government-response-to-consultation.

[73] Hansard, HC Deb 1 February 2023, vol 727, cols 152WH–168WH.

because the law would more closely reflect their normative expectations, but because it would increase clarity about what was permitted without requiring community members to navigate complex or expensive processes. Similarly, the strengthening of moral rights, particularly the right of attribution, would also likely bring benefits to the CUGC environment as it would align with the strong norms against false attribution. Clarity could also be improved by the requirement for formalities, particularly in how they may be able to provide a solution to orphan works problems if requiring registration means that users would have better access to identifying information to seek permission.[74]

Secondly, the book has highlighted widespread confusion and frustration at the complexities of copyright law for CUGC community members, as well as their difficulties in accessing reliable legal advice. As such, simplifying the law could increase its accessibility, with positive effects for the CUGC environment. For example, chapter five, section V highlighted that inaccurate understandings of copyright law created difficulties for creators and users when negotiating over an alleged misuse of a work. Simplification could help to avoid such problems.

Thirdly, reforms focused specifically on making copyright less restrictive, such as by shortening copyright duration, could also benefit the communities; it could help the law to respond to creativity critique about copyright's failure to recognise the importance of creative source material in the creative process and could lead to increased access to creative works. Relatedly, strengthened moral rights would provide stronger rights for creators, and in doing so would represent an improved place for creators (rather than corporate copyright holders) within the copyright system. It also seems that if the aim of reintroducing formalities is partly to increase the number of works accessible in the public domain, then it is possible this aim could align with broader critiques of the extent of copyright.

Strengthened moral rights would provide stronger rights for creators, and in doing so would represent an improved place for creators (rather than corporate copyright holders) within the copyright system. In relation to creating law that supports creativity, lawmakers would need to take care as giving creators too much control over their works, particularly in relation to the right to integrity, could also restrict future uses.

However, despite seeming to offer benefits on the face of things, these suggestions often seem impractical, unlikely or unpragmatic. Many of the suggestions require extensive, structural reform, of the sort that would be highly controversial and would take significant time and money to implement. Furthermore, many would require reform of the Berne Convention itself, for example reforms to the duration of copyright terms and the reintroduction of formalities. What might be nice in theory is unlikely to be achievable in practice.

Furthermore, on closer inspection, some of the options are not practical solutions for the CUGC context. For example, more accessible enforcement

[74] van Gompel (n 28).

procedures such as the Copyright Claims Board for individual creators proposed by Olson[75] are positive in theory, but are still likely to be inaccessible in practice due to the level of effort required, making it only worthwhile where the misuse of a work carries a sufficient level of financial gain to warrant pursuing a claim. In terms of formalities, such reforms are unlikely to be of practical benefit to these communities.

Elkin-Koren is critical of reintroducing formalities and highlights the inherent commercial bias within the suggestions as meeting formality requirements will require there to be sufficient commercial value to the work to justify cost and effort.[76] Consequently, she argues that formality requirements would disadvantage creators of UGC and position them within the public domain, regardless of the creator's wishes or the wider creative and social value of the work.[77] Any formal processes of registration or notice would therefore likely have a negative effect for CUGC creators; it was clear in chapter five that they wanted to retain control over their work, but may not have the resources to pursue formal copyright processes. Furthermore, while registration might assist with legal certainty and address the orphan works problem, this could remain ineffective where creators wished to retain anonymity, or if the system was not responsive enough for the CUGC context.

In light of this, it is most likely that CUGC issues would be addressed by UGC exceptions or limitations. This is the focus of most UGC-specific reform suggestions, and the fact that it has already been implemented in Canada indicates that it is a more realistic proposition than some of the more significant reforms detailed above. It is also clear that the type of proposals put forward for a UGC exception would be of value to the CUGC environment to the extent that they would remove liability for the use of copyright protected work in UGC. This would benefit CUGC creators who use remix practices in their work, as well as potential users of CUGC who wanted to create new UGC to share. Furthermore, it would be a positive step towards a copyright system that more fully recognised the importance of access to existing works and the cumulative nature of the creative process.

Nonetheless, the UGC exceptions as currently proposed and/or existing are problematic as they leave some significant gaps. In particular, the focus of this area of reform discussion is too narrowly on remix practices and the use of commercial works by those who share UGC. This means that current debates do not fully reflect the range of acceptable uses under CUGC norms and again overlook the fact that CUGC creators are themselves copyright holders.[78] The wider copyright reform developments are also guilty of this, with provisions that cover issues

[75] Olson (n 24).

[76] N Elkin-Koren, 'Can Formalities Save the Public Domain? Reconsidering Formalities for the 2010s' (2013) 28 *Berkeley Technology Law Journal* 1537, 1552–54.

[77] ibid 1555–58.

[78] See also, Maguire (n 47) 165–67.

that are very relevant to CUGC but that are written in ways that seem to alienate CUGC creators from benefiting from them.

The focus on remix practices goes some way to reflect permissive normative expectations around the non-commercial remix of CUGC. However, it is clear from chapter four, section III.A that non-commercial non-transformative use is also acceptable without permission. For example, resharing CUGC is a normal part of interacting on Reddit, although it is best practice to provide appropriate credit. That most of the UGC reform proposals, and the Canadian exception, specify a requirement for transformativity is sometimes argued to be an essential element of the exception in order to meet the requirements of the three-step test.[79] However, a requirement of transformativity means that such an exception would not adequately recognise the value of non-transformative sharing within the creative ecosystem. As such, there would remain a gap. This author has elsewhere argued against the interpretation that transformativity is the only way to meet the three-step test requirements. Indeed, while there is the possibility that this can be met by the simultaneous existence of a statutory licensing and remuneration system, more simply, the three-step test can be satisfied by framing the (C)UGC environment as a 'certain special case' in and of itself. This would be based on its significant value as a creative space.[80]

Furthermore, there is an inherent assumption within the various forms of the UGC exception that the UGC sharer is a user of commercial copyright works, and not a copyright holder themselves. While it is arguable that there is nothing to prevent these exceptions applying to CUGC, it is clear that there is a focus on commercial copyright holders in the proposals for fair compensation and/or equitable remuneration.

These provisions lead to some incoherencies, and to a failure to recognise the relevance of copyright law to non-commercial creativity. Fundamentally, the inclusion of compensation and remuneration provisions within the proposals demonstrates the assumptions made about the value of CUGC. The provisions are an attempt to address the 'value gap' between the money UGC platforms make from the sharing of content and the money that the relevant copyright holders receive, but CUGC creators and their works also make money for platforms and are themselves therefore disadvantaged by the value gap.[81] The financial burden of remunerations systems is placed on the platforms themselves but is likely to be passed down to the platform users, either as subscription or advertising models.[82]

[79] Senftleben (n 48) 149; the three-step test requires limitations or exceptions to rights under copyright law to apply to certain special cases, not conflict with normal exploitation of the work and not unreasonably prejudice the legitimate interests of the author (see Berne Convention, Art 9(2); TRIPS, Art 13; and WIPO Copyright Treaty, Art 10(1)–(2)).

[80] Maguire (n 47) 166.

[81] Maguire (n 47) 166; K Weatherall, 'The Relationship between User-Generated Content and Commerce' in D Hunter et al (eds), *Amateur Media: Social, Cultural and Legal Perspectives* (London, Routledge, 2012) 59.

[82] Angelopoulos and Quintais (n 50) 170.

The assessments used to calculate compensation or remuneration are also more likely to benefit commercial rather than amateur creators. While for other exceptions such as private copying, fair compensation has been calculated based on the harm caused to the copyright owner, it has been argued that in the case of a UGC exception it should be based on the value the exception has for the user, in order to reflect the absence of a functioning market for UGC works and to recognise the creative effort of the user.[83] In either approach, the amount is likely to be low for uses of amateur creativity. Even if compensation or remuneration were due, amateur creators are far less likely to benefit when these processes are run through collective management organisations or formal licensing schemes that would be less accessible to CUGC creators. Although it is possible they could take advantage, this would face the same barriers as for copyright registration: knowledge of such schemes and how they work; and time and effort to sign up.

Article 17 CDSM Directive is another example of this issue. Inherent in the provision is the assumption that UGC is the use of commercial copyright protected works, and that platforms must therefore compensate those rightsholders for its use. There is no acknowledgement that UGC creators themselves may warrant compensation for their efforts in populating the platform. Furthermore, it is clear that CUGC creators could not be the beneficiaries of Article 17 remuneration provisions because it is not feasible to negotiate licences with individual creators. Instead, the provision relies on platforms making best effort to obtain licences.[84] In the German UrhDaG, this means that CUCG creators would either have to approach the platforms, have a representative rights-holder or be a member of a collecting society or rights management organisation.[85] This replicates the access problems flagged above. The exception to this would likely be where CUGC was being reshared/remixed within the same platform, as terms of service usually provide platforms with a licence to sublicence as they wish.

Similarly, the EU's TDM exception[86] is very relevant to the CUGC context, and chapters four and five showed that CUGC creators hold strong feelings about wanting to restrict use of their works by generative AI models. However, the opt-out option does not provide adequate protection for CUGC works. That the AI Act has put in place further support for the opt-out demonstrates the importance that is placed on the opt-out option, but where platform terms of service widely permit them to sublicence, they will not be adequately available to CUGC.

We can therefore see that copyright reform has not sufficiently recognised CUGC creators as copyright holders themselves. This is a significant gap in the proposals as it further entrenches the misconception about copyright's applicability to the CUGC environment. It also highlights the fact that copyright reform

[83] ibid 168; Senftleben (n 48) 160.
[84] CDSM Directive, Art 17(4).
[85] UrhDaG, s 4(1).
[86] CDSM Directive, Art 4.

needs to go further if it wants to properly respond to the points highlighted at the start of this chapter.

B. How and why to Fill the Gap

The final piece of this puzzle then is to consider how to fill the gaps identified above. The discussion makes three straightforward suggestions that can be used to supplement existing proposals or to help guide future ones. The chapter finishes with a brief argument as to why this is the preferred approach.

The final piece of this puzzle then is to consider how to fill the gaps identified above. The discussion puts forward three straightforward guidelines that can be used to supplement existing proposals or to help guide future ones. The chapter finishes with a brief argument as to why this is the preferred approach.

The first guideline to address gaps in reform narratives is to ensure that any CUGC-specific exceptions include express provisions permitting not just transformative uses of CUGC but also non-commercial, non-transformative uses of CUGC, subject to sufficient credit. This would help to provide a more thorough representation of CUGC community norms and would help to improve clarity and coherence between the norms and copyright law.

The second guideline is that such provisions should also be clear in their drafting that it is use of CUGC specifically that is being addressed, rather than CUGC's use of other copyright works. Making this clear in provisions will ensure that the law recognises CUGC creators as copyright holders and also that CUGC creators recognise the applicability of the legal provisions to them.

The third guideline is that more general reform provisions also take careful steps to consider the extent to which proposals may be relevant to the CUGC context and to ensure that their drafting does not unnecessarily exclude them or inadvertently prevent them from benefiting from provisions. This could be applied in the case of the EU TDM exception, and perhaps addressed through obligations placed on platforms to provide user-friendly opt-out options regardless of any pre-existing user agreements if they use CUGC to train their own generative AI models or license others to do so.

Using these guidelines to supplement and guide copyright reform proposals relevant to CUGC would provide benefits to creators and users, is preferable to non-legal solutions and would help to diffuse the anonymous creativity critique as it allows the law to better reflect and facilitate creativity and so leads to more coherent law.

The guidelines are valuable to creators and users because they provide a solution to the risk to users, and an indirect benefit in relation to the risks to creators of sharing. The first guideline would deal with that risk by removing the conflict between restrictive law and permissive community norms. In doing so it significantly reduces the *risk to users* by providing clear understandings of expectations, so that users can avoid the difficulties of negotiating use or asking for permission in the anonymous online environment. It would improve ex-ante enforcement, as messaging over unacceptable uses would be clearer, thus preventing misuses where users thought they were acting within the rules. It would also improve enforcement should misuse occur, as certainty over acceptable uses would reduce the difficulties individuals and community members had in navigating complex rules in formal and informal ex-post mechanisms. The guidelines could also indirectly help to reduce the *risk of sharing* in relation to commercial misuse, where creators have limited access to legal solutions. By clearly defining the boundaries of what use is legally allowed in relation to CUGC, it highlights and draws attention to the often overlooked existence of copyright protection over this content. In doing so it disproves any assumption by commercial users that CUGC 'belongs to the internet'. Similarly, by making sure that the protection of CUGC is adequately considered in provisions, it helps to minimise the risk of sharing as it can reduce particular creator concerns that might lead to selective sharing. In particular, concerns about text and data mining might be better addressed.

Why is a legal solution preferable when individual, community or platform-level approaches that do not require law reform are also available? For example, creators could be more explicit about their expectations when sharing CUGC, communities could post more detailed rules or platforms could provide drop-down options for creators to label their shared CUGC according to which uses they want to restrict. Legal reform, however, provides a much clearer and simpler solution that provides far more reliable certainty to potential users about what uses are permitted. It also provides a more comprehensive solution that is not restricted by platform and/or community will or resources. Instead, a legal solution applies to all relevant works and uses without further requirement. As such it is a preferable response to non-legal reform solutions.

The reform proposal is therefore generally beneficial to creators and users. However, we should consider that there was not a unanimous position on norms within or across the communities studied. Roundtree argues one reason that graffiti norms should not be incorporated into mainstream law is because they are not unanimous.[87] In our context, this could cause issues as the first guideline would limit some existing rights held in copyrighted works, as it would create a more permissive copyright landscape. This could conflict with creator wishes. However, within the specific context of this research it is argued that there is consensus,[88] and in the context of CUGC creators and users more generally, there seems to be an indication of similar viewpoints, as demonstrated by the well-established suggestions for UGC exceptions that align with the CUGC creator views set out in this book. As the guideline diverges from those suggested reforms in focusing

[87] A Roundtree, 'Graffiti Artists Get Up in Intellectual Property's Negative Space' (2012) 31 *Cardozo Arts & Entertainment Law Journal* 959, 989–91.

[88] McAdams explains that a consensus requires only that 'the majority of those who hold an opinion share the same opinion': RH McAdams, 'The Origin, Development, and Regulation of Norms' (1997) 96 *Michigan Law Review* 338, 358.

specifically on the use of CUGC and suggests exemptions in relation to the sharing of works with no or limited remix elements, these proposals are also unlikely to face significant challenge as they would have little impact on the interests of traditional copyright holders.

While the minority of creators who seek stronger controls over their CUGC will see their positions sidelined, it is argued that this is acceptable because of the benefits the provision will provide to creativity and copyright law more generally. These provisions benefit creativity in several ways: facilitating an external network of sources; reflecting the creative reality of these communities; and reducing conflict between law and anonymity. Chapter three, sections II.B.ii and III.B.iii, outlined that existing literature shows us that creativity requires rich external networks of sources, information and influences so that the brain can make new connections leading to creativity. We can view the CUGC environment as a very explicit example of such external networks because it provides widespread and easy access to huge amounts of creative content. This was seen in practice; some community members highlighted the role of inspiration from online creative communities in their creative process.[89]

It also highlighted that copyright law has the ability to limit the fertility of these networks by restricting what can be made available within them, and so the law needs to be configured correctly to avoid over-protection. The suggested guidelines mean that copyright's over-protection of works in this context would be resolved by making it clear that these types of creative works can be used and shared without risk of infringement. In removing the restrictions of copyright in this context, the law is therefore better able to support creativity and the creative process. This is also the case where the guidelines ensure that CUGC itself is adequately protected, thereby helping to find a better equilibrium.

The provisions also in part diffuse the specific anonymity critique of copyright law. These provisions allow copyright law to work more harmoniously alongside anonymity in this online creative environment, which is important considering the creative benefits attributed to online anonymity practices in chapter three, section III.B. Where expectations are clearer and more coherent, then users are less likely to need to contact CUGC creators to ask permission and CUGC creators are less likely to need to identify and pursue misuse, both of which are challenging where anonymity is pervasive.

The guidelines further support creativity by helping the law to better reflect the needs, practices and norms of CUGC creators. It has been argued in this book that copyright's focus on incentives does not align with motivations for

[89] Participant 4 (Paul) explained: 'Well, scrolling through large numbers of pictures I'll get an idea for a composition, then sketch based on that and either continue from there and finish or set it aside, that's the visual part anyway. I'll also sometimes be inspired by a poem in r/ocpoetry or a writing challenge. It's … well, it's filled with more thoughts, pictures and ideas than anyone could possible see or reflect on individually – but as an amalgamation it can help create a basis for creative thought'.

creativity in this context. Furthermore, copyright was considered largely inaccessible and considered irrelevant to creators.[90] The conflicts between copyright law and community norms created problems where both systems were applicable at once, and this caused difficulties for the creative process as it created confusion about what uses were allowed. By bringing the law in line with the creative reality for these communities, this would both improve the situation for creativity by reducing the risk of using and the risk of sharing that arose from this confusion. It would also improve the legitimacy of the law by reducing cases of technically infringing but practically tolerated uses of creative content.

As previously argued, supporting creativity is a positive aim in itself due to its cultural and social value, but it is also imperative to coherent copyright law. It is creativity rhetoric that supports copyright policy. As has been argued repeatedly, without adequately representing and facilitating creativity, copyright law lacks a compelling narrative of justification and social value. Therefore, it is essential that copyright law adapts to better reflect this rhetoric. Guiding reform in this way therefore offers the opportunity not only to fix a specific problem for anonymous CUGC communities, but also to make the law more reflective of its purpose – creativity.

IV. Conclusion

This chapter has explored issues of copyright reform in relation to creative user-generated content (CUGC). It started by putting forward an argument for reform based on the needs and specifics of the CUGC environment as well as on a wider critique of copyright's relationship with (anonymous) creativity. It then went on to outline the landscape of copyright reform, highlighting relevant proposals and implemented provisions and focusing particularly on those suggesting an exception or limitation for user-generated content. The various provisions were analysed and evaluated for their ability to address issues with copyright law identified in the argument for reform. The discussion highlighted that a user-generated content (UGC) exception is the most practically feasible of many approaches that could bring potential benefit to the UGC context. It also highlighted that while proposals were able to address issues with copyright law being overly restrictive in relation to the transformative use of works for non-commercial purposes, existing proposals and recent reforms did not properly recognise the value of non-transformative uses, nor of the CUGC creator's status as copyright holder.

As such, the chapter provided three guidelines to help supplement and inform copyright reform proposals relevant to CUGC. These ensure that there

[90] See chs 4 and 5.

is sufficient permissibility for transformative uses of CUGC; that the status of the CUGC creator as copyright holder is adequately clear in drafting; and that where reform provisions may be relevant to the protection of CUGC that provisions do not unnecessarily or inadvertently exclude them from benefiting from it. These guidelines will help to address the critiques outlined at the beginning of the chapter, with the overall effect that they will assist copyright law in optimising creativity.

7

Concluding Remarks

I. Summary

This book began by highlighting its aims of exploring how copyright law, creativity and anonymity interact in order to better understand copyright law in practice in the specific context of the anonymous creative user-generated content (CUGC) environment, and of engaging with existing copyright debates by interrogating narratives and rhetoric in copyright theory, and by exploring whether reform is required.

The first two substantive chapters looked to explore the interrelationship between anonymity, creativity and copyright law from two angles. Chapter two described the CUGC environment, both in terms of CUGC and interactions with CUGC, but also anonymity, and in doing so provided context for the rest of the book. The discussion defined and categorised CUGC and identified a variety individuals who can interact with CUGC in a variety of ways (remixing, re-sharing, utilising, or giving feedback) in a variety of 'locations' (intra-community, extra-community, extra-platform or offline). It identified that there are various ways that anonymity manifests itself in this creative environment, including through names, contact information, patterns of behaviour, or typification and geographic information. It also argued that anonymity is pervasive in this environment both because some communities (such as 4chan and Reddit) have strong cultures of anonymity practices, and more broadly because the scale and ephemerality of online participation undermines reliable traceability.

The chapter then demonstrated that copyright subsists in user-authored content and may subsist in user-derived content, depending on levels of originality. Additionally, interactions with that content corresponded to relevant rights under copyright law, and so could constitute infringement if conducted without authorisation. Despite in theory applying to the CUGC environment, copyright law is undermined as a system of regulation there by anonymity. Anonymity makes it inefficient for creators as copyright holders to locate and pursue infringers and for potential users (remixers, re-sharers or utilisers) to locate creators to negotiate permission to use their CUGC. Where copyright owners cannot be found, CUGC can be framed as an orphan work but orphan work provisions are not designed for this online context. Anonymity also muddies an already complex international copyright landscape where choice of law issues are exacerbated by not knowing where a creator or locator is located. As such, anonymity and copyright law could be understood as being incompatible on practical grounds.

Chapter three then explored the interrelationship between anonymity, creativity and copyright law from a different angle, by looking at the comparative relationships between copyright law and creativity and anonymity and creativity. It highlighted that the law relies on creativity rhetoric to justify its existence and expansion, but that there is extensive scholarly critique of this rhetoric. Qualitative findings from 4chan and Reddit supported much of this critique, identifying that for these anonymous creators, as with others, the law does not seem to reflect their activities and creative processes, instead focusing too narrowly on corporate interests and beneficiaries, particularly in relation to facilitating access to source material and incentivising creativity.

The chapter also demonstrated that CUGC community members had a variety of positive, neutral and negative experiences of anonymity, and argued that these correlated with an ability to foster an environment where creativity could thrive. In particular, anonymity can provide practical benefits to creators seeking honest feedback to help them to improve and can encourage the sort of risk-taking and experimentation that benefits creativity when reputational risks are reduced. Furthermore, anonymity can benefit the creative process as it can lead to an enhanced sense of community belonging, while increasing a sense of security, and in doing so encourages sharing and collaboration. Anonymity also creates the right conditions for some of the reputational and intrinsic motivators that lead to 4channers and Redditors to create, particularly by enhancing the validating effect of positive feedback. As such, it was argued that anonymity can have a more positive effect on creativity than copyright law in these communities, shining extra light on the initial creativity critique in the first half of the chapter and raising questions about copyright justifications. These findings also indicated that if we need to reform copyright law so it better serves creativity, then the law also needs to find a way to work alongside anonymity.

While the critiques of the law identified in chapters two and three clearly put forward some broad considerations for reform, it was also necessary to consider how anonymous communities go about regulating uses of CUGC. This would allow us to assess if and how the law fits into this system and to identify any specific flaws that the law might need to address. Therefore, chapters four and five moved away from broader questions of the interrelationship between anonymity, creativity and copyright law to specifically consider how 4chan and Reddit communities approached 'ownership' of creative content and how they regulated uses of content, considering in particular the respective roles of community norms and the law. Chapter four explored ownership norms and explained that, despite several reasons to expect that anonymity could mean that creators were forfeiting ownership this was not the case and CUGC shared by anonymous creators or merely within the anonymous online environment did not usually 'belong to the internet'. Community members were, on the whole, supportive of a copyright system but not necessarily of the one we currently have. There were many criticisms of a bloated, impenetrable or corporate-focused legal regime, and also a commonly held view that copyright law was about commercial works and uses and not relevant to their amateur efforts or non-commercial interactions.

Despite this view of copyright law as not particularly relevant to them, most creators wanted to retain control of some sort over their content. The chapter therefore looked to explore how 'ownership' of creative content is constructed within these communities in comparison with copyright law to understand whether there is a conflict of values that would mean that the law could never align with community norms. Despite the fact that unanimity on these points was not established, and that there were minority positions that deviated from them, there was some consensus on each of the elements of the construction of ownership (originality, authorship, rights and justifications) within community norms. There were also overlaps between these positions of consensus and the position of the law. For example, the criteria for a work to be considered original mostly fit within the broad themes of originality within copyright law, particularly the focus on creative choices, self-expression, labour and skill. Creators were seen as the originators of works, and there was a normative expectation that this restricted how others could use those works, particularly in terms of commercial uses and in terms of attribution, just as copyright law does. Some of the reasons given for these restrictions centre on the idea of justice and fairness (the creator getting a just reward for their work), the idea of respecting the creator and their personal link to the work, and also, very occasionally, supporting commercial creators to make a living. These align with copyright justification narratives of desert theory, personality theory and the economic incentive/utilitarian theory.

However, the consensus on norms was not without its conflicts with copyright and inherent critiques of the law. Positions on the standard of originality required for ownership deviated between 'you're a hack', 'good artists borrow, great artists steal' and 'no rules just tools'. Mostly expectations were that creative content would inevitably incorporate ideas and elements from other works, and that the only requirement to legitimise this was that the creator 'made it their own'. In this, there was no rejection of the role of originality as a criterion for ownership of works, but a slight deviation from the idea of the creator-genius as originator in copyright law to reflect a middle ground between the total rejection of originality in some of the creativity critique and copyright's Romantic author.

Furthermore, a significant difference between the legal and normative conceptions of 'ownership' was identified in the sort of uses of works that were permitted or restricted. I highlighted that copyright law operates from a default position of restriction – uses are 'infringing unless' – whereas within the communities, the default position was 'permitted unless'. As such, most non-commercial uses of works, including re-sharing, utilising and remixing, were all acceptable without seeking the permission of the creator, subject to appropriate attribution. Finally, there was a significant reason given to justify these restrictions that did not mirror the copyright narratives. This was artistic integrity and morality. Acts such as falsely claiming a work as one's own or profiting from someone else's work was described in terms more naturally associated with criminal than private law mechanisms, such as 'evil', 'stealing' or 'unethical'. Here we saw that where this applied, these restrictions could be framed less as individual creator 'rights' but as community 'public' mechanisms to protect the creative community and creativity itself, and so there is an additional role that these norms play in comparison to the law.

Consequently, we saw that it was not impossible for copyright law to adapt to community norms as they were not so fundamentally different. However, the analysis did provide critical perspectives on the practical set up of the law (too restrictive) and on its broader narratives (originality is too narrowly conceived and there is limited relevance of economic incentives). These findings led on to chapter five, which focused on understanding and evaluating the system of enforcing those norms in order to assess if there was any identifiable need for law reform specifically for these communities. If non-legal enforcement mechanisms were sufficient, reform could not be justified using their specific needs.

Chapter five identified that CUGC communities on 4chan and Reddit use a variety of approaches to enforce control over how works that are shared within them are used. It explored four stages of this process: communicating and negotiating norms; deterrence of transgression; detection of transgression; and remedies and sanctions for transgression. It was clear in each stage that both community-led and individual-led approaches were available, and that there were several problems with these approaches, and that the system of norms is not capable of fully supplanting the legal system. First, the simultaneous existence of ownership norms and copyright law as potential regulatory forces over the CUGC environment creates a problem of contradictory messages about what types of uses are permitted, and this is exacerbated by discussions of copyright law as a potential solution in many cases of misuse, despite the limits on its suitability. Seeking permission to use each work often carries high transaction costs or is unreliable, something made worse by anonymity. This creates risk for potential users of works.

Secondly, finding and responding to misuse once it occurs is similarly troubled by difficulties. Formal legal solutions are either only accessible in certain limited circumstances (of high-value commercial misuse) or are inflexible in meeting creator wishes (for example, for attribution rather than takedown). Direct negotiation and non-legal approaches face problems of reliability and predictability. Community approaches focus on shaming and ostracism, which similarly lack predictability, and sometimes lack proportionality. Furthermore, these approaches often respond not to the harm to the individual creator's control, but rather to the collective harm to the community. This creates risk for creators in sharing their CUGC.

Without a reliable means of dealing with misuse ex post, the most effective means available to individual creators is to use ex-ante measures to limit how their creative content can be used. The most reliable of these is selective sharing, whereby creators only share what they are happy to lose some control of.

While this is an effective strategy for individual creators, it is not the preferable approach for a flourishing creative environment since this relies on a fertile network of sources for creators to build on.

Furthermore, this chapter demonstrated that anonymity plays a complex role in this process, both undermining individual approaches by increasing the transaction costs of negotiating use or negotiating misuse, and by supporting community approaches by helping to communicate norms, heightening the fear of sanctions, encouraging normative behaviour, and in the case of strong anonymity, insulating creators from the risk of misuse by those both within and outside the community. Although, to add to the complexity, there are also possibilities that anonymity might make community sanctions disproportionate and unpredictable. This further sets anonymity and copyright in opposition for the purposes of critique of the law.

Having identified that there is scope for improvement in the system, chapter six then focused on considering how the previous findings could help us to build a specific and general critique of the law and respond to and engage with ongoing debates about copyright reform. It argued that the law fails to meet the needs of or reflect the creative practice of anonymous creative communities, despite the fact that it could adapt to do so without undermining its values or internal logic. Instead, as demonstrated in chapter five, copyright law seems to make things more difficult for the communities by confusing the messaging about permitted uses, and therefore seemingly contradicts its own creativity rhetoric.

It also outlined a specific anonymous creativity critique of the law that supports and develops existing critique of copyright law's relationship with creativity. By understanding anonymity's conflict with copyright, we are able to further accentuate the law's flaws. The choice to perpetuate anonymity through their own individual practices highlights the limited relevance amateur creators place on copyright law on their activity. Furthermore, failure to respond or adapt to the anonymous online environment highlights copyright's disconnect with creative reality, further undermining its own creativity rhetoric. It argued that faced with misleading creativity narratives underpinning copyright law, the aim should be to seek reform of the law to enable it to live up to its claims.

These critiques then formed the basis of an analysis of copyright reform, first by considering ongoing trends in copyright debates, and secondly by considering specific reform proposals for CUGC communities. By considering the communities as stakeholders in the debates the chapter argued that generally there were a range of copyright reform proposals that seemed to align with the needs and desires of CUGC communities and that would address the creativity-based critique of copyright law, but that many of these were far-fetched, impractical or a poor fit for the CUGC context. Instead, it was argued that the most realistic reform proposals are those that outline a specific exception for UGC.

The chapter then highlighted that even though such reforms would partially address the critiques of the law set out earlier in the chapter, there were some significant gaps in the proposals that meant they could not fully respond to the critique. These focused mainly on the fact that reforms largely overlook the role of CUGC creator as copyright holder and thereby risk entrenching many of the problems reform needs to address. As such, three guidelines for supplementing and informing UGC-focused copyright reform were proposed. The first was to ensure that provisions reflected norms around non-transformative and non-commercial uses, not just transformative ones. The second was to ensure that provisions were carefully drafted so that CUGC creators were not only framed as user of others' copyright works, but also as potential rights-holders themselves. The third was to ensure that provisions that could apply more generally to UGC are careful to avoid unnecessarily or inadvertently excluding CUGC creators from benefiting from them.

It was argued that this would then reduce some of the difficulties facing anonymous CUGC communities and would help address some of the issues underlying the anonymous creativity critique. Furthermore, it would help the legitimacy and coherency of the law. In this way, the law's conflict with anonymous creativity could be solved and the anonymous creative environment would thrive even more.

In short, this book has argued that creativity should be at the heart of how we frame copyright law. Using the lens of anonymity and the specific context of CUGC communities in an anonymous online environment, it has created a wide-ranging critique of how the law currently addresses creativity, highlighting the often misleading nature of its own creativity rhetoric. To address this critique, it has argued that the law needs to take a more comprehensive approach to reform to better reflect creative reality and the complexities of the CUGC environment.

II. Practical Suggestions for Navigating the Creative User-Generated Content Environment

This book has concluded that the most effective solution for some of the problems identified is legal reform. The reality is, however, that such a solution takes time and effort, and may never come at all given the reticence policymakers have shown towards UGC reform generally. It therefore seems sensible to spare a little space here to think pragmatically about how to navigate those challenging areas of the CUGC environment and how those who are participating in it can perhaps make things a little easier for others. This certainly does not constitute legal advice but is informed by what has been learned from the process of researching and writing this book.

CUGC creators who are concerned about their work being misused should think carefully about what they share and where they share it. Once it is online, it can be difficult to control how it is used, so if it is something particularly precious, it might be better kept offline. That being said, if there is a way to reduce its value to misusers so that it can still be shared, that is better in terms of the community. They can consider sharing partial works, drafts or low-resolution images. This is certainly not a fail-safe solution but is probably the best compromise for still allowing community participation.

The particular platform or website chosen for sharing also has an impact on what might happen to it, as would the community itself. Considering how well they understand the norms of that particular sharing community and to what extent they mirror their own is important: if they want control but it seems like anything goes in a particular community, then it probably is not the right fit. Similarly, if they strongly want to avoid their CUGC becoming AI training data then some platforms will be more appropriate than others.

CUGC creators can also help themselves and make things easier for potential users by being explicit about their expectations when sharing content. Using clear, straightforward language to explain if, for example, they are happy for anyone to do anything with the work or want people to ask permission for certain uses, will be very helpful.

CUGC communities could also contribute to making it easier to navigate them. If the structure of the community makes it possible, explicit rules about using CUGC can help with clarity. Similarly, another important role for moderated communities who want to encourage participation is to carefully monitor shaming and ostracism responses to ensure they are not disproportionate.

The number one rule for users of CUGC is: do not claim credit for someone else's CUGC! The second rule is: 'it doesn't belong to the internet'. Beyond this, potential users of CUGC should take their time to understand the norms of the community where the CUGC is posted. Generally speaking, if the use is non-commercial it will likely be acceptable to use the CUGC as long as adequate credit is given, but if it is commercial then permission will be needed. If there is any ambiguity or the user is unsure, then the first step is to try to find out from the creator whether the intended use is acceptable to them. If they cannot find out from the creator for whatever reason, and it is a commercial use, then it should be left alone.

III. The Future of Creative User-Generated Content

Chapter one highlighted that the CUGC environment is not static. It has already changed from the early days of copyright literature exploring the digital age, and it will continue to transform as technology and society changes. While it is never possible to definitively predict what the CUGC environment will look like in the future, it is clear that generative AI is likely to have a significant impact on creative practice and copyright law policy. What exactly that impact will be is yet to be seen, but as a more substantial body of legislation, regulatory efforts and case law emerges in the next few years, we will get a better picture.

The book touched briefly and intermittently on some generative AI issues relevant to the CUGC environment, but this has not been a comprehensive exploration. Instead, it looked to give a flavour of the questions and problems that are emerging to see whether they have had much impact on its findings. In chapter two, section III, questions about copyright subsistence in AI-generated and assisted CUGC and about the potential for generative AI to infringe its training data were answered, albeit with some grey areas remaining. Chapter four, section III, highlighted the very strong distaste the CUGC communities had for their creative work being used to train AI models, but also that there was generally very little that could be done about it. Chapter six, section III.A.i. also flagged the limitations of some of the protections against text and data mining now that platforms have started to cooperate with generative AI businesses. While there are still many questions about what the impact of AI will or should be, the findings in the AI study supported the findings in the main (pre-AI) study, and this suggests perhaps that things will not change too much for CUGC communities.

However, more apocalyptic visions of the future of generative AI might be concerned about the threat to creative jobs. If copyright policy does not respond to this hypothetical threat appropriately, then commercial creative practice may become a thing of the past for humans. In that world, perhaps CUGC thrives, as non-commercial creativity – all the art, literature, photography made for fun, enjoyment, or any of the other many motivations identified in chapter three – becomes the only remaining human creativity. Alternatively, if copyright law does not develop adequate protections against text and data mining for generative AI training models, there is a significant risk that people will be less inclined to participate in the CUGC environment and it will decline.

However, in either version of the future of CUGC, and any of the in-betweens, the question at the centre of this book will remain valid: is copyright law optimising creativity, and if not, how can we fix it?

APPENDIX

Table 1 Subreddit selection for main study observational work

Art subreddits	Photography subreddits	Writing subreddits
r/Art r/ArtistLounge r/comics r/comicbookcollabs r/comiccrits r/photoshopbattles	r/itookapicture r/photography r/photocritique r/pics	r/writing r/writingprompts r/writers r/producemyscript r/screenwriting

Table 2 Subreddit selection for AI study observational work

Art subreddits	Photography subreddits	Writing subreddits
r/Art r/ArtistLounge	r/photography r/photocritique r/askphotography	r/writers r/writing

Table 3 Interview participant information

Participant	Platform	Creativity type
1	Reddit	Art
2	Reddit	Art
3	Reddit	Art
4	Reddit	Art
5	Reddit	Art
6	Reddit	Art
7	Reddit	Art
8	Reddit	Writing
9	4chan	Art; Writing
10	4chan	Art
11	4chan	Photography
12	4chan	Art

BIBLIOGRAPHY

Aoki, K, 'Adrift in the Intertext: Authorship and Audience Recoding Rights – Comment on Robert H Rotstein, Beyond Metaphor: Copyright Infringement and the Fiction of the Work' (1993) 68 *Chicago-Kent Law Review* 805.

Amabile, TM, *Creativity in Context*, 2nd edn (New York, Routledge, 2018).

Angelopoulos, C and Quintais, P, 'A Better Solution to Online Infringement' (2019) 10 *Journal of Intellectual Property, Information Technology and E-Commerce* 147.

Arnold, R, 'The Need for a New Copyright Act: A Case Study in Law Reform' (2015) 5 *Queen Mary Journal of Intellectual Property* 110.

Aufderheide, P and Jaszi, P, *Reclaiming Fair Use: How to Put Balance Back in Copyright*, 2nd edn (Chicago, IL, University of Chicago Press, 2018).

Bachmann, G, Knecht, M and Wittel, A, 'The Social Productivity of Anonymity' (2017) 17 *ephemera: theory & politics in organization* 241.

Barnett, JM, 'Copyright without Creators' (2014) 9 *Review of Law & Economics* 389.

Barron, A, 'Copyright Law and the Claims of Art' (2002) 4 *Intellectual Property Quarterly* 368.

Benhamou, Y and Andrijevic, A, 'The Protection of AI-Generated Pictures (Photograph and Painting) under Copyright Law' in R Abbott (ed), *Research Handbook on Intellectual Property and Artificial Intelligence* (Cheltenham, Edward Elgar Publishing, 2022) 198–217.

Benkler, Y, *The Wealth of Networks: How Social Production Transforms Markets and Freedom* (New Haven, CT, Yale University Press, 2007).

Bently, L and Sherman, B, *Intellectual Property Law*, 4th edn (Oxford, Oxford University Press, 2014).

Bently, L et al, *Intellectual Property Law*, 6th edn (Oxford, Oxford University Press, 2022).

Bernstein et al, '4chan and /b/: An Analysis of Anonymity and Ephemerality in a Large Online Community', *Proceedings of the Fifth International Conference on Weblogs and Social Media* (2011).

Bertoni, A and Montagnani, ML, 'Foodporn: Experience-Sharing Platforms and UGC: How to Make Copyright Fit for the Sharing Economy' (2017) 39 *European Intellectual Property Review* 399.

Biagioli, M, Jaszi, P and Woodmansee, M, *Making and Unmaking Intellectual Property: Creative Production in Legal and Cultural Perspective* (Chicago, IL, University of Chicago Press, 2011).

Bodle, R, 'The Ethics of Online Anonymity or Zuckerberg vs Moot' (2013) 43 *ACM SIGCAS Computers and Society* 22.

Bonadio, E, 'Street Art, Graffiti and Copyright: A UK Perspective' in E Bonadio (ed), *The Cambridge Handbook of Copyright in Street Art and Graffiti* (Cambridge, Cambridge University Press, 2019) 159–74.

Bowrey, K, *Law and Internet Cultures* (Cambridge, Cambridge University Press, 2005).

Boyle, J, Shamans, *Software, and Spleens: Law and the Construction of the Information Society* (Cambridge, MA, Harvard University Press, 1997).

—— *The Public Domain: Enclosing the Commons of the Mind* (New Haven, CT, Yale University Press, 2008).

Brown, CS, 'Copyleft, the Disguised Copyright: Why Legislative Copyright Reform Is Superior to Copyleft Licenses' (2010) 78 *UMKC Law Review* 749.

Bruns, DA, 'The Future Is User-Led: The Path towards Widespread Produsage' (2008) 11 *Fibreculture Journal*.

Bunce, A, 'British Invasion: Importing the United Kingdom's Orphan Works Solution to United States Copyright Law' (2013) 108 *Northwestern University Law Review* 243.

Campus, G, 'Generative AI: Main Copyright Issues and Some (Partial) Answers in the EU AI Act' (2024) 46 *European Intellectual Property Review* 434.

Carroll, MW, 'One for All: The Problem of Uniformity Cost in Intellectual Property Law' (2005) 55 *American University Law Review* 845.

Castronova, E, 'Theory of the Avatar' (2003) No 863 CESifo Working Paper 31.

Chon, M, 'New Wine Bursting from Old Bottles: Collaborative Internet Art, Joint Works, and Entrepreneurship' (1996) 75 *Oregon Law Review* 257.

Cohen, JE, 'Creativity and Culture in Copyright Theory' (2007) 40 *UC Davis Law Review* 1151, 1152.

—— *Configuring the Networked Self: Law, Code and the Play of Everyday Practice* (New Haven, CT, Yale University Press, 2012).

Colangelo, G and Lincesso, I, 'Law versus Technology: Looking for a Solution to the Orphan Works' Problem' (2012) 20 *International Journal of Law and Information Technology* 178.

Coombe, RJ, *The Cultural Life of Intellectual Properties: Authorship, Appropriation, and the Law* (Durham, NC, Duke University Press, 1998).

Cordell, N, Potts, B and Dickens, R, 'Ownership of AI-Generated Content in the UK' (2024) 46 *European Intellectual Property Review* 470.

Davis, G, 'When Copyright is Not Enough: Deconstructing Why, as the Modern Music Industry Takes, Musicians Continue to Make' (2017) 16 *Chicago-Kent Journal of Intellectual Property* 373.

Darling, K, 'IP without IP: A Study of the Online Adult Entertainment Industry' (2013) 17 *Stanford Technology Law Review* 709.

Darling, K and Perzanowski, A (eds), *Creativity without Law: Challenging the Assumptions of Intellectual Property* (New York, NYU Press, 2017).

De Choudhury, M and De, S, 'Mental Health Discourse on Reddit: Self-Disclosure, Social Support, and Anonymity', *Proceedings of the Eighth International AAAI Conference on Weblogs and Social Media* (2014).

Dent, C, 'Decisions around Innovation and the Motivators that Contribute to Them: Patents, Copyright, Trade Marks and Know-How' (2016) 6 *Queen Mary Journal of Intellectual Property Law* 435.

Depoorter, B, Holland, A and Somerstein, E, 'Copyright Abolition and Attribution' (2009) 5 *Review of Law & Economics* 1063.

Derclaye, E, 'Debunking Some of UK Copyright Law's Longstanding Myths and Misunderstandings' (2013) 1 *Intellectual Property Quarterly* 1.

Deuze, M, 'Participation, Remediation, Bricolage: Considering Principal Components of a Digital Culture' (2006) 22 *The Information Society* 63.

Dibbell, J, 'Radical Opacity' (2010) 113 *Technology Review* 82.

Donat, GS, 'Fixing Fixation: A Copyright with Teeth for Improvisational Performers' (1997) 97 *Columbia Law Review* 1363.

Drassinower, A, 'A Note on Incentives, Rights, and the Public Domain in Copyright Law' (2011) 86 *Notre Dame Law Review* 1869.

Dusollier, S, '(Re)Introducing Formalities in Copyright as a Strategy for the Public Domain' in L Guibault and C Angelopoulos (eds), *Open Content Licensing: From Theory to Practice* (Amsterdam, Amsterdam University Press, 2011) 75–105.

Dworkin, G, 'The Moral Right of the Author: Moral Rights and the Common Law Countries' (1994) 19 *Columbia-VA Journal of Law and the Arts* 229.

Elkin-Koren, N, 'Can Formalities Save the Public Domain? Reconsidering Formalities for the 2010s' (2013) 28 *Berkeley Technology Law Journal* 1537.

Ellickson, RC, *Order Without Law: How Neighbours Settle Disputes* (Cambridge, MA, Harvard University Press, 1991).

Fagundes, D, 'Talk Derby to Me: Intellectual Property Norms Governing Roller Derby Pseudonyms' (2011) 90 *Texas Law Review* 1093.

Farrand, B, 'Lobbying and Lawmaking in the European Union: The Development of Copyright Law and the Rejection of the Anti-Counterfeiting Trade Agreement' (2015) 35 *Oxford Journal of Legal Studies* 487.

Faulkner, SL and Trotter, SP, 'Data Saturation' in *The International Encyclopedia of Communication Research Methods* (Hoboken, NJ, John Wiley & Sons, 2017) 1–2.

Fiesler, C, 'Everything I Need to Know I Learned from Fandom: How Existing Social Norms Can Help Shape the next Generation of User-Generated Content' (2007) 10 *Vanderbilt Journal of Entertainment and Technology Law* 729.

Fiesler, C and Bruckman, AS, "Creativity, Copyright, and Close-Knit Communities: A Case Study of Social Norm Formation and Enforcement" (2019) 3 *Proceedings of the ACM on Human–Computer Interaction* 241.

Fiesler, C, Feuston, JL and Bruckman, AS, 'Understanding Copyright Law in Online Creative Communities', *Proceedings of the 18th ACM Conference on Computer Supported Cooperative Work and Social Computing* (New York, ACM Press, 2015).

Fiesler, C et al, 'Reddit Rules! Characterizing an Ecosystem of Governance' [2018] *Proceedings of the Twelfth International AAAI Conference on Web and Social Media* 72.

Fischmann Afori, O, 'Implied License: An Emerging New Standard in Copyright Law' (2009) 25 *Santa Clara Computer & High Technology Law Journal* 275.

Fisher, WW, 'Theories of Intellectual Property' in SR Munzer (ed), *New Essays in the Legal and Political Theory of Property* (Cambridge, Cambridge University Press, 2001) 437–68.

—— 'Recalibrating Originality' (2016) 54 *Houston Law Review* 437.

Fromer, JC, 'A Psychology of Intellectual Property' (2010) 104 *Northwestern University Law Review* 1441.

Froomkin, AM, 'Legal Issues in Anonymity and Pseudonymity' (1999) 15 *The Information Society* 113.

Frosio, G, 'Reforming the C-DSM Reform: A User-Based Copyright Theory for Commonplace Creativity' (2020) 51 *IIC – International Review of Intellectual Property and Competition Law* 709.

—— 'Four Theories in Search of an A(I)uthor' in R Abbott (ed), *Handbook of Intellectual Property and Artificial Intelligence* (Cheltenham, Edward Elgar Publishing, 2022) 156–78.

Ganley, P, 'The Internet, Creativity and Copyright Incentives' (2005) 10 *Journal of Intellectual Property Rights* 188.

Gates, TM, 'Providing Adequate Protection for Comedians' Intellectual Creations: Examining Intellectual Property Norms and Negative Spaces' (2014) 93 *Oregon Law Review* 801.

Geiger, C, 'Promoting Creativity through Copyright Limitations: Reflections on the Concept of Exclusivity in Copyright Law' (2009) 12 *Vanderbilt Journal of Entertainment and Technology Law* 515.

Gervais, D, *(Re)Structuring Copyright: A Comprehensive Path to International Copyright Reform* (Cheltenham, Edward Elgar Publishing, 2017).

—— 'The Machine as Author' (2020) 105 *Iowa Law Review* 2053.

—— 'AI Derivatives: The Application to the Derivative Work Right to Literary and Artistic Productions of AI Machines' (2022) 52 *Seton Hall Law Review* 1111.

—— 'The Human Cause' in R Abbott (ed), *Research Handbook on Intellectual Property and Artificial Intelligence* (Cheltenham, Edward Elgar Publishing, 2022) 22–39.

Ginsburg, JC, 'The Concept of Authorship in Comparative Copyright Law' (2002) 52 *De Paul Law Review* 1063.

Ginsburg, JC and Budiardjo, LA, 'Authors and Machines' (2019) 34 *Berkeley Technology Law Journal* 343.

Goldstein, P, *International Copyright: Principles, Law and Practice* (Oxford, Oxford University Press, 2001).

Guadamuz, A, 'The Monkey Selfie: Copyright Lessons for Originality in Photographs and Internet Jurisdiction' (2016) 5 *Internet Policy Review* 1.

—— 'Living in a Remixed World: Comparative Analysis of Transformative Uses in Copyright Law' in L Edwards, B Schafer and E Harbinja (eds), *Future Law: Emerging Technology, Regulation and Ethics* (Edinburgh, Edinburgh University Press, 2020) 343–63.

—— 'Do Androids Dream of Electric Copyright? Comparative Analysis of Originality in Artificial Intelligence Generated Works' in J-A Lee, R Hilty and K-C Liu (eds), *Artificial Intelligence and Intellectual Property* (Oxford, Oxford University Press, 2021) 147–76.

Hargreaves, I, 'Digital Opportunity: A Review of Intellectual Property and Growth: An Independent Report' (2011).
He, K, 'The Concept of Originality in Copyright Law in China and Europe' in N Lee, N Bruun and M Li (eds), *Governance of Intellectual Property Rights in China and Europe* (Cheltenham, Edward Elgar Publishing, 2016) 91–106.
Hennessey, BA and Amabile, TM, 'Creativity' (2010) 61 *Annual Review of Psychology* 569.
Hesse, C, 'The Rise of Intellectual Property, 700 BC–AD 2000: An Idea in the Balance' (2002) 131 *Daedalus* 26.
Hetcher, S, 'User-Generated Content and the Future of Copyright: Part One – Investiture of Ownership' (2007) 10 *Vanderbilt Journal of Entertainment and Technology Law* 863.
Heymann, LA, 'The Birth of the Authornym: Authorship Pseudonymity and Trademark Law' (2005) 80 *Notre Dame Law Review* 1377.
—— 'A Tale of (at Least) Two Authors: Focusing Copyright Law on Process over Product' (2008) 34 *Journal of Corporation Law* 1009.
Hine, C, *Virtual Ethnography* (London, SAGE Publications, 2000).
Hogan, B, 'Pseudonyms and the Rise of the Real-Name Web' in J Hartley, J Burgess and A Bruns (eds), *A Companion to New Media Dynamics* (Chichester, Wiley-Blackwell, 2013) 290–307.
Horowitz, SJ, 'Copyright's Asymmetric Uncertainty' (2012) 79 *University of Chicago Law Review* 331.
Hudson, E and Burrell, R, 'Abandonment, Copyright and Orphaned Works: What Does It Mean to Take the Proprietary Nature of Intellectual Property Rights Seriously?' (2011) 35 *Melbourne University Law Review* 972.
Iljadica, M, *Copyright Beyond Law: Regulating Creativity in the Graffiti Subculture* (Oxford, Hart Publishing, 2016).
—— 'User Generated Content and its Authors' in T Aplin (ed), *Research Handbook on Intellectual Property and Digital Technologies* (Cheltenham, Edward Elgar Publishing, 2020) 163–85.
Jaszi, P, 'On the Author Effect: Contemporary Copyright and Collective Creativity' (1991) 10 *Cardozo Arts & Entertainment Law Journal* 293.
—— 'Toward a Theory of Copyright: The Metamorphoses of "Authorship"' [1991] *Duke Law Journal* 455.
Johnson, EE, 'The Economics and Sociality of Sharing Intellectual Property Rights' (2014) 94 *Boston University Law Review* 1935.
Johnson, P, 'Dedicating Copyright to the Public Domain' (2008) 71 *Modern Law Review* 587.
Judge, EF and Gervais, DJ, 'Of Silos and Constellations: Comparing Notions of Originality in Copyright Law' (2009) 27 *Cardozo Arts & Entertainment Law Journal* 375.
Justin, B, 'The EU's Trouble with Mashups' (2014) 5 *Journal of Intellectual Property, Information Technology and E-Commerce* 172.
Kahan, DM, 'Gentle Nudges vs Hard Shoves: Solving the Sticky Norms Problem' (2000) 67 *University of Chicago Law Review* 607.
King, N and Horrocks, C, *Interviews in Qualitative Research* (London, SAGE, 2010).
Klein, B, Moss, G and Edwards, L, *Understanding Copyright: Intellectual Property in the Digital Age* (London, SAGE Publications, 2015).
Klonick, K, 'Re-Shaming the Debate: Social Norms, Shame, and Regulation in an Internet Age' (2016) 75 *Maryland Law Review* 1029.
Knuttila, L, 'User Unknown: 4chan, Anonymity and Contingency' (2011) 16 *First Monday*.
Kozinets, R, *Netnography: Redefined* (London, SAGE Publications, 2015).
Kozinets, R, Dolbec, P-Y and Earley, A, 'Netnographic Analysis: Understanding Culture Through Social Media Data' in U Flick (ed), *The SAGE Handbook of Qualitative Data Analysis* (London, SAGE Publications, 2014) 262–76.
Ku, RSR, 'The Creative Destruction of Copyright: Napster and the New Economics of Digital Technology' [2002] *University of Chicago Law Review* 263.
Ku, R, Sun, J and Fan, Y, 'Does Copyright Law Promote Creativity? An Empirical Analysis of Copyright's Bounty' (2009) 62 *Vanderbilt Law Review* 1667.

Lambrecht, M and Cabay, J, 'Remix Allowed: Avenues for Copyright Reform Inspired by Canada' (2016) 11 *Journal of Intellectual Property Law & Practice* 21.
Landes, WM and Posner, RA, 'An Economic Analysis of Copyright Law' (1989) 18 *Journal of Legal Studies* 325.
—— 'Indefinitely Renewable Copyright' (2003) 70 *University of Chicago Law Review* 471.
Larsson, S and Svensson, M, 'Compliance or Obscurity? Online Anonymity as a Consequence of Fighting Unauthorised File-Sharing' (2010) 2 *Policy & Internet* 75.
Lastowka, G, 'Digital Attribution: Copyright and the Right To Credit' (2007) 87 *Boston University Law Review* 41.
Lea, M, Spears, R and de Groot, D, 'Knowing Me, Knowing You: Anonymity Effects on Social Identity Processes within Groups' (2001) 27 *Personality and Social Psychology Bulletin* 526.
Lee, E, 'Warming up to User-Generated Content' [2008] *University of Illinois Law Review* 1459.
Lessig, L, *Free Culture: The Nature and Future of Creativity* (New York, Penguin Books, 2005).
—— *Remix: Making Art and Commerce Thrive in the Hybrid Economy* (New York, Bloomsbury Academic, 2008).
Levy, P, *Cyberculture*, R Bononno trans (Minneapolis, MN, University of Minnesota Press, 2001).
Li, Y, 'The Age of Remix and Copyright Law Reform' (2020) 12 *Law, Innovation and Technology* 113.
Litman, JD, *Digital Copyright* (Amherst, NY, Prometheus Books, 2006).
—— 'Real Copyright Reform' (2010) 96 *Iowa Law Review* 1.
Loshin, J 'Secrets Revealed: Protecting Magicians' Intellectual Property without Law' in CA Corcos (ed), *Law and Magic: A Collection of Essays* (Durham, NC, Carolina Academic Press, 2010) 123–42.
McAdams, RH, 'The Origin, Development, and Regulation of Norms' (1997) 96 *Michigan Law Review* 338.
Macmillan, F, 'Cultural Diversity in an Era of Corporate Dominance: A Clash of Rights?' (2007) DIME Working Papers on Intellectual Property Rights, Working Paper No 29.
MacQueen, HL, 'Copyright Law Reform: Some Achievable Goals?' in F Macmillan (ed), *New Directions in Copyright Law*, Vol 4 (Cheltenham, Edward Elgar Publishing, 2007) 55–84.
Madison, MJ, 'Rewriting Fair Use and the Future of Copyright Reform' (2005) 23 *Cardozo Arts & Entertainment Law Journal* 391.
—— 'Beyond Creativity: Copyright as Knowledge Law' (2009) 12 *Vanderbilt Journal of Entertainment and Technology Law* 817.
Maguire, R, '"It Doesn't Belong to the Internet": Copyright Reform for User-Generated Content' [2022] *Intellectual Property Quarterly* 141.
Mandel, GN, 'To Promote the Creative Process: Intellectual Property Law and the Psychology of Creativity' (2011) 86 *Notre Dame Law Review* 1999.
Manivannan, V, 'Attaining the Ninth Square: Cybertextuality, Gamification, and Institutional Memory on 4chan' [2012] *Enculturation.*
Markham, A, 'The Methods, Politics, and Ethics of Representation in Online Ethnography' in NK Denzin and YS Lincoln (eds), *Collecting and Interpreting Qualitative Materials*, 3rd edn (Thousand Oaks, CA, SAGE Publications, 2008) 247–84.
Marwick, AE, 'Online Identity' in J Hartley, J Burgess and A Bruns (eds), *A Companion to New Media Dynamics* (Chichester, Wiley-Blackwell, 2013) 355–64.
Marwick, AE and boyd, d, 'I Tweet Honestly, I Tweet Passionately: Twitter Users, Context Collapse, and the Imagined Audience' (2011) 13 *New Media & Society* 114.
Marx, GT, 'What's in a Name? Some Reflections on the Sociology of Anonymity' (1999) 15 *The Information Society* 99.
—— 'Internet Anonymity as a Reflection of Broader Issues Involving Technology and Society' (2004) 11 *Asia-Pacific Review* 142.
Matteson, JD, 'Unfair Misuse: How Section 512 of the DMCA Allows Abuse of the Copyright Fair Use Doctrine and How to Fix It' (2018) 35 *Santa Clara High Technology Law Journal* 1.

Matulionyte, R, 'The Law Applicable to Online Copyright Infringements in the ALI and CLIP Proposals: A Rebalance of Interests Needed' (2011) 2 *Journal of Intellectual Property, Information Technology and E-Commerce Law* 26.

McIntyre, TJ, 'Online Anonymity: Some Legal Issues' (2004) 11 *Commercial Law Practitioner* 90.

Meese, J, '"It Belongs to the Internet": Animal Images, Attribution Norms and the Politics of Amateur Media Production" (2014) 17 *M/C Journal*.

—— 'User Production and Law Reform: A Socio-Legal Critique of User Creativity' (2015) 37 *Media, Culture & Society* 753.

Meese, J and Hagedorn, J, 'Mundane Content on Social Media: Creation, Circulation, and the Copyright Problem' (2019) 5 *Social Media + Society* 1.

Merges, RP, 'The Concept of Property in the Digital Era' (2008) 45 *Houston Law Review* 1239.

Morse, JM, 'Critical Analysis of Strategies for Determining Rigor in Qualitative Inquiry' (2015) 25 *Qualitative Health Research* 1212.

Murray, LJ, Piper, ST and Robertson, K, *Putting Intellectual Property in Its Place: Rights Discourses, Creative Labor, and the Everyday* (Oxford, Oxford University Press, 2013).

Mysoor, P, *Implied Licences in Copyright Law* (Oxford, Oxford University Press, 2021).

Nagle, A, Kill *All Normies: Online Culture Wars from 4Chan and Tumblr to Trump and the Alt-Right* (Lanham, John Hunt Publishing, 2017).

Nelson, E, 'Unacknowledged Legislators: The Contemporary Poetry Community's Quasi-Regime of Intellectual Property' (2015) 91 *North Dakota Law Review* 633.

Netanel, NW, 'Copyright and a Democratic Civil Society' (1996) 106 *Yale Law Journal* 283.

Nissenbaum, H, 'The Meaning of Anonymity in an Information Age' (1999) 15 *The Information Society* 141.

Ohly, A, 'Choice of Law in the Digital Environment: Problems and Possible Solutions' in J Drexl, R Hilty and J Straus (eds), *Intellectual Property and Private International Law: Heading for the Future* (Oxford, Hart Publishing, 2005) 241–56.

Oliar, D and Sprigman, CJ, 'There's No Free Laugh (Anymore): The Emergence of Intellectual Property Norms and the Transformation of Stand-Up Comedy' (2008) 94 *Virginia Law Review* 1787.

Olson, KK, 'The Copyright Claims Board and the Individual Creator: Is Real Reform Possible?' (2020) 25 *Communication Law and Policy* 1.

Opdenakker, R, 'Advantages and Disadvantages of Four Interview Techniques in Qualitative Research' (2006) 7 *Forum: Qualitative Social Research* Art 11.

Osborne, D, 'User Generated Content (UGC): Trade Mark and Copyright Infringement Issues' (2008) 3 *Journal of Intellectual Property Law & Practice* 555.

Ostrom, E, 'Collective Action and the Evolution of Social Norms' (2000) 14 *Journal of Economic Perspectives* 137.

Pallante, MA, 'The Next Great Copyright Act' (2013) 36 *Columbia Journal of Law & the Arts* 315.

Parchomovsky, G and Stein, A, 'Originality' (2009) 95 *Virginia Law Review* 1505.

Patry, *How to Fix Copyright* (Oxford, Oxford University Press, 2011).

Perkel, D, 'Share Wars: Sharing, Theft, and the Everyday Production of Web 2.0 on DeviantArt' [2016] *First Monday*.

Pham, H, 'Standing Up for Stand-Up Comedy: Joke Theft and the Relevance of Copyright Law and Social Norms in the Social Media Age' (2019) 30 *Fordham Intellectual Property, Media and Entertainment Law Journal* 55.

Pihlajarinne, T, 'Should We Bury the Concept of Reproduction – Towards Principle-Based Assessment in Copyright Law?' (2017) 48 *IIC-International Review of Intellectual Property and Competition Law* 953.

Post, DG, 'Pooling Intellectual Capital: Thoughts on Anonymity, Pseudonymity, and Limited Liability in Cyberspace the Law of Cyberspace' (1996) 1996 *University of Chicago Legal Forum* 139.

Postmes, T et al, 'Social Influence in Computer-Mediated Communication: The Effects of Anonymity on Group Behavior' (2001) 27 *Personality and Social Psychology Bulletin* 1243.

—— 'Individuality and Social Influence in Groups: Inductive and Deductive Routes to Group Identity' (2005) 89 *Journal of Personality and Social Psychology* 747.

Raustiala, K and Sprigman, CJ, 'The Piracy Paradox Revisited' (2009) 61 *Stanford* Law Review 1201.

—— 'When Are IP Rights Necessary? Evidence from Innovation in IP's Negative Space' in B Depoorter, P Menell and D Schwartz (eds), *Research Handbook on the Economics of Intellectual Property Law, Vol 1: Theory* (Cheltenham, Edward Elgar Publishing, 2016) 309–29.

Raymond, ES, *The Cathedral & the Bazaar* (Cambridge, MA, O'Reilly Media, 2001).

Reed, C, *Making Laws for Cyberspace* (Oxford, Oxford University Press, 2012).

Reuveni, E, 'Copyright, Neuroscience and Creativity' (2013) 64 *Alabama Law Review* 735.

Rigamonti, CP, 'Deconstructing Moral Rights' (2006) 47 *Harvard International Law Journal* 353.

Robertson, K, 'No One Would Murder for a Pattern: Crafting IP in Online Knitting Communities' in LJ Murray, ST Piper and K Robertson (eds), *Putting Intellectual Property in its Place: Rights Discourses, Creative Labor, and the Everyday* (Oxford, Oxford University Press, 2013) 41–62.

Rose, CM, *Property and Persuasion: Essays on the History, Theory, and Rhetoric of Ownership* (Boulder, CO, Westview Press, 1994).

Rosenblatt, EL, 'A Theory of IP's Negative Space' (2011) 34 *Columbia Journal of Law & the Arts* 317.

—— 'Fear and Loathing: Shame, Shaming, and Intellectual Property' (2013) 63 *DePaul Law Review* 1.

Rosenthal Kwall, R, 'Originality in Context' (2007) 44 *Houston Law Review* 871.

Rotstein, RH, 'Beyond Metaphor: Copyright Infringement and the Fiction of the Work' (1993) 68 *Chicago-Kent Law Review* 725.

Roundtree, A, 'Graffiti Artists Get Up in Intellectual Property's Negative Space' (2012) 31 *Cardozo Arts & Entertainment Law Journal* 959.

Samuelson, P, 'Preliminary Thoughts on Copyright Reform' [2007] *Utah Law Review* 551.

Sarid, E, 'Don't Be a Drag, Just Be a Queen – How Drag Queens Protect Their Intellectual Property Without Law' (2014) 10 *FIU Law Review* 133.

Senftleben, M, 'User Generated Content: Towards a New Use Privilege in EU Copyright Law' in T Aplin (ed), *Research Handbook on Intellectual Property and Digital Technologies* (Cheltenham, Edward Elgar Publishing, 2020) 136–62.

Schuler, AG, 'Insta-Appropriation: Finding Boundaries for the Second Circuit's Fair Use Doctrine after Campbell' (2016) 85 *Fordham Law Review* 367.

Shavell, S, 'Should Copyright of Academic Works Be Abolished?' (2010) 2 *Journal of Legal Analysis* 301.

Sieman, JS, 'Using the Implied License to Inject Common Sense into Digital Copyright' (2006) 85 *North Carolina Law Review* 885.

Silbey, J, *The Eureka Myth: Creators, Innovators, and Everyday Intellectual Property* (Stanford, CA, Stanford University Press, 2015).

Simon, DA, 'Culture, Creativity and Copyright' (2011) 29 *Cardozo Arts & Entertainment Law Journal* 97.

Singh, A, 'Anonymity, Authorship, and Blogger Ethics' (2009) 16 *symploke* 21.

Smiers, J, 'The Abolition of Copyright: Better for Artists, Third World Countries and the Public Domain' (2000) 62 *Gazette* 379.

Smith Ekstrand, V, 'The Many Masks of Anon: Anonymity As Cultural Practice and Reflections in Case Law' (2013) 18 *Journal of Technology Law & Policy* 1.

Spinello, RA and Bottis, M, *A Defense of Intellectual Property Rights* (Cheltenham, Edward Elgar Publishing, 2009).

Sprigman, C, 'Reform(Aliz)Ing Copyright' (2004) 57 *Stanford Law Review* 485.

—— 'Conclusion: Some Positive Thoughts about IP's Negative Space' in A Perzanowski and K Darling (eds), *Creativity without Law: Challenging the Assumptions of Intellectual Property* (New York, NYU Press, 2017) 249–69.

Stamatoudi, I and Torremans, P, *EU Copyright Law: A Commentary* (Cheltenham, Edward Elgar Publishing, 2014).

Suhl, NC, 'Moral Rights Protection in the United States under the Berne Convention: A Fictional Work' (2001) 12 *Fordham Intellectual Property, Media & Entertainment Law Journal* 1203.

Svantesson, DJB, *Private International Law and the Internet*, 3rd edn (Alphen aan den Rijn, Kluwer Law International, 2016).
Tan, C, *Regulating Content on Social Media: Copyright, Terms of Service and Technological Features* (London, UCL Press, 2018).
Towse, R, 'Partly for the Money: Rewards and Incentives to Artists' (2001) 54 *Kyklos* 473.
—— 'Creativity, Copyright and the Creative Industries Paradigm' (2010) 63 *Kyklos* 461.
—— 'The Quest for Evidence on the Economic Effects of Copyright Law' (2013) 37 *Cambridge Journal of Economics* 1187.
Trammell, M, 'User Investment and Behavior Policing on 4chan' (2014) 19 *First Monday*.
Tushnet, R, 'Legal Fictions: Copyright, Fan Fiction, and a New Common Law' (1996) 17 *Loyola of Los Angeles Entertainment Law Journal* 651.
—— 'User-Generated Discontent: Transformation in Practice' (2007) 31 *Columbia Journal of Law & Arts* 497.
—— 'Economies of Desire: Fair Use and Marketplace Assumption' (2009) 51 *William & Mary Law Review* 513.
Tuters, M, Jokubauskaitė, E and Bach, D, 'Post-Truth Protest: How 4chan Cooked Up the Pizzagate Bullshit' (2018) 21 *M/C Journal*.
Van der Nagel, E and Frith, J, 'Anonymity, Pseudonymity, and the Agency of Online Identity: Examining the Social Practices of r/Gonewild' (2015) 20 *First Monday*.
Van Dijck, J, 'Users like You? Theorizing Agency in User-Generated Content' (2009) 31 *Media, Culture & Society* 41.
van Gompel, S, 'The Orphan Works Chimera and How to Defeat It: A View from across the Atlantic' (2012) 27 *Berkeley Technology Law Journal* 1347.
—— 'Copyright Formalities in the Internet Age: Filters of Protection or Facilitators of Licensing' (2013) 28 *Berkeley Technology Law Journal* 1425.
Waldron, J, 'From Authors to Copiers: Individual Rights and Social Values in Intellectual Property' (1993) 68 *Chicago-Kent Law Review* 841.
Weatherall, K, 'The Relationship between User-Generated Content and Commerce' in D Hunter et al (eds), *Amateur Media: Social, Cultural and Legal Perspectives* (London, Routledge, 2012) 59–70.
Weisberg, RW, 'On the Usefulness of "Value" in the Definition of Creativity' (2015) 27 *Creativity Research Journal* 111.
Wilson, AN, 'Jet-Setting Orphan Works: The Transnational Making Available of Works of Unknown Authorship, Anonymous Works, or Lost Authors' (2009) 23 *Emory International Law Review* 783.
Woodmansee, M, 'On the Author Effect: Recovering Collectivity' (1991) 10 *Cardozo Arts & Entertainment Law Journal* 279.
—— *The Author, Art and the Market: Rereading the History of Aesthetics* (New York, Columbia University Press, 1996).
Wu, T, 'Tolerated Use' (2007) 31 *Columbia Journal of Law and the Arts* 617.
Zelenkauskaite, A et al, 'Shades of Hatred Online: 4chan Duplicate Circulation Surge during Hybrid Media Events' [2021] *First Monday*.

INDEX

www.ingramcontent.com/pod-product-compliance
Ingram Content Group UK Ltd.
Pitfield, Milton Keynes, MK11 3LW, UK
UKHW020819290926
15470UKWH00003B/1245

9 781509 982325